P9-CKX-467

DYKEMAN RONALD MYERS MAIN

GILLIAM FRATER TALLMAN ALBERTSON GAY

Superior court judges in 1911, the first year judges were permitted robes.

FROM PROFANITY HILL
King County Bar Association's Story

Marc Lampson

Documentary Book Publishers Corporation
Kirkland, Washington

FROM PROFANITY HILL
King County Bar Association's Story
Copyright© 1993 by King County Bar Association.
All rights reserved. Printed in the United States of America.
No part of this book may be used or reproduced in any
manner whatsoever without written permission except in the
case of brief quotations embodied in critical articles or reviews.
For information, write Documentary Book Publishers Corporation,
Suite 272, 135 Lake Street South, Kirkland, WA 98033.

Author: Marc Lampson
Editor: Barry Provorse
Copyeditor: Judy Gouldthorpe
Cover and book design: Amy Hines Design
Library of Congress Cataloging-in-Publication Data
LC # 93-071147
Lampson, Marc
From Profanity Hill: King County Bar Association's Story
ISBN 0-935503-10-2
1. King County Bar Association—History
2. Seattle, Washington—History
3. Washington State—History
4. Law—History

TABLE OF CONTENTS

Considered to be the first photograph taken in King County, this image of
Seattle, in 1860, shows the "city's" above-ground water system and
Sarah Yesler sitting on her front porch.

ACKNOWLEDGMENTS

For my mother, Helen Lampson

Many people made the writing of this book possible. Alice Paine, the Executive Director of the Seattle-King County Bar Association, believed in the project and believed in my ability to write the book. Barry Provorse, the publisher and editor, was always patient, understanding, and encouraging. Kelly Kunsch, the Reference Librarian at the University of Puget Sound School of Law, was always friendly and helpful, as were the other librarians at the school. Mary Louderback, the Circulation Librarian at the University of Washington's Gallagher Law Library, was singularly helpful, friendly, and willing to bend the rules.

The book, intended as a popular history, is heavily indebted to secondary rather than primary sources. The author wishes to acknowledge here the many fine historians whose works, listed in the endnotes, were major resources: Jerold S. Auerbach, Richard C. Berner, Norman Clark, Ivan Doig, Lawrence M. Friedman, Morton J. Horwitz, Murray Morgan, Roger Sale, Jane Sanders, and Charles H. Sheldon. None of the people listed above are responsible for any perceived shortcomings in the book; they are responsible, however, for whatever the reader finds helpful and interesting.

Marc Lampson

FOREWORD

It was my privilege to become a member of the State and King County bars in 1952, many years after the last curse was uttered by a lawyer struggling up Seattle's "Profanity Hill." Thanks to the art, skill, and thoroughness of Marc Lampson, the experiences of the men and women who acted out that and other eras in the life of the King County Bar Association are now available to us all for inspection, reflection, and just plain enjoyment. Many of the lawyers in the book are my contemporaries.

My father was born to Scandinavian immigrants in King County shortly after statehood. His birthplace, Newcastle, is now popularly referred to as one of those "affluent Seattle suburbs"; then it was a rough coal mining camp. I was born in Auburn. It was natural that, after serving as an armored infantryman in wartime Europe and receiving a law degree from the University of Washington, I would start my career as an attorney in King County.

Marc Lampson's book is about lawyers, but it is not just a lawyer's book. There is something in it for everyone: legal scholars, politicians, armchair historians, and those who are simply interested in a good story. And there are lessons to be learned. Mr. Lampson's book focuses on the role of King County Bar members in important social, legal, and political events in our ever-changing society. He tells how lawyers have fought in the finest traditions of advocacy for what they believed to be right and just.

The account reminds me well of the time when a handshake was a lawyer's bond—no triple-signed copies of agreements were needed. Those were also the times when opposing counsel might well join each other—and often the judge—for refreshments at a nearby bar while waiting for a verdict. And the days when a court reporter would write up a transcript and trust you for payment.

For those of us born in King County, as well as those who saw it, liked it, and adopted it as their home, the book is rich in nostalgia and liberally laced with names of people we know or knew. Over the years, many of King County's and the state's most influential citizens have been members of the King County Bar Association.

Our state is still in its youth. Those in our profession who preceded us in the King County Bar Association did their work well. They were builders and doers. This well-founded book is about those lawyers and the legal heritage they bequeathed us. May we always do it honor.

James A. Andersen, Chief Justice
State of Washington Supreme Court
April 13, 1993
Olympia, Washington

From Rough
to Tough Justice

When the fog and mist lifted high enough above the climax forests on the cliffs above Elliott Bay, one could see Seattle taking shape in the winter of 1851-52. The hills above the deep-water harbor, including one later called Profanity Hill by lawyers who swore at its steepness as they lumbered up its face to the courthouse, provided panoramic views of the Olympic Mountains to the west and the Cascade Mountains to the east. Profanity Hill was also a place from which to view the dock where the Duwamish Indians, and later Chinese laborers, would be expelled, and to view the town's center, where protest would shape the local culture.

Natives, Invaders, and Lawyers

The Denny party, probably the most important group of whites who came to stay, landed at Alki Point on the schooner *Exact* on November 13, 1851. This group of twenty-two people were mostly from Illinois; they were tired, they were wet, and upon seeing their new home, some of them wept.

By February, most of the group had moved inland around the bay to a clearing they hoped would provide some shelter from the gales that raced along Alki Point. The area was near deep anchorage, which would help

"Tribe follows tribe and nation follows nation" lamented Chief Sealth when he and his followers boarded boats for the Indian reservation on the Kitsap Peninsula at Suquamish.

the community's hoped-for maritime trade. On this new site, they staked land claims to what, a few years later, would become the center of the town: Seattle. The already cleared land they settled on was a winter fishing village of the Duwamish Indians.

"Duwamps" is apparently how the invading midwesterners mispronounced the native people's tribal name, and for a short while Duwamps is what they called the new settlement: at least until a soon-to-be lawyer, Dr. David S. Maynard, convinced them otherwise.

Maynard came down-sound in a flat-bottomed boat loaded with merchandise from his store in Olympia, in the spring of 1852. He was a doctor, store owner, and promoter, and he later became Seattle's first justice of the peace and one of its first lawyers. He also became the central figure in one of its most famous legal battles: the suit to settle his and his two wives' land claims to part of downtown Duwamps.

Maynard came to town at the suggestion of an acquaintance, one of the principal leaders of the Duwamish tribe, Chief Sealth. Maynard thought it would be a nice gesture, given that they were settling in on one of the tribe's villages, to change the name of Duwamps to Sealth to honor the respected chief. He also knew that white folks didn't like having to pronounce either Duwamish or Sealth because they thought both names sounded unpleasant. So in the interest of harmony, and promoting future settlement, he argued for the name Seattle. It was the least they could do, but it was not everything they would do.

On March 2, 1853, Washington became a territory of the United States, and Isaac Ingalls Stevens was appointed both governor and superintendent of Indian affairs for the new territory. In a quick tour of the territory that year, Stevens convened a meeting of the native people who lived in the area around Seattle.

They all gathered on the shore of Elliott Bay in front of Doc Maynard's log cabin, which housed his drugstore and real estate office, at Front (First Avenue) and Main streets. Stevens told the natives how the Great Chief in Washington loved the Indians and that, because of this love, the Great Father was soon going to buy their lands and give them new homes. Chief Sealth then delivered his most famous speech, one often taught to Washington schoolchildren and quoted by environmentalists as a model of ecological thinking. Unmoved, Stevens was soon back in the nation's capital.

Claiming to respect and admire the native people, Stevens returned to the Pacific Northwest in 1854, made treaties with more than seventeen thousand natives, and extinguished their title to the more than sixty-four million acres of land that made up the territory of Washington, Idaho, and Montana. As part of this effort, between December 1854 and January 1855, six thousand Puget Sound natives, by treaty, ceded to the United States most of the Puget Sound area and the Olympic Peninsula.

Often at Stevens' side during the treaty making was the first lawyer whose written words had lasting consequences for Seattle, George Gibbs. Lawyer, cartographer, surveyor, translator, ethnologist, Gibbs, in 1855, was Territorial Governor Stevens' assistant in negotiating and drafting the Medicine Creek and Point Elliott treaties regarding the land inhabited by the region's native tribes, which included the Duwamish.

Because Governor Stevens, by Gibbs' and other accounts, was often dead drunk during treaty negotiations, Gibbs' drafting role was critical: Chief Sealth could not understand English and Governor Stevens, even when sober, could not understand any native dialect, including Chinook, the trade jargon that developed between the natives and traders.

Over a century later, in the landmark Boldt decision, United States District Court Judge George Boldt was still trying to decide what Gibbs meant in the treaty with the words: "The right of taking fish, at all usual and accustomed grounds and stations, is further secured to said Indians, in common with all citizens of the Territory."[1]

Gibbs had received his legal training at Harvard, taking his degree in 1838. He then practiced in a Wall Street firm, but he spent much of his time involved with the New York Historical Society, where, after hearing a lecture by another lawyer and anthropologist, Lewis Morgan, he became intensely interested in Indian culture.

Heading west on horseback, Gibbs arrived in Oregon City, Oregon, in 1848. He practiced law in Oregon, but had many other interests. He began to compile dictionaries of the various tribal languages in the Northwest and in California, and he helped negotiate many treaties in Oregon and California before coming to Washington, in March 1853, to do surveys for the government and the railroads.

He appeared before the Washington Territorial Supreme Court on December 4, 1854, and was admitted to practice in the territory. Three days later he accepted an offer from Governor Stevens to be the surveyor for the Indian Commission charged with drafting and negotiating treaties with the Territory's native tribes. The commissioners decided that Gibbs should prepare the treaty program. He devised the treaty format, containing fifteen articles, and in three days he had fixed a schedule for treaty conferences. As his biographer Stephen Beckham wrote, "Gibbs' handiwork shaped the course for Indian policy for the entire western section of Washington Territory."[2]

In December 1854, he left Olympia for nearby Medicine Creek, where the first treaty along Puget Sound was to be negotiated. In his diary, he described the scene of the negotiations:

Thin temporary huts of mats with the smoke of their numerous camp fires, the prows of canoes hauled up upon the bank and protruding from among the huts, the horses grazing on the marsh, the gloom of the firs & cedars with their long depending moss & the scattered & moving groups of Indians in all kinds of odd and fantastic dresses present a curious picture.[3]

On December 26, 1854, the Medicine Creek treaty was signed, and the following week Gibbs sailed for Elliott Bay to negotiate with four Seattle-area tribes. When Governor Stevens arrived in Seattle later in January, he named Gibbs secretary for the commission. In that capacity, Gibbs wrote the Point Elliott treaty. On January 22, Chiefs Sealth of the Duwamish, Patkanim of the Snohomish, Goliah of the Skagit, and Chowitshoot of the Lummi signed the treaty. The natives, who had previously gathered in front of Doc Maynard's general store, this time gathered north of Seattle at Mukilteo, near the town of Everett.

Gibbs was familiar with the natives' concept of property rights, and for about three hundred thousand dollars to be paid over twenty years, he convinced the natives to surrender their lands. In an extensive study for the United States Geographical and Geological Survey entitled "Tribes of Western Washington and Northwestern Oregon," Gibbs wrote:

Property—As far as I can gather the views of the Sound tribes, they recognize no individual right to land except actual occupancy. This seemed to be respected to this extent, that if a man has cleared a spot of land for cultivation, he can hold it on the return of the season for planting from year to year, as long as he sees fit. So in their villages, the site of a house pertains to the individual as long as he leaves any vestige or evidence of a building on it.[4]

The whites' claims to the land occupied by the Duwamish were made initially under the authority of the Donation Land Act of 1850, which provided that each adult United States citizen could receive 320 acres merely by staking a claim to it. Both husband and wife could each claim 320 acres. That same year Congress passed the Indian Treaty Act, which authorized purchase of lands from various Northwest Coast tribes and the removal of the Indians to areas that were not wanted by settlers. The treaties and the removal were backed up by the threat of military power.

George Gibbs had compiled dictionaries of various tribal languages in the Northwest and in California, and had helped negotiate treaties in Oregon and California before coming to Washington in 1853. In 1854, he negotiated the Medicine Creek treaty, and one month later the Point Elliott treaty.

An Early Capital Crime and the Removal of the Natives

The Point Elliott treaty was not the local natives' first lesson in the rule of law. Two years earlier, in 1853, several white men had lynched a native named Massachie Jim. They did this because he had allegedly killed his wife, and, more importantly, he had a good chunk of property the settlers had always admired. Eighteen months after the lynching, the first district court in King County was convened in Seattle and the three white men were tried for the lynching.

Doc Maynard was not yet a lawyer, but he was the court clerk when Territorial Supreme Court Chief Justice Edward Lander came to preside over the trial. One of the accused, David Maurer, admitted to the court that he had helped in the lynching. The court quickly appointed an attorney for him who changed the plea to not guilty. Maurer was soon thereafter acquitted, as was a second man, William Haebner. After that, J. T. Ronald, the prosecutor, gave up and dropped charges against the third, Luther Collins. Ronald would later serve as a King County Superior Court judge.

Despite this curious introduction to the rule of law, the Duwamish, for the most part, remained friendly, even through the Indian Wars of 1855-56, which visited Seattle only briefly. After several skirmishes between natives and settlers around the territory, blockhouses and a stockade were constructed in Seattle and the war ship *Decatur* arrived in the bay in anticipation of an attack by the natives. In a scene foreshadowing the deportation of the Chinese, East Indians, and Gypsies, and the internment of the Japanese in later decades, Doc Maynard helped load many of the Duwamish, and other natives still not openly hostile to the whites, onto a boat bound for the new reservations across the bay. In Chief Sealth's reluctant departure he noted the inevitability of displacement: "Tribe follows tribe and nation follows nation, like the waves of the sea. It is the order of nature, and regret is useless."[5]

On January 26, 1856, nearly one year to the day after the Point Elliott treaty was signed, several groups of natives attacked Seattle, firing from the trees still standing on First Hill and Capitol Hill. The battle began in the morning and lasted only that day; numerous buildings were destroyed, but only two whites and apparently no natives were killed. The war was soon concluded throughout the territory, and the original inhabitants of Duwamps were finally extracted from the land.

Professors in the Science of Glorious Uncertainties: Pioneer Lawyers, Judges, and Courts

While the natives were being introduced to different ideas about justice and property rights, the whites set up other rudimentary legal institutions to assure order and regularity in affairs between the settlers themselves. The first official legal ceremony reported occurred on November 19, 1852, when Doc Maynard, who had just been appointed justice of the peace, presided over the marriage of John Bradley and Mary Relyea.

The United States Congress established such structures of legitimacy when it created the Washington Territory by the Organic Act of 1853. President Fillmore appointed Isaac Stevens as governor of the territory, Edward Lander as chief justice, and Victor Monroe and O. B. McFadden as judges of the territorial supreme court. The Organic Act provided for judicial power to be vested in a supreme court, district courts, probate courts, and justice courts. The supreme court justices served both as justices of the supreme court and as judges for the three district courts.

The territorial supreme court heard all appeals from the district courts, and the supreme court's important decisions were reviewable by the United States Supreme Court. The district courts had original jurisdiction in all cases arising under the United States Constitution and the laws of the Washington Territory, so they were, in essence, both federal and state courts. The territory was divided into three judicial districts, and the supreme court justices were required to reside within the districts to which they were assigned as district judges. Seattle was usually the headquarters for the third judicial district.

The probate judges and the justices of the peace were at first appointed and later elected. The probate courts had original jurisdiction over the probate of wills and the administration of estates, and they were empowered to appoint guardians and conduct adoption and insanity hearings. The justices of the peace heard petty criminal and civil cases in which less than one hundred dollars in damages or debt was involved. They frequently heard the original complaint in a case and referred it on to a district court.

From 1854, when the first district court convened, to the time of statehood in 1889, when the court system changed considerably, the largest number of the district courts' 6,834 criminal cases involved substance abuse: selling liquor to the native people and opium smoking. Fewer than half the cases involved crimes of violence such as murder, rape, or assault, and contrary to the image of gun-slinging westerners, only 110 cases charged a defendant with exhibiting a weapon.

In the same period, the district courts heard over twenty-five thousand civil cases, the majority involving collection of debts. Disputes over property and foreclosures significantly increased after 1880. Personal damage suits, on the other hand, declined in the latter part of the period. The evidence from the early court records shows, from the beginning, that the people of Washington Territory relied heavily upon the law and the courts. Of the over thirty-seven thousand district and probate court cases recently catalogued by the Frontier Justice Records Project, 70 percent were civil, 20 percent criminal, and 10 percent probate. On a per capita basis, the civil cases rose fairly consistently with the population, while the criminal and probate cases did not keep pace.

In 1864, Seattle was still a village. It had more houses than people, its principal industry was a sawmill owned by Henry Yesler, and down the street were Doc Maynard's store and a miscellany of other shops, saloons, and two hotels. It had a livery stable and a blacksmith shop, a bowling alley, two churches, and a university.

Seattle's first telegraph line arrived in 1864, which allowed the first local newspaper, the *Gazette*, to carry news of some of the final battles of the Civil War as they occurred. When news of the assassination of President Lincoln arrived,

This Suquamish reservation Indian protest, which was held in Olympia in 1864, was an expression of Indian frustrations with the realities of reservation life and constant encroachment by the white man.

the flag on the tall fir flagpole in front of the Occidental Hotel was lowered to half staff as all of Seattle's citizens gathered for a memorial service. It would be another entire year before Seattle had its first bawdy house.

Seattle's First Houses of Legal Repute

Even though the first term of the district court in Seattle began on February 13, 1854, with Chief Justice Edward Lander presiding, it wasn't until 1864 that an attorney came to permanently reside in Seattle: John J. McGilvra. (Twenty-two years later he became the King County Bar Association's first president.) Many of the attorneys who first arrived in Seattle were either federal appointees, new graduates, apprentices, or legal practitioners from the East. They came in part to assist with the heavy federal involvement in establishing the new Washington Territory.

John McGilvra rode into town as the Lincoln-appointed United States attorney for the Washington Territory. Like Seattle's founders, he was an Illinois transplant, and while practicing in Illinois, he had been at least acquainted with Lincoln, if not the good friend that some claim.

From 1861 to 1864 his U.S. attorney offices were in Vancouver, Washington. During that time he fought at least

two losing battles. First, he tried to halt the wholesale logging of timber on government lands, logging that made many company owners millionaires at what McGilvra considered the expense of the government. Second, he tried to get the United States government, and its army, to enforce treaties and keep invading miners and others off lands that had been reserved for the native people.

Before the arrival of whites in the fur trade, the native population had had no contact with alcohol. Then the whites began to use alcohol to facilitate trade, both as an exchange item and as a way of impairing the judgment of the Indian traders. Though for many decades the native people were resistant to the detrimental effects of alcohol, after time some of them succumbed. After the decline of the fur trade, alcohol no longer served its essential economic role, and the whites passed laws to make it illegal to sell liquor to the Indians.

In his first year as United States attorney and in a pattern that was similar throughout his tenure, McGilvra vigorously prosecuted two types of cases: cutting timber on public land, a boondoggle by some loggers and local mills he

John J. McGilvra, in 1864, was the first attorney to permanently practice in Seattle, and in 1886, became the first president of the King County Bar Association.

Having spent the last two weeks upon said Reservation I have seen and know something of the real Condition of affairs there. I find that the Indian Intercourse Act is being flagrantly and openly violated in almost every particular. The lands of the Indians, even in some instances their little farms are being taken from them, their stock is being stolen, intoxicating liquor is being sold and given to them without measure, and in one instance at least one of their number was shot down in cold blood by one of these white Robers [sic]. Their condition is indeed wretched and they are almost in despair.[6]

Little action was forthcoming on either complaint.

White people were not immune to alcohol's deleterious effects either, as previous mention of Governor Stevens might attest, and a temperance movement soon arose in Seattle. Prominent among those members of the bar who joined in temperance rallies and meetings opposed to the proliferation of saloons in the 1870s were such people as Judges Thomas Burke and Roger Greene, as well as at least two attorneys, Everett Smith and Austin E. Griffiths. Both of these latter two men later became King County Superior Court judges, and Griffiths was known as the "temperance lawyer" for his help in shutting down saloons throughout the Northwest.

A year after his move from Vancouver in 1864, after completing his four-year term as U.S. attorney, John McGilvra opened a private practice in Seattle.

McGilvra was a contentious man and his voice was heard on many subjects during his nearly forty years in Seattle: issues concerning the railroads, or the ship canal between Seattle's two major lakes and Puget Sound, or the Cedar River watershed, which would supply Seattle with its water, or what parks and streets would most benefit the city. He was anti-corporate, though he was never anti-business. And he believed that treaties were legitimate contracts that should be enforced.

Late in his life, during a speech at a state bar meeting, McGilvra reminisced about the early days: "When I selected Seattle as my home, in 1864, there was no resident attorney at that place. Isaac M. Hall, afterwards probate judge, and a man of sterling qualities, with only generous faults, was the next arrival. James McNaught came next; then Waldo M. York, John Leary, Thomas Burke and a host of others until the Seattle bar now numbers about three hundred disciples of Blackstone and the later professors in the science of glorious uncertainties."[7]

By some accounts, Jaspar Johnston and Isaac M. Hall may have already been practicing law when McGilvra arrived. One historian states that Johnston opened an office in 1859, and to supplement his income he became county auditor,

was intent on stopping, and selling liquor to Indians. Of the 114 cases in his first year, 39 were for timber cutting, 39 for selling liquor, and 36 other cases involved a variety of 19 other crimes.

Not many liquor-selling convictions resulted, however, partly because the white defendants would often disappear and partly because the witnesses were often other native people and the courts were reluctant to grant their testimony any conclusiveness, especially because in all cases other than liquor-selling prosecutions Indians were completely prevented by statute from giving testimony in court.

In light of the military's unwillingness to prevent either the selling of liquor or the intrusion by whites upon Indian reservations, McGilvra demanded action in an angry letter he wrote to the army officer who he suspected was in charge of these matters:

sleeping in the little county building on the hill. C. C. Hewitt, another account has it, had practiced for a brief time in Seattle but had, by 1864, moved on to become the chief justice of the territorial supreme court. Doc Maynard and Edward L. Bridges are believed to have begun practice in 1865. Other historians believe that George N. McConaha was the first lawyer in Seattle; but there wasn't much business, so he had a partnership with J. W. Wiley, of Olympia, and practiced in both places. He spent additional time in Olympia as the chair of the first territorial legislature. McConaha's child is believed to have been the first white child born in Seattle: Eugenie McConaha, on September 18, 1853.

McConaha later drowned en route from Olympia by way of Vashon Island. A storm came up and his canoe capsized on May 4, 1854. Some later historians claim that what contributed to the drowning was McConaha's over-indulgence in spirits at the close of the first legislative session.[8]

Isaac Hall entered the city's legal community in 1864 or 1865. Though Hall was hailed by McGilvra as a man of "sterling qualities," Judge Orange Jacobs had reservations about him. Jacobs described Hall as "the wit of the [King County] bar. He possessed two abilities. The ability to utter the most witty expressions, and also the ability, I will say the 'absorbing' ability, which was his great weakness.... He was a man of dissipated habits, but they were periodical."[9]

In his autobiography, Jacobs told many stories about Isaac Hall. One occurred when Jacobs was presiding over the district court, sitting that day in Port Townsend. Prior to adjourning, Jacobs asked if there were any further matters, and Hall rose and put forth "an able and finished argument, as he always could" regarding the construction of a particular statute. Rather than hear opposition to the motion, Jacobs told Hall that the two other justices of the supreme court, of which Jacobs was the third member, had already decided the question contrary to Hall's position. Jacobs rendered his opinion in accord with the justices' unanimous interpretation, allowing that Hall could appeal if he wished to take an exception to the ruling on the record. Jacobs cautioned him that because all three justices were against him it was unlikely his appeal would be successful.

Jacobs continued his story: "It seemed to nonplus the man for a moment or two. He dropped his head in meditation. The whole bar was looking at him intently. Finally, he raised his head and said: 'Your Honor, I believe I will take the exception anyhow; the tenure of office is very uncertain in this country." As it turned out, Hall was right: when his appeal was heard, the supreme court sustained his exception and ruled in his favor.[10]

Orange Jacobs lived in Oregon for seventeen years before President Grant appointed him as an associate justice of the Supreme Court of Washington Territory. He came to

The new King County Courthouse, built in 1881, was a wood-frame structure located at Third Avenue and Jefferson Street with courtrooms above and a jail in the basement.

Seattle in 1869, after which he served in various political positions, including, after 1889, state legislator and as the city's mayor. In 1890, he was one of fifteen framers of the Seattle Charter.

Jacobs was known to lecture Hall on temperance and to lecture others about many things. McGilvra recalled that Jacobs, "having been a pedagogue in early life...sometimes lectured the boys of the bar on the subject of pleading and practice."[11] One day while Jacobs was again serving as judge in the territorial court, he began lecturing Obadiah B. McFadden, who had been one of the first two justices of the territorial supreme court, about the science of legal pleading. Jacobs intimated that a boy who had swept a law office for six months could have done better.

When Jacobs finally finished, McFadden rose and in a bland and courteous manner stated, "Your honor, when I was up on the Bench where your honor now sits, I never had any difficulty in determining what the law was, but I find it a very different matter down here."[12] Jacobs' face reddened and he called the next case.

James M. McNaught was another notable early Seattle lawyer. He and John McGilvra formed a law partnership several years after McGilvra had arrived in the city. McGilvra described McNaught as "a fastidious young man from Bloomington, Illinois, who wore eye-glasses and a plug hat, and whose dandy appearance generally made him the butt of a portion of the local press."[13]

Orange Jacobs recalled McNaught's dapper appearance:

The first place he landed was at Port Townsend. He had a stove-pipe hat and he had it on his head. Let me say that in those times nobody had character enough except a show man or a minister to wear a stove-pipe hat. McNaught with a swallow tail coat, which was no doubt a reminiscent revellation [sic] to the inhabitants of that section, with his stove-pipe hat on his head—he was near sighted, and his spectacles across his nose—in this condition he went out to view the town…as though he expected to gather a glimpse of the golden wings of a flock of angels hanging over that spiritual town. Well, everybody noticed it.[14]

Jacobs also noted that after McNaught moved to Seattle he soon changed his habit of dress to match the "barbarous habits that existed on the Sound at that time."[15]

The partnership between McGilvra and McNaught was short-lived, as were many in that era, contrary to our contemporary view that today's firms are far more transitory than those of the past. McNaught later formed partnerships with, among others, Selucius Garfielde, known as "the silver

James M. McNaught, who was described by McGilvra as "a fastidious young man…whose dandy appearance generally made him the butt of a portion of the local press," became the local counsel for the Northern Pacific and one of Seattle's most prominent lawyers.

tongued orator," and other notables such as his younger brother Joseph McNaught, John Leary, and Elisha P. Ferry.

In August 1868, when local book lovers met in Yesler's Pavilion to form a library association, McNaught was elected the association's first president. McNaught was an avid reader, especially of his contemporaries the Romantic poets. Because of his bad eyes, though, it is said that he had to hold whatever he read four inches from his face. Despite this limited eyesight, he was able to foresee the value of working for the railroads, and he soon became counsel to the Northern Pacific Railroad in the Northwest.

When he arrived in Seattle in 1867, he had barely enough money to pay for one week's board and room. When he moved to Northern Pacific's headquarters in Minnesota twenty years later, McNaught left behind a mansion that he had built for himself and his wife, Agnes, and their two children at Fourth Avenue and Spring Street in 1883 at a cost of fifty thousand dollars. (The site today is the location of Seattle's public library.)

After McNaught and his family had vacated their mansion, his old friends and associates started a new social organization there: the Rainier Club.

Another McNaught law associate, John Leary, fared equally well. Leary was a Canadian lumberman turned attorney, banker, and newspaperman. He served as president of Seattle National Bank (a part of what became Seafirst Bank) and was a founder and director of Peoples Savings Bank (now U.S. Bank of Washington). He also founded *The Post*, which later merged to become *The Seattle Post-Intelligencer*. His obituary in 1905 stated that after his arrival in Seattle in 1869, there were few major transactions in the city that did not involve Leary in some manner.

Another Leary interest was real estate. The Yesler-Leary building, near the site of one of Seattle's most infamous lynchings, was built as a cooperative venture with Henry Yesler in 1883 at Yesler's Corner (now Pioneer Square). The building was soon destroyed in the Great Seattle Fire of 1889, but it stood for a time as a symbol of Seattle's rising metropolitan ambitions.

Leary's mansion, at 1551 Tenth Avenue East, was built in 1903-04, just prior to his death. (Today it is the home of the Episcopal Diocese of Washington.) It is an example of the English Tudor Arts and Crafts Style of architecture, which was popular from the early 1900s to 1920. The original fifteen-acre site was designed as a deer park.

Thomas Burke was, arguably, Seattle's most prominent early lawyer. Following his arrival in 1875, he came to dominate the Seattle legal and business community for years. Burke's crowning achievement, getting the Great Northern Railroad's James Jerome Hill to choose Seattle as the railroad's western terminus, would not finally be attained until 1893.

When he first arrived, Burke joined the city's dominant attorney, John McGilvra, as a partner. Toward the end of his career, Burke took in, as an associate, another attorney who would dominate the legal arena in a different way in a different era: George Vanderveer.

Even though the McGilvra & Burke firm was short-lived, the two would have a lifelong association, at least in part because Burke married McGilvra's oldest daughter, Caroline.

Burke was short, stocky, and Irish. His clients included common laborers, who saw him as their champion, as well as bankers and business people, who saw him as their champion, too. He maintained a benevolent if not entirely beneficent or nonracist attitude toward other immigrants or natives, notably the Chinese, the Japanese, and the native people of the area.

He read widely, traveled widely, and was revered by most at his death on the evening of December 4, 1925. He was popularly known, even before his death, as "the man who built Seattle."

Burke's primary contribution was as counsel and promoter of the Great Northern Railroad, but he was involved in many other civic and transportation projects, including the canal between the lakes and the Seattle Lake Shore and Eastern Railroad, a concern that was supposed to link Seattle to transcontinental railroads at Spokane Falls in the east and to the Canadian Pacific in the north. Those who joined as incorporators of this effort included many Seattle notables: John Leary, David Denny, George Kinnear, and, most actively, Burke himself and another lawyer, Daniel Gilman. (Today's Burke-Gilman trail, where lawyers and law students, among many others, jog, literally follows the route of the old Seattle Lake Shore and Eastern Railroad.)

Burke was probably the most notable of John McGilvra's partners. McGilvra entered seven partnerships in his career, three while he was in Illinois and four after arriving in Seattle. This was not an unusual number at that time. Despite much talk in the press recently that lawyers no longer have any loyalty to their firms, firm-hopping seems to have long been customary.

From 1885 until the end of his active career in the law, McGilvra practiced with Elbert F. Blaine, a lawyer who became closely allied with Seattle's founding families and entrepreneurs, especially A. A. Denny and Dexter Horton. This final partnership was the most successful for McGilvra.

Though McGilvra's partners went on to represent major clients, his own practice always depended on small estate cases, bill collections, and the other sorts of matters that are even today the bread-and-butter of small firm practice: drafting wills and contracts, serving as a notary public, handling small civil cases. Bill collecting was even more

important after 1877, when he became the attorney for Dexter Horton & Company, the major banking firm in the area. McGilvra did a steady business with them, including a lot of debt collection. He retained 7.5 percent of the collection until the late 1880s, when he raised it to 10 percent.

A look at McGilvra's firm provides some insight into the history of the day-to-day practice of law in King County. By 1886, the firm of McGilvra & Blaine had begun having documents prepared on a typewriter rather than by longhand, and by 1889 they had purchased a "Yost Writing Machine" for $97.50 from a San Francisco supplier. Their offices at this time were three rooms in the Boston Block Building. An inventory of his office then shows that he had several chairs aside from his oak "tilt-back" chair, a desk, a table, a sofa, a safe, and a folding screen. McGilvra, an avid reader of poetry, put on his walls pictures of the poets Henry Wadsworth Longfellow and John Greenleaf Whittier. When he moved to Washington, McGilvra had shipped sixty-one law books; by 1890 his law office was lined with well over two hundred books, a large collection for a personal law office at the time.

Though today the McGilvra family has all but disappeared from Seattle, the name still is around: McGilvra Street, McGilvra Boulevard, and the McGilvra Elementary School, near where he built his large home beside Lake Washington, Laurel Shade. Madison Street, a route he had cleared through the forest from his home at Laurel Shade to his law office downtown, still is a major thoroughfare.

In his later years, members of the bench and bar generally referred to McGilvra as "Judge." It was purely an honorary title, McGilvra never having served on the bench.

Doc Maynard's Land Claims

McGilvra's seniority brought him some enviable cases: one of them occurred in 1875, when the city retained him and Thomas Burke to press its claim for half of Doc Maynard's donation claim.

Maynard, as had most of the other early settlers, staked his claim to the land on Elliott Bay under authority of the Donation Land Act. The act allowed all settlers to claim 320 acres, and their spouses could claim an additional 320 acres. Maynard was married when he arrived in Seattle to his first wife, Lydia A. Ricky. Though she had not accompanied him from Illinois, he filed their combined claim for 640 acres of prime Seattle real estate south of Yesler's skid road. His claim was divided between equal eastern and western halves. Much of Seattle was subsequently built on plots Maynard sold to the city from the western half of the tract.

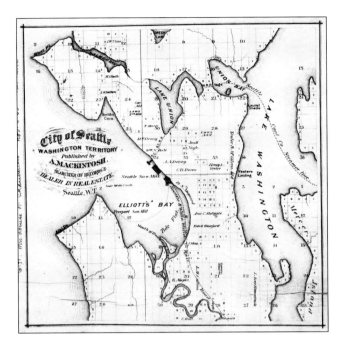

The contested D. S. Maynard claim is shown on this real estate map of the city of Seattle that was drawn during the 1870s.

Maynard divorced and remarried, and he and his second wife, Catherine Broshears, sold the remaining portion of the western half for five hundred dollars. C. H. Larrabee, another lawyer, however, bought from Maynard's first wife her right and title in the claim and began negotiating with those who held portions of the Maynard claim who thought they were buying it under clear title.

The land office ruled that Maynard and his second wife had no claim to the land, and his first wife was awarded the eastern half of the claim. The United States Secretary of the Interior affirmed Maynard's original title to the western half, but ruled that neither of his wives had any title to the contested eastern half, which was subsequently resurveyed. In the hope that this eastern half would revert to the government, the city of Seattle, in 1875, applied for the 320 acres, but the territorial land office refused the application.

The city hired Burke and McGilvra to press its claim to the eastern half, and McGilvra left, in September 1876, for Washington, D.C., to represent the city's interests. The claim was rejected there, too, on several levels. The secretary of the interior found that Seattle never was entitled to a claim for any land in the Maynard Donation Claim because, despite the city's argument that the town-site acts entitled it to the land, the site was wholly located on private land and "is not, therefore, such a town as was contemplated by the said laws."

Despite this defeat, the city in 1877 elected McGilvra to a one-year term as city attorney, and he immediately sought a legislative remedy for the decision against the city's claim. McGilvra urged both Orange Jacobs, then a territorial delegate to the U.S. Congress, and Sen. John J. Mitchell of Oregon to introduce legislation that would override the decision against the city. In 1878, the proposed act became law and confirmed that the city of Seattle had a legal existence. It was a significant contribution to the city by its first resident lawyer, John McGilvra.

Ruffian Justice—1881-1882

After thirty years of growth, Seattle was still rough-hewn: literally, in that most of its buildings were still made of wood, and figuratively, in that its residents were of all types. In an 1882 photograph by Thomas Prosch, his caption details what there was of the city's skyline: "Seattle in 1882 from Dearborn Street and Twelfth Avenue South looking Northwest. Among the buildings are Stetson and Post Sawmill, Gas Works, County Courthouse, Catholic, Episcopal, and Methodist churches, Squire's Opera House, Post Building, and Yesler's Mill Co."[16]

In 1880 Seattle's population stood at 3,553, but the strength of its economy and the rumor of a transcontinental railroad increased its numbers dramatically to 42,837 by 1890. In the eighties Seattle's industries—coal and timber and its port—all grew. Added to this mix were breweries, banks, and bakeries, retail stores, doctors' offices, and law offices.

The people, too, were increasingly divided between the early settlers, many of whom were landed, if not wealthy, by the 1880s, and the newly arrived people, who usually were neither. Looking for a better life wherever one could be found, the new arrivals often were transient and had recently emigrated from Europe, living by customs and traditions the more established citizenry could not quite condone. No doubt it was in part this increased population and activity that led many to feel a general sense of lawlessness at the beginning of Seattle's fourth decade, and some events bore the feeling out.

In October 1881, Seattle police officer David Sires was killed, and Benjamin Payne was arrested for the killing. A few months later, on January 17, 1882, at about 6:00 p.m., a respected and popular merchant, George B. Reynolds, was robbed, shot, and killed at Third and Marion, near his home. The irate citizenry, having had enough of such lawlessness, formed a vigilante committee that soon found two suitable suspects hiding in some hay on the wharf at the foot of Washington Street. Through the forceful intervention of King County Sheriff Louis Wyckoff, the committee turned the two men, James Sullivan and William Howard, over to the court.

At 10:00 the next morning the court arraigned the two suspects, but the vigilante committee had already determined their guilt. Overnight, some members of the committee had taken the shoes of the two men and found that the shoes matched mud prints near the Reynolds murder scene. Court in those days was held in Yesler Hall, also known as Yesler's Pavilion, at First and Cherry. Since the mid-1860s the Hall had been the center for local meetings and celebrations, as well as touring performers and lecturers and for court.

Judge Roger Sherman Greene had been sick with tonsillitis the night the mob first seized the two men. C. H. Hanford, his next-door neighbor, a lawyer and later a federal judge, had come late that evening to tell him of the events. Greene decided he had to be in court the next morning. When he arrived at his office that morning he met James McNaught and the two of them went to Yesler's Pavilion. Justice of the Peace Coombs was on the platform and Judge Orange Jacobs was a little to the rear of him to his right. When Coombs committed the two to jail to await trial, the mob began shouting and advancing on the suspects.

As the mob advanced, Jacobs tried to stop them, but a sheet was thrown over his head and he was held this way for about five minutes. The mob seized other officers of the court and took the prisoners out the rear entrance of the Pavilion.

The suspects were taken a short distance away, to the street next to Henry Yesler's home, on the northeast corner of Front (now First Avenue) and James streets. (Today this is where many people begin the underground tour of Seattle shortly after leaving an establishment called Doc Maynard's.) Within five minutes of being taken from the courthouse, and despite the efforts of several citizens, including Sheriff Wyckoff, the two men were hanged from the maple trees along Henry Yesler's side lawn on James Street. In some photographs of Yesler's house, the scaffolding or scantling over which the hanging ropes were thrown can be seen spanning the two trees.

Wyckoff was in the midst of the melee, living only a block from the scene, at Second and Cherry. But he was helpless. Judge Greene, too, had arrived at the scene and with his pocket knife had partly cut the rope that held up Howard. But amid screams to hang him with the others, he was seized by members of the mob and pulled aside, unable to save either of the two suspects' lives.

Later that same day the mob of two to five hundred vigilantes went directly to the jail, chopped off the bolt on the outer door, smashed the second door, beat down a third door, and seized Benjamin Payne, the man accused of murdering the police officer in October. The mob marched Payne to the same trees and hung him next to the other two. Before dying, Payne told the mob, "You hang me and you hang an innocent man."

Though steps were taken to punish the mob, the effort came to nothing. Judge Greene later said the whole incident was an "outburst of lawlessness" and "an explosion of savagery." Sheriff Wyckoff died of a heart attack three days later. The legend is that he was brokenhearted over the outburst of savagery. Seattle's first significant historian, Charles Bagley, quotes Orange Jacobs regarding the incident: "As a member of Judge Greene's Court, I feel terribly indignant; as a private citizen, I think I shall recover."[17]

Later in 1882, perhaps as a subconscious response to this outbreak of mob rule, a new county courthouse was built at Third Avenue and Jefferson Street. From the start the building had a variety of nicknames: the Tower of Despair, the Gray Pile, the Cruel Castle. In March 1883, shortly after the new courthouse went up, a meeting of lawyers passed resolutions asking Congress for additional judges for Washington Territory.

Expelling the Chinese

By the middle of the 1880s, all of the ingredients were present in Seattle to create a cataclysm: an economic downturn, particularly in the timber and railroad business in the Northwest; an established, wealthy class of early settlers and their well-to-do professional associates; an insurgent class of people, laborers or small business people, feeling closed off from the promise of wealth the land had once held; and finally, a group that could serve as a scapegoat for everyone else's perceived bad luck: the Chinese.

On one day all these people and social currents converged in the center of town, near where the city had begun: on Yesler, Washington, and Main streets, between Commercial and Third avenues.

The Chinese had been imported wholesale into the Pacific Northwest from their homeland to help build, at a discount, the great railroads as the tracks moved into the West. After the railroads were completed—the Northern Pacific in 1883, the Canadian Pacific in 1885—or were stalled, the Chinese people began to take jobs in the timber and coal industries. They settled in Seattle up and down Washington Street.

The street was bordered on the western end by the wharf, where the Duwamish had been loaded onto boats and sent to their reservations in the 1850s. It was bordered on the eastern end by Third Avenue, with a number of businesses leading up to the corner, including laundries, cigar stores, and Lew's Restaurant, where today the Washington State Trial Lawyers Association has its office. A few stores, the Wah Chong Co. and the King Cheung Restaurant, were a block over on Main Street.

Main Street, between Second and Fourth, would later be the site, separated by four decades, of the murders of leaders of the Alaska cannery workers' union: two officials were murdered in a Chinese restaurant on this street in the 1940s; two other officials, Silme Domingo and Gene Viernes, were murdered at the union's headquarters in 1981. A civil trial in the federal district court in Seattle toward the end of the 1980s resulted in former Filipino president Ferdinand Marcos and his wife, Imelda, being found liable for conspiring to kill Domingo and Viernes.

The area south of Yesler encompassed most of the area that was originally part of Doc Maynard's land claim. Historically, this was home to the poor whites. North of Yesler was for the well-to-do. When the Chinese began to reside in Seattle, they lived south of Yesler, near the railroad depot, from where many of them would be taken into the mountains by train to work on the railroads.

A growing sector of the white community, many of them laid-off timber or mining workers, joined the nationwide agitation that began in the 1880s against Chinese immigration. This movement was fueled by the Chinese Exclusion Act, passed in 1882 by the United States Congress. The act prohibited further immigration of the Chinese into the United States, except for a small group of ministers, scholars, and merchants, and prohibited the Chinese already here from becoming United States citizens. Anti-Chinese riots occurred throughout the West, in Rock Springs, Wyoming, in Newcastle, Oregon, and in Black Diamond, Squak Valley (near Issaquah), and Tacoma, Washington.

Seattle's divisions, too, were widening. White citizens who were involved with the issue comprised two groups, neither one of which could be said to be pro-Chinese. On the one hand there was the vigilante group, which advocated direct action and deportation. This group was known variously as the Anti-Chinese Party or the "Committee of Fifteen." The second faction was known as the "Law and Order" group, and its leaders advocated legal means to limit and expel the Chinese population.

Lawyers were conspicuous among the leadership in both groups. George Venable Smith and Junius Rochester were among the most vociferous of the vigilantes. They championed white laborers and their unions against the perceived incursions by the Chinese into an already saturated labor market.

Judges Thomas Burke and Roger Greene were among the most conspicuous of the Law and Order advocates. They represented the more established citizens and were primarily concerned that vigilante action would hurt the reputation and hence the economic well-being of the growing city.

Both groups met feverishly throughout the last months of 1885 and the first months of 1886, sometimes apart and sometimes contentiously together. Tensions were running so high that on November 8, 1885, the United States Secretary of War issued an order for federal troops to be sent to Seattle. When they arrived, however, they treated the Chinese almost as badly as had Seattle's citizens. Though some calm was restored finally in February, the inevitable confrontation exploded on the streets.

In the early morning hours of February 7, 1886, the vigilante group rousted from their beds hundreds of the Chinese living south of Yesler along Washington and Main, and marched them toward a ship at the end of Washington Street, the *Queen of the Pacific*, bound for San Francisco.

It was not until mid-morning that the Law and Order group was able to marshal its forces. A Chinese man had rushed to Burke's house for help. Burke contacted the United States attorney, W. H. White, and the two of them rushed toward the dock. Territorial Governor Squire happened to be staying in town at the time, and at the urging of Seattle's better citizens, the Law and Order group, he issued a proclamation warning that the people who had marched the Chinese to the ship would be punished. The vigilantes gave no ground, and they maintained control over the Chinese on the dock.

At the courthouse at Third and Jefferson, a Chinese man appeared before Judge Greene and asked that a writ of habeas corpus be issued against the ship's captain because the Chinese were being unlawfully detained aboard the ship. The judge issued the writ, and it seemed to end the possibility of the deportation for that day.

The next day the Home Guard, the local militia, met little resistance from the tired vigilantes and it took control of the dock. The Chinese went before the court of Judge Greene. Though the judge told them they need not go aboard the ship, most of them, having just marched several blocks through lines of angry Seattle citizens, were very willing to do so.

The group was then marched back to the dock. In a scene reminiscent of the expulsion of the Duwamish, and one foreshadowing the expulsion of the Japanese in the 1940s, about 350 Chinese were loaded onto the dock at the end of Washington Street. The ship, however, could only take 196. Because another ship was not expected for several days, George Venable Smith suggested that the Chinese remain on the dock.

The Home Guard decided to the contrary, and the Chinese people returned to their homes. Unfortunately, as they began to march through the angry crowd, pushing, shoving, and fights erupted. Eventually, rifles were fired and five men were wounded. One of the injured, a logger, died of his wounds several days later. Though it is perhaps apocryphal, it was rumored that Thomas Burke, somewhere in the crowd, had fired the shot that killed the logger.

Order was restored later the same day when Governor Squire proclaimed martial law, and President Cleveland made it official that evening. Though some of the vigilante group were later tried, no one was ever convicted of any crime arising from the anti-Chinese riots.[18]

Founding the King County Bar Association

Out of the social rubble that resulted from the riots rose the King County Bar Association. As early as 1870, Seattle lawyers met in informal meetings, usually to eulogize a recently deceased colleague, and John McGilvra often chaired these meetings. But no formal bar association existed. In 1884, Seattle lawyers Orange Jacobs, Roger Sherman Greene, I. M. Hall, C. H. Hanford, W. H. White, and McGilvra were appointed to formulate plans for a bar association.

But it was not until 1886, after the anti-Chinese riots, that the association was organized, in part to condemn and censure those attorneys who had participated in the vigilante action against the Chinese. It was the feeling of many in the bar that the lawyers who were vigilante leaders should be punished in some manner for their participation in the illegal riots and other activities surrounding the expulsion of the Chinese.

In keeping with this sentiment, in May 1886 charges of unprofessional conduct during the anti-Chinese riots were preferred against Junius Rochester and George Venable Smith, and their suspension from practice was demanded.[19]

The bar eventually passed a strong resolution against the anti-Chinese agitation in general and in favor of law and order. By a 37 to 1 vote, the bar passed a resolution condemning all members of the bar who had acted with the mob. George Venable Smith's was the lone dissenting vote. Afterward, Smith went off to help found a utopian community at Port Angeles. Junius Rochester continued to practice law in Seattle and later became one of the first University of Washington School of Law instructors.

The founding twenty-four members of the King County Bar Association drafted its constitution and by-laws, along the lines suggested by the informal committee in 1884. The venerable John J. McGilvra was elected the Association's first president.

In 1886, lawyers were conspicuous among the leadership of both pro-Chinese and anti-Chinese groups. Shown are members of Tacoma's Chinese community boarding a southbound Northern Pacific train.

A City and a Profession Ascendant

The Statue of Liberty, inscribed "Give me your tired, your poor, your huddled masses yearning to breathe free...," was dedicated at the entrance of New York harbor in 1886, the year the Chinese were shipped out of Seattle's harbor and the year that a band of defeated and weary Apaches, with their leader, Geronimo, surrendered to the United States government in the Southwest. On May 4, shortly after a nationwide strike for the eight-hour day, a bomb exploded in Haymarket Square in Chicago during a labor rally for the shorter workweek. On May 10, the United States Supreme Court, in a victory for the growing corporations, especially the railroads, held that a corporation had to be considered a "person" within the protections of the due process clause of the Fourteenth Amendment: that no "person" may be deprived of life, liberty, or property without due process of law.

These forces, primarily labor and capital, as well as the majority and the nation's minorities, would shape the era stretching from the founding of the King County Bar Association, in 1886, to the founding of the Seattle Bar Association, in 1906.

As legal scholar Alfred Z. Reed noted, this was a time of extreme social tension in the United States, with "widespread outbreaks of labor militancy, agrarian crusades for free silver, demands for progressive

The King County Courthouse, between Seventh and Eighth avenues and Terrace and Alder streets, on "Profanity Hill," replaced the county's wood-framed Third Avenue and Jefferson Street courthouse in 1891.

taxation of large incomes, and incessant agitation against the 'trusts.' "[1]

These disparate forces and tensions were reflected as well in the legal profession and its associations. The Law and Order faction and the lawyers within it during the anti-Chinese agitation in Seattle were convinced that those advocating forced expulsion of the Chinese were "outside agitators" stirring up the "honest working-people" of Seattle. As one attorney noted, King County Bar member George Venable Smith was "engaged in organizing communists clubs...and...was head of the anarchists troubles in Seattle."[2]

Thomas Burke wrote the first resolution passed by the King County Bar. It put forth a dream of unity in the face of disharmony (the Chinese riots):

In a community like this, where there are no privileged classes and very little fixed capital, and where all are workers in some industry or calling, and where the prosperity of one class is intimately associated with the prosperity of all, there is no occasion for jealousy, animosity, or strife, and those pestilential agitators who, abandoning every useful calling, have for months past, and at a time when Western Washington was to human view about entering an era of prosperity unprecedented in her history, devoted themselves to arraying one class against another, by lies and incendiary appeals, are the worst enemies of society, and are especially the enemies of our honest workingmen, who they are striving to dupe and trick into becoming lawbreakers, and whose livelihood they already have imperiled by frightening capital out of the country.[3]

Through Burke's words, the Bar Association, while unflinchingly recognizing class divisions, expressed at least two ideals: one, that the law, as an institution, is and should be neutral in any conflict between the classes and, two, that a harmony between the classes would bring prosperity to all. The Association had been organized in part to discipline attorneys Junius Rochester and George Venable Smith, whose actions were antithetical to those ideals. This marked a new chapter in the legal profession in Washington.

Up until the 1880s, the legal profession throughout the United States, as well as in Washington, had been informally organized. Admission to the bar had been a haphazard affair, and expulsion even more random. For most of the nineteenth century no organization anywhere attempted to speak for, or organize, the bar. Lawyers had formed associations that were mainly social. General bar groups did not arise until the last third of the century.

Similarly, Washington newspapers, during the middle decades of the 1800s, described meetings of members of the bar as social gatherings, often for the purpose of eulogizing a recently deceased judge.

In 1870, lawyers in New York City formed the first "modern" bar association. It was a reaction to "a thirty-year era of decadence and vice for the New York bench and bar."[4]

Bar associations were not necessarily open to every lawyer, and the 450 attorneys who joined the City of New York Bar Association in 1870 represented the " 'decent part' of the profession. They were primarily well-to-do business lawyers, predominantly of old-American stock."[5]

Between 1870 and 1878, eight state and eight city bar associations were founded in twelve different states, most of them with a reform ideology and a desire to improve the competency and the image of the bar. With few exceptions, however, these associations extended invitations for membership only to the "decent part" of the bar.[6]

The American Bar Association (ABA) was organized in 1878 to "advance the science of jurisprudence, promote the administration of justice and uniformity of legislation...uphold the honor of the profession...and encourage cordial intercourse among the members of the American Bar."[7] But the founding members numbered only 75 "gentlemen," out of 60,000 lawyers in the country, and by 1902 membership had risen only to 1,718.

In the opinion of the well-respected legal historian Lawrence Friedman, the ABA prior to 1900 was "never much more than a gathering of dignified, well-to-do lawyers, enjoying the comfort and elegance" of their meeting place in Saratoga, New York.[8]

With the growth of America's industrial economy came the rise of social tension. Organization became a cardinal virtue, and lawyers were quick to heed the general trend.[8] Though the anti-Chinese incidents in Seattle had provided the final impetus for organizing the King County Bar Association, it had long been in the air.

The King County Bar Association, in its first several years, took on the business of disciplining fellow lawyers, as well as the business of the legal profession. These concerns were similar to those of other bar organizations throughout the country.

In 1887, the important questions before the King County Bar included such matters as determining the best length of the terms of the probate court, implementing plans for a law library, providing rooms for bar meetings, and establishing a municipal court in Seattle. The Association decided that each of the six terms of the probate court should last two weeks and that Judge Cornelius H. Hanford, prosecutor J. T. Ronald, and attorney Harold Preston should draft a bill regarding the formation of a municipal court.[9]

The following year, at what became an annual meeting of the King County Bar Association, the members elected Orange Jacobs as the Association's second president and Judge Hanford as its vice president. Outgoing president McGilvra urged, in his address to the members, that they work to establish a law library under the auspices of the Bar Association, and he announced that he had authorized James McNaught to represent the Washington Territorial Bar at a national convention of attorneys in Washington, D.C., probably a meeting of the American Bar Association.

Jacobs would serve as president of the King County Bar Association for many years and, though he provided a welcome link with the traditions of the past, his long reign was symbolic of the bar's resistance to recognizing the major changes that were occurring in society generally and in their profession in particular.

Washington State Bar Association[10]

In 1913, the Secretary of the Proceedings for the Washington State Bar Convention wrote:

In territorial days, all cases appealed to the Supreme Court were set down for argument as of the first day of the term. For that purpose, then, or arguing their cases, lawyers were required to be on hand at the beginning of the term in which they had cases and to remain until their cases were called, waiting sometimes for two or three weeks before their cases were reached on the calendar. This gave the territorial lawyers opportunity to become well acquainted with each other…

It was during such an occasion that a group of lawyers met in the supreme court chambers in Olympia on January 19, 1888, to form the Washington Bar Association. After statehood, the name was changed to the Washington State Bar Association (WSBA). The founding membership consisted of thirty-five lawyers, and its first president was B. F. Dennison of Vancouver. It was not open to all, though the requirements for membership were probably not stringent. By the WSBA's twenty-fifth anniversary, its membership totaled about six hundred lawyers.

As the population of lawyers grew in the state, there was much debate regarding the form and purposes of the WSBA. Should its membership be made up of representatives of city and county bar associations, or should it be open to all lawyers in the state? What should its purposes be?

The Washington Bar Association, which was formed in 1888, became the Washington State Bar Association following statehood in 1889. Shown is the state's capitol during Washington's statehood celebration on November 18, 1889.

In 1914, WSBA President Ira P. Englehart, of North Yakima, argued that there were three reasons for "a strong organization":

> First, to observe and discuss proposed legislation.... Second, for social intercourse.... Third, for the government and discipline of members of the bar, to require members to live up to the ethics and traditions of the profession.

At the 1918 annual convention, a proposal was made to "amalgamate" the local bar associations with the WSBA. Specifically, all members of county and city bar associations in Washington would automatically become members of the WSBA. The local bars would collect dues and pass on a portion ($2.00) to the state bar. That proposal was supported by local bar associations, including the Seattle Bar Association, and was approved by its membership.

By 1930, as more lawyers were admitted to practice, it was proposed that the WSBA have a paid executive secretary and a paid representative in Olympia when the legislature was in session, that it have an official publication, and that it be incorporated. George McCush of Bellingham was appointed chairperson of the Incorporation Committee. That committee reported back with a draft of a Bar Association Act, to be proposed to the legislature.

This proposal was widely debated over the next few years. One issue was whether the bar should be established by legislative or court rule. Ultimately, the drafting was taken up by Seattle attorney Alfred J. Schweppe, former dean of the University of Washington School of Law. He argued forcefully and successfully for legislative establishment of the WSBA. In 1933, the State Bar Act (RCW ch. 2.48) was enacted.

During this period, Schweppe also agreed to serve, briefly, as the first executive secretary of the Association. He was soon succeeded by Clydene Morris, who had been his secretary, and she held that position until 1955, when Alice O'Leary Ralls, a bar member, became executive secretary.

Today, the WSBA has more than 17,500 active and 600 honorary and judicial members.

The Attorney's Image

The image of the attorney in the United States through the 1850s had often been either that of the aristocrat or the country lawyer. Lawyers then (and now) were fond of quoting Alexis de Tocqueville's book *Democracy in America*:

> If I were asked where I place the American aristocracy, I should reply without hesitation that it is not among the rich who are bound by no common tie but that it occupies the judicial bench and the bar.[11]

They were less apt to quote de Tocqueville's next paragraph:

> The more we reflect upon all that occurs in the United States, the more we shall be persuaded that the lawyers, as a body, form the most powerful, if not the only, counterpoise to the democratic element.[12]

The lawyer as aristocrat was probably best represented by Daniel Webster. Locally, the lawyer as aristocrat may best have been seen in James McNaught, John Leary, or Judge Roger Greene: men of property, often with an eastern education and family, who represented the business elite and who were often themselves the business elite.

The country lawyer, represented nationally in many Americans' memory by Abraham Lincoln, was probably represented best in Seattle by Lincoln's appointee and acquaintance John McGilvra and by McGilvra's successor as president of the King County Bar Association, Orange Jacobs. Both McGilvra and Jacobs had indeed been country lawyers, circuit riders who lugged books on horseback and in canoes. By 1887, the country lawyer was becoming extinct, even in outlying provinces such as Seattle. Both the image and the reality of the law and the legal profession were in transition.

Lawyers' numbers increased dramatically in the final half of the nineteenth century. In 1850 there were about 22,000 of them; after the Civil War, the Gilded Age, and the transformation of the American economy from agrarian to industrial capitalism, the number of lawyers reached 60,000 by 1880, and 114,000 by 1900.[13]

Another significant change in the legal profession was the replacement of complex and technical rules of pleading and procedure by more easily understood codes and simpler procedures for pleadings. These changes demystified the courtroom and ensured that it would not remain the province of an aristocratic few.

At the same time, however, in part as a result of the simpler procedures, and in part due to the changing nature of the economy, fewer lawyers actually practiced in court. The Wall Street lawyers, who were generally richer and enjoyed more prestige than other lawyers, rarely saw a judge except in social situations.

More and more, attorneys came from the middle class, the offspring of shopkeepers, clerks, and small business people, rather than predominantly from the families of wealth and status, as they had in the early 1800s.[14]

The legal profession became layered: some aristocrats and lawyer-politicians, some country lawyers, some corporate lawyers, and some who came from merchant families or more impoverished backgrounds, looking for status and wealth.

In Seattle, Thomas Burke was probably the best representative of the type who came from the ranks of the middle class. Eventually, he represented some of the country's most powerful capitalist interests, including James J. Hill and the Great Northern Railroad.

Burke was born of immigrant Irish parents in New York on December 22, 1849. He was the oldest of four children. His father was apparently a failed farmer and shopkeeper. After the children's mother died, the family moved to Iowa, where Burke received a standard public education for the time. He moved to Ypsilanti, Michigan, to attend the Ypsilanti Seminary, and he taught there in order to afford furthering his education. In 1870, he entered the University of Michigan in Ann Arbor, and the following year entered the department of law.

Burke was not able to complete the two-year law course, probably for financial reasons. He entered a nearby Michigan law firm, where he worked and studied law for bar admission. He was admitted to the Michigan bar close to his twenty-fourth birthday, in 1873. During his time in Michigan, he became friendly with the Bagley family, and they convinced him to move to Seattle.

The Bagley family, like Burke and his family, became well-known Seattle citizens. Clarence Bagley's histories of King County and Seattle have, for decades, been the principal sources for local historians' work.

Following Bagley's advice, Burke left Michigan for San Francisco, where he boarded a Seattle-bound ship. He arrived in May 1875, with his certificate of admission to the Michigan bar and about ten dollars. One year later he wrote to a friend that "the man with a capital of from five thousand to ten thousand dollars, if he understands or has made a study of the 'dynamics of cities,' can in a very few years make a millionaire of himself [in Seattle]."[15]

By 1878, Burke had twice been elected county judge of probate. He left public service and entered practice with John J. McGilvra, and soon thereafter married McGilvra's daughter, Caroline. He began investing heavily in local real estate and business concerns. His clients included a wide variety of people: laborers with their wage claims, businesses with their debt collections, and real estate investors with their paperwork.

He purchased a large tract of land on Lake Washington, as well as land along the waterfront, in Ballard, and elsewhere. By 1883, he was quite wealthy, and he purchased property that year at Second and Marion, where in 1891 he began construction of the Burke Building. Burke's own office and a private power plant were in the building, which stood on that site until 1960, when it was razed for the construction of the Federal Building. Arched entranceways from the Burke Building still stand today outside the Federal Building.

Judge Thomas Burke moved from Michigan to Seattle in 1875. During his career he represented some of the country's most powerful capitalists, including James J. Hill and the Great Northern Railroad.

Perhaps Burke's most lasting achievement on behalf of the city was bringing outside investment capital to Seattle, particularly intercontinental railroads and light rail for local transportation.

Burke thus was a figure who bridged the gap between the old image of the attorney as aristocrat or country lawyer and the new image of the attorney as corporate confidant and advisor. His accomplishments earned him recognition in newspapers and in several local history books as the man "who built Seattle."

Burke did much to reinforce for some, to dispel for others, the negative image of the attorney. Americans had always had, at best, an ambivalent attitude toward the law and its practitioners, whether aristocrats, country lawyers, or corporate advisors. Folk heroes such as Davy Crockett and novelist James Fenimore Cooper's character Natty Bumppo, representing natural, simple, unlettered adventurers, scorned the artificial, complex, urbane forces of civilization represented most often and aptly by the law and its institutions. Early American novelists cast their heroes into direct conflict with the law over these same issues.

In one such encounter, when the prototypical pioneer Natty Bumppo is sentenced to a month in prison for poaching and threatening a constable, he rebukes the sentencing judge by invoking the American distrust of the law:

> Talk not to me of law, [Judge] Marmaduke Temple.... Did the beast of the forest mind your laws, when it was thirsty and hungering for the blood of your own child!... I've travelled these mountains when you was no judge, but an infant in your mother's arms; and I feel as if I had a right and a privilege to travel them ag'in afore I die.[16]

Gradually, however, as the wilderness became more a place in the mind than a place just over the horizon, most Americans resolved to live, if unhappily, with the law. Cooper, in a later novel, had Bumppo express this ambivalence, too: "The law—'tis bad to have it, but I sometimes think it is worse to be entirely without it."[19]

Americans, by the final decade of the 1800s, had become resigned to having law and lawyers. Seattle's attorneys, for the most part, were prospering in this atmosphere as 1890 approached.

Seattle Burning

On June 6, 1889, though, the glow in the sky was not from the sunny future but from the Great Fire, which was destroying the entire core of what had been pioneer Seattle. The city built by the Yeslers and Maynards and Dennys consisted largely of wooden buildings connected by wooden sidewalks. The business district, between Yesler and Marion and between Front (or Commercial, today First) and Fourth, burned, with few exceptions, to the ground. Mythically at least, its cause was a boiling glue pot in a building at Front and Madison.

Henry F. McClure, a young Seattle lawyer, witnessed the destruction and wrote a letter to his brother Edgar at the University of Oregon describing what he saw:

> As I telegraphed you...I am burned completely out of office and room. About 2 o'clock yesterday afternoon the fire bell rang and after awhile I thought I would walk up the street and see if the fire would amount to anything. It was then under full headway in the block above my room.
>
> After the main portion of the town had burned the wind changed to the northeast and the fire ceased to spread east but between Fourth street and the waterfront in South

> Seattle there is not a building standing. The "PI" issued a small sheet this morning and stated that eighty acres of business property has been destroyed and forty acres more of wharfage and small establishments in addition. You can imagine the loss. There is not a dry goods store left in the city, nor a grocery store of any size, only one bank and that one recently organized, three restaurants and only two buildings used by professional men; the Colonial block in which I am writing and the Boston Block across the street from this in which is the post office and the land office. The court house and the auditor's office were saved. Newlin, Fenton and Stratton saved nearly all their books. But many a man in this city last afternoon saw all of many years' savings go up in a few minutes flames.[17]

Everyone watching the fire expected the old courthouse at the southeast corner of Third and Jefferson to go up in flames. It, too, was a wooden structure, built in 1872. The courthouse held important property records in the upstairs offices and 120 prisoners in its downstairs jail. As the fire approached, clerks began hurriedly bundling up the records, and jailers began shackling prisoners and removing them to the nearby armory.

Inside the courthouse, Judge Cornelius Hanford was holding court, a murder trial, and he did not want to adjourn and disrupt the sequestered jury, despite the smoke pouring in the windows and the deafening fire bells clanging outside.

When Hanford saw the flames in the bell tower of Trinity Church across the street, he relented. He adjourned and let the jurors leave except for a few he recruited to help save the courthouse. Judge Hanford later recalled the scene:

> We got a ladder from somewhere, but it was too short to reach the eaves of the building. It was long enough, however, so that if some of us held it perpendicular, an agile fellow could reach from the top end of the roof and pull himself up. The name of the agile young fellow who did that is Lawrence S. Booth. He climbed up and stood on the roof. It was still smoking then. In a few seconds it would have been blazing. We used the halyards on the flagstaff to haul buckets of water up to him. He dashed the water on the roof where it was smoking. The courthouse was saved.[18]

In the end, 116 acres of Seattle lay in ashes in the area that had once been a Duwamish fishing village.

From Ash to Cash

Thomas Burke had always been aware of the commercial potential of Seattle. Fourteen years after his arrival, when the core of the city as he had known it lay in ashes all around him, Burke had still not changed his opinion. Neither had many other Seattle residents.

On the day after the disaster the *Seattle Morning Journal* appealed to the "Seattle Spirit":

Yesterday was a dark day indeed in the history of the city, but the future is full of hope and every one, fortunately, seems disposed to take that cheerful view. There is no use repining when immediate action offers relief, and that is the Seattle way of looking at this fearful visitation.[19]

That same day the *Seattle Post-Intelligencer* printed a similar view:

We believe that it will be comparatively but a short time until the immediate loss which has befallen us will prove to be indirectly a great and permanent blessing. From the ruins of Seattle there will spring a new Seattle, just as from the ruins of Chicago there spring [sic] a new and mightier Chicago.[20]

To add to the upbeat mood, Washington was about to become a state, the intercontinental railroads seemed to be inevitably on their way to Seattle, the city's population was growing rapidly, business was expanding, and new banks, with capital and growing deposits, were opening wherever there was space: some opened for business in tents, while others shared space.

Since Burke had purchased property at Second and Marion, he had been planning to construct the Burke Building and another brick office building. Even before the fire, office and retail space had been in short supply. After the fire, Burke heartily went forward with the plans. With equal enthusiasm he encouraged railroads to join in building Seattle's future.

Attracting a Railroad[21]

Seattle was quick to recover from the fire, and persistent rumors of a transcontinental railroad, destined for Seattle, braced the city's spirit. Seattle had always seen itself as a logical transcontinental railroad terminus. A transcontinental railroad was essential to any city with hope of a future, because railroads were central to all commerce and travel, providing the vital link between isolated frontier towns and the rest of the world. Without the railroad, markets for Pacific Northwest timber and coal were tethered to slow maritime transportation, and without the railroad, the export potential of a city's harbor was dormant.

Within days of Seattle's Great Fire of June 1889, Judge Burke announced the construction of his "fire-proof" brick building at Second Avenue and Marion.

In 1864, Congress granted the Northern Pacific Railroad Company (NP) rights to public lands across the territories of the United States. The NP, in turn, made promises, sold stock, and began building west.

Once it was established along the Columbia River, the NP planned its western terminus north on Puget Sound. Promoters gathered money and pledges, politicians set aside prime waterfront and city lots, and rival cities around Puget Sound began a bidding war. Seattle's few thousand citizens offered the NP sixty thousand dollars cash, plus 2,500 acres of raw land, 450 city lots within one mile of the city's waterfront, and other rights-of-way. Tacoma presented itself as a developer's dream thirty miles closer than Seattle to the Columbia River, and its offer prevailed.

Building the railroad remained a major challenge, and it was not until 1873 that the NP steamed into Tacoma, in the rain, deep in debt.

On the rebound in 1874, Seattle's citizens, including John McGilvra and James McNaught, formed their own railroad company, the Seattle & Walla Walla (S&WW). They planned an inter-mountain line that would connect Seattle's waterfront commerce to Renton's coal mines and then go on to the agriculture-rich region east across the Cascade Mountains. Once there, the planners hoped to link up with the Union Pacific, or another transcontinental railroad.

Everybody turned out for the May Day ground-breaking of the S&WW line and helped lay three miles of track that day. Three years later the rest of the sixteen-mile narrow-gauge line to Renton was completed. From there the railroad

The south King County town of Franklin was one of several coal towns serviced by the Columbia and Puget Sound Railroad, which began in 1874 as the Seattle & Walla Walla Railroad.

eventually linked the coal mines of Black Diamond, Newcastle, and Franklin with a steamboat landing on the Duwamish River, south of Seattle. The S&WW was never completed to Walla Walla, but it did become profitable.

In 1880, Henry Villard, through the Oregon Improvement Company, purchased the line as part of his plan to take over the NP, and the S&WW was renamed the Columbia and Puget Sound (C&PS). Villard promised Seattle's citizens that he would lay standard-gauge track parallel to that of the existing line, and link Seattle to the outside world. But the nation's economy plunged, the prices of lumber and coal fell sharply, and Villard's plans, and his railroad, began to rust.

Still trying to attract a mainline rail service to Seattle, the city granted to the NP the rights-of-way along its waterfront in 1882. Other rights were acquired from individual property owners. By the time the owners who were willing to grant the rights had been separated from those who were not, the completed right-of-way was a winding, tortured affair that became known as the Rams Horn Right of Way. The NP's Seattle line operated for only a month before it stopped abruptly, in part because of the NP's poor financial condition.

C. H. Hanford described the situation as exasperating:

Villard, who promised to give the City railroad service, was shorn of power; that service was discontinued; the grant of the rams horn right of way was irrevocable and it was regarded as a nuisance; residents of the City had parted with control of the narrow guage [sic] railroad and there was no hope of any extension of it beyond coal mines in King County....

Despite frustration, Seattle boomed, and as it grew it became a real threat to Tacoma and to the NP's vast real estate holdings in that city. NP withheld scheduled services to Seattle and, for a time, all service was stopped. Those bound for Seattle walked, or took passage on Puget Sound steamers. Mail took longer than necessary to reach Seattle, and lumber cut in Seattle's mills cost more to ship east by rail. All of this ferment was fertile ground for lawyers on both sides of the issues. James McNaught represented the Northern Pacific, Burke represented the Great Northern and others.

The rail link south was never satisfactory. In 1883, Burke and fellow attorney Daniel Hunt Gilman proposed that the city snub Tacoma and the NP and look northward to link up with the Canadian Pacific Railroad, which had just completed its transcontinental link that year with Vancouver, British Columbia.

Thomas Burke had become professionally, financially, and personally involved in Seattle's quest for a railroad. He, along with John Leary and others, joined Gilman in 1885 in a plan to build the Seattle, Lake Shore, and Eastern Railroad (SLS&E) to make the northern link. They raised $1 million from eastern financiers.

Access to the city from the north was assured by the creation of Railroad Avenue, an idea of C. H. Hanford's and Judge Burke's. The Northern Pacific had not taken quite all of the rights-of-way remaining along the waterfront, and the SLS&E was able to obtain these rights in order to build its tracks into the city. The start-up company built a passenger terminal at the foot of Columbia Street.

From Seattle the track ran along the waterfront, through Interbay to Ballard, then east along the north end of Lake Union, then along the south and east sides of the University of Washington campus, around Union Bay to a logging town known as Yesler (which became Laurelhurst), then along Lake Washington and Lake Sammamish to Gilman (now Issaquah). It is this track, known as the Burke-Gilman trail that many run and jog along today.

Seattle's attempts to seduce a transcontinental railroad continued. Finally, in late 1889, James J. Hill, of the Great Northern, at the encouragement of his agent, Thomas Burke, chose Seattle as the railroad's western terminus. In July 1893, the first Great Northern train steamed into the city, and the link to the rest of the world was complete.

Seattle's Attorneys Prosper

Only two years after the fire that destroyed Seattle, *The Spectator* proclaimed that the law profession was doing very well indeed:

ATTORNEYS WHO MAKE MONEY
There are 307 lawyers in Seattle. Just think of it! Three hundred seven lawyers in a town of less than 50,000 people; or about one lawyer to every 170 population, men, women, and children. Judging from this, the popular impression would be that the lawyer business was slightly overdone, and that not very many of them can be deriving very handsome income from the practice of their profession. But this is a mistake. The truth of the matter is, that while a large number of them do not make anything at all, there are many who are in receipt of handsome incomes.

Lawyer H. G. Sutton, who became a partner with Day Karr and George Gregory, is shown in the firm's office in the early 1900s with his secretary, Sadie Miller.

Although there are not more than fifty thousand people in Seattle, it is a great legal centre. There are a great many admiralty cases to be tried, and an extensive Land Office business. Then all the legal business of King County is done in the city, and as a large number of the principal corporations of the State have their headquarters located here, they offer very profitable employment for a number of attorneys.

There are a number of firms in this city, who have an annual income of ten thousand dollars and over. Among them is the firm of Burke, Shepard & Woods, composed of Thomas Burke, T. R. Shepard, and Andrew Woods. They do a large corporation practice, and among other wealthy companies are attorneys for the Great Northern Railroad.[22]

The article continued to chronicle many firms in Seattle in the "over ten thousand dollars per year" bracket, including many firms that had been founded as early as 1879 and that have continued in existence in some form or another up until the present.

The oldest firm at the time, one that existed into the 1980s, was that of Struve & Leary, consisting of Henry G. Struve and John Leary. Struve, like his partner Leary, was interested in banking and real estate. This firm is believed to have been founded in 1879. In 1891, it was known as Struve & McMicken. The *Spectator* article notes that the firm members "are attorneys for several of our largest corporations and are kept busy almost entirely with their affairs." The firm eventually became known as Schweppe, Krug & Tausend before it was dissolved in 1989.[23]

The Preston Thorgrimson firm was founded around 1885 as Carr & Preston. Its founding principals were Harold Preston and E. M. Carr. *The Spectator* noted that this firm too had a large commercial practice and represented, among others, Puget Sound Savings Bank, which in 1992 became a part of Key Bank.

McGilvra & Blaine was formed in 1885 by John McGilvra and E. F. Blaine. In 1891, the firm was renamed Blaine & DeVries, and it represented Dexter Horton & Company (now Seafirst Bancorporation) and other businesses. Later, in the 1960s, it became known as Elvidge, Watt, Veblen, Tewell & Venables. It conducts its business today as Tewell & Findlay.

Richard A. Ballinger and Alfred Battle founded Ballinger & Battle in 1897. Ballinger went on to be mayor of Seattle in 1904-06 and the first president of the Seattle Bar Association in 1906. Later, he was United States Secretary of the Interior. Today the firm is known as Helsell, Fetterman, Martin, Todd & Hokanson.

Judge Charles H. Paul researched the history of several of Seattle's oldest law firms as part of his address to the 1968 Lawyers' and Judges' Luncheon. His list included the firm of Pritchard & Grosscup, which was founded in 1890 and merged in 1900 to become Peters and Powell. Today the firm is known as Lane Powell.

W. H. Bogle began his practice in 1895, in a depressed Tacoma economy, in partnership with Charles Richardson and in 1898 they moved their practice to Seattle. Near the turn of the century Bogle became ill with Tuberculosis and moved to the dryer climate of Yakima, Washington, where he practiced law with Harry Rigg. Rigg became a superior court judge, and with renewed health Bogle moved to Seattle in 1905. In 1906 Bogle joined with Thomas Hardin and Charles Spooner and their firm became known as Bogle, Hardin & Spooner. Bogle became an expert in maritime law as did his son Lawrence, who joined the firm shortly after its founding. Today the firm of Bogle & Gates is nationally recognized for its maritime law expertise.

Many who practiced law in Seattle often wished they had not—after having to climb the steep hill up to the new courthouse built around 1888 and occupied sometime in 1891. The new courthouse was between Seventh and Eighth avenues and Terrace and Alder streets (approximately where Harborview Medical Center stands today), and most of the attorneys had their offices much farther down the hill, along Second Avenue. Torn down in 1930, the courthouse once dominated its portion of the Seattle skyline with an elaborate dome and Greek temple decorations. The hill upon which it sat became known as Profanity Hill because of the words the attorneys blurted out as they climbed it.

Judge Paul remembered the indignity of climbing Profanity Hill:

There was, it is true, a cable car but, even though you caught it, the last trek up a precipitous dirty slope carrying a dozen strap-bound volumes, mostly out-of-state reports, was, I can tell you, not compatible with the dignity which I thought I had acquired by passing the bar examinations.

The Law School

A key development in the late 1800s was the organization of corporations as essential institutions in the industrial economy. Out of this grew a general social trend to organize and to institutionalize other aspects of society.

One institution that grew during this period was the professional school: pharmaceutical schools, medical schools, and law schools. Law schools were a good way of furthering the bar's often-stated goal of ensuring competence in the legal field by requiring some standard of legal education. As early as 1879, the American Bar Association's Committee on Legal Education and Admissions had advocated an expansive program for standardization of legal education.[25]

Many of the early practitioners in Seattle and King County had received some sort of formal legal education in the East or Midwest, but many others became attorneys by the apprentice system, working in a law office as a law clerk and "reading" the law in preparation for some sort of bar admission procedure. This was similar to the system in England for barristers and solicitors and, in fact, was the way the overwhelming majority of attorneys were trained in the United States prior to the 1860s.[26] Even the elite lawyers of the East, working in Wall Street firms in the 1890s, though they may have graduated from Yale College or Harvard Law School, would often spend the first few years afterward working for a firm to learn practical skills.[27]

The more typical lawyer, however, often began practice with little or no institutional training. Abraham Lincoln's legal training came this way, and he wrote that "the cheapest, quickest and best way" to become an attorney was to study the Constitution and "read Blackstone's *Commentaries*, Chitty's *Pleadings*, Greenleaf's *Evidence*, Story's *Equity* and Story's *Equity Pleading*, get a license, and to the practice and still keep reading."[28]

It was a system that depended heavily upon books, and books in the West were often hard to come by. Even when books were available, the lawyers and judges who rode the circuit of the courts often had the unenviable task of packing along a great number of the heavy volumes mentioned by Lincoln. Law libraries were a rarity, and when several sizable private collections began to develop in Seattle, civil cases were often transferred to the city from the remote areas in

The University of Washington School of Law officially opened on this site in September 1899, on the original site of the university in downtown Seattle.

order to be closer to the books. Of the early lawyers, both Burke and McGilvra began to develop good collections.

Perhaps it was the need to house such collections, as well as regulating legal training and ensuring competence, that led local attorneys to advocate a law school at the Washington Territorial University at Seattle. In the entire country there were only fifteen law schools in 1850; by 1890, there were sixty-one, and in the final decade of the nineteenth century, forty more were opened.

Still, nowhere was a law degree or a college degree required to practice law between 1850 and 1900, and the usual degree, a bachelor of laws, was a minor undertaking compared to today's requirement, which is essentially a postgraduate degree. Most of the law schools in the final half of the nineteenth century did not require any prior college work for admission, and many law schools merely existed alongside their parent institutions. Most law programs were two-year courses, and the faculty were usually members of the local bar, teaching part-time. Full-time instructors were rare.[29]

In Washington, as early as 1885, the Board of Regents of the Washington Territorial University in Seattle established a department known as the Washington Law School, with a degree of bachelor of laws to be conferred upon the successful completion of a two-year course.[30] The faculty was

to consist of some familiar names: Roger Greene, Orange Jacobs, Thomas Burke, and J. C. Haines, as well as the president of the university, L. L. Powell, Elisha P. Ferry, Elwood Evans, and John B. Allen. The sole instructor who was to receive compensation was another familiar name: Junius Rochester.

This first law school does not seem to have prospered, and not a single degree was awarded during the life of the school, which ended in 1894, when the Board of Regents rescinded the resolution that had founded the school.

But the bar did not give up on the idea. In the same year that the first school was abolished, representatives of the Washington State Bar Association appeared before the Board of Regents and discussed details of a proposed law college, as part of the University of Washington. It was another year, however, before the board adopted a resolution in favor of the new law school. It was to operate out of the old University Building at Fourth and Union, today the site of the Four Seasons Olympic Hotel.

Another four years passed before members of the Washington State Bar Association and the Board of Regents met at the Seattle Chamber of Commerce's building to again consider a law school. This meeting passed a resolution to

John T. Condon, first dean of the University of Washington School of Law

found a department of law at the University of Washington and granted twenty-five hundred dollars for that purpose.

A week later the board selected John T. Condon of Seattle to be the dean of the school, at an annual salary of fifteen hundred dollars. The school was housed in two rooms in the old University Building at Fourth and Union.

The law school was officially opened in September 1899. The faculty included Dean Condon and George McKay, as well as Burke and Allen. To this list was added Cornelius H. Hanford, judge of the United States Circuit and District Court; John T. Hoyt, former chief justice of the Washington Supreme Court; and Theodore L. Stiles, another former chief justice. Also teaching were the following, many of whom were Seattle attorneys: James Hamilton Lewis, Edward Whitson, Charles E. Shepard, Frederick Bausman, William Hickman Moore, George E. Wright, John Arthur, John W. Pratt, Victor E. Palmer, Tyman O. Abott, and William A. Peters.

The first class consisted of twenty-six students, including two men who would become superior court judges and eventually Washington Supreme Court chief justices: Walter M. French and Walter B. Beals. Beals married a law school classmate, Othelia Carroll, and during World War I she was elected justice of the peace of King County, though she resigned at the war's conclusion, when the "boys" returned home. Vivian M. Carkeek, a professor at the law school in the 1930s, was also in the first class.

Class photographs of these early students still hang along the walls of the current law school. The photographs show that in 1901 two other women joined Othelia (Carroll) Beals in the small law school: B. Rosenbaum and Adele M. Parker. In the class of 1902 was an African-American, W. M. Austin. Austin and Parker were joined there by a man who was probably Japanese, T. Yamashita, and by another woman, Grace Mitchell. By 1903, however, Adele Parker is the only woman photographed, by 1904 E. H. McGee is the only person of color, and from 1905 forward for many years, the photographs usually reflect a white male exclusivity.

The school itself was literally on the move. It remained only a short while in the old university building, soon moving to a dormitory on the same grounds. In 1903 the law school left the center of town, as had its parent, and moved to the present university campus, first occupying the attic of Denny Hall. The cornerstone of Denny Hall had been dedicated in 1894 by Phi Beta Kappa graduate Adele Parker, who later graduated from the university's School of Law.

The requirements for admission into the law school when it first opened were that the candidate either satisfactorily pass an exam on required subjects or have a certificate of graduation from high school or college. These requirements remained the same through 1906, and the course was two years long. To graduate in 1905 the student had to both pass an exam on the law and have a standing in general scholarship equal to that of a sophomore in the college of liberal arts. In 1906 this standing was raised so that one had to rank as a junior in the college of liberal arts. A thesis of at least forty pages was also required for graduation in these years.

Tuition fees in 1899 were twenty-five dollars per year in advance or ten dollars per term in advance, or five dollars per course. From 1902 to 1907, the fee was twenty dollars per semester, with a five dollar graduation fee.

The American Bar Association had long been concerned about institutionalizing and standardizing legal training, and throughout its first several decades announced many recommendations for this training. In 1896, the ABA approved the requirement of a high school diploma and two years of law study for bar admission, and by 1897 it recommended that the period of study be three years. In 1899 the

ABA called for the organization of "reputable law schools," and as a result in 1900 the Association of American Law Schools (AALS) came into existence. It and the ABA continued to promulgate increasingly higher standards for a permissible legal education. The continued pressure on states to adopt these standards has been viewed by several social historians as an effort to control the market rather than to control the quality of lawyers.[31]

The efforts to raise standards, standards that involved more pre-law education as well as a law degree itself, all of which cost money, were primarily concerned, in social historian Jerold Auerbach's analysis, with keeping out Jews, blacks, immigrants, and in so doing, radicals.[32] Auerbach quotes the president of the Carnegie Foundation deploring the low bar admission standards as opening the gates of the law to "the poorly educated, the ill-prepared, and the morally weak candidates."[33] Perhaps this, better than anything, explains the absence of photographs of women and people of color in the class photographs of many law schools after 1905.

African-American Attorneys[34]

Shortly after the Civil War and the passage of the federal Civil Rights Act and the Fourteenth and Fifteenth amendments, life for African-Americans in the United States generally improved. In Seattle the Original Georgia Minstrels, a black traveling musical show, stayed at the posh Occidental Hotel in 1876, a clear sign that discrimination in Seattle was minimal.

Washington became a state in 1889, just twenty-four years after the end of the Civil War. Upon adoption of the Washington Constitution in 1890, the Public Accommodations Act became effective. The act was to guarantee to all people the equal enjoyment of all public transportation, theaters, public amusement facilities, and restaurants. The act in fact criminalized discrimination, making it a misdemeanor for a person to deny public accommodation to another person on the basis of "race, color, or nationality."

Slowly, however, the rights granted by federal and state legislatures were being taken back—directly or through segregation laws known as "Jim Crow." Whites who wanted to go back to the pre-Civil War days made frenzied and racist attacks. A South Carolina politician stated it succinctly: "Whenever the Constitution comes between me and the virtue of white women of the South, I say to hell with the Constitution."[35]

Historian Lerone Bennett, Jr., has described the retrenchment in this way:

> Brick by brick, bill by bill, fear by fear, the wall grew taller and taller. The deaf, the dumb and the blind were separated by color. White nurses were forbidden to treat Negro males.

University of Washington law school class of 1901

> White teachers were forbidden to teach Negro students. South Carolina forbade Negro and white cotton mill workers to look out the same window. Florida required "Negro" textbooks and "white" textbooks to be segregated in warehouses. Oklahoma required "separate but equal" telephone booths. New Orleans segregated Negro and white prostitutes. Atlanta provided Jim Crow Bibles for Negro and white witnesses.
>
> In the last decade of the nineteenth century and the first decades of the twentieth, the wall went higher and higher. The thrust came from fear, from economic competition and political needs, from frustration, from an obsession with the cult of White Womanhood. In only two other countries— South Africa and Nazi Germany—have men's fears driven them to such extremes.[36]

In 1895, the retreat from equality was in full force in Washington, too. In that year Washington's Public Accommodations Act was amended, on the one hand adding eating houses and barber shops to the list of public accommodations, but on the other hand completely omitting the teeth of the act: the criminal penalty provision. Throughout the period, however, sporadic incidents of discrimination were reported, usually the denial of services to black people. Operators of restaurants were the chief offenders, though hotels continued to accommodate nonwhites. But from 1898 on, each term of the Washington State Supreme Court heard a restaurant discrimination case.

Into this atmosphere came the first person of African descent to practice law in Washington, Robert O. Lee. He was granted admission to the bar here on March 20, 1889. He had graduated from Columbia Law School in South Carolina and had taken postgraduate law at Badden Institute in North Carolina. Following in the footsteps of other Seattle residents, the Dennys and the McGilvras, Lee moved, after finishing his legal training, to Lincoln's hometown, Springfield, Illinois, where he was admitted to practice in the superior court. He soon thereafter left for Seattle. The record on Lee is scant after his admission to the Washington bar in 1889.

By 1891, another black lawyer, Allen Garner, was carrying on a thriving civil and criminal practice. He was active in Republican politics in the area, and in 1892 he moved for the admission of another black attorney, James A. Scott. Scott and Garner shared office space at 612 Second Street in 1892.

Conrad Rideout arrived in Seattle not to promote his law business but to promote a group of wealthy farmers from the South who sought to immigrate to the Northwest. Rideout had graduated from Ann Arbor University (in Arkansas), and beginning in 1882 had served as a Democratic legislator for two terms in the Arkansas legislature.

Rideout married a widow who had returned from the Alaska Gold Rush with a sizable amount of valuable gold dust. Shortly thereafter, in 1897, Rideout and another prominent African-American attorney, J. E. Hawkins, became promoters and board members of the Seattle and Klondike Grubstake and Trading Company.

While practicing law and promoting business in Seattle for nearly ten years, Rideout often sought political office, but was frustrated in his efforts. In 1899 he left for South Africa "to attend to business for a syndicate" he represented. By May 1900 Mrs. Rideout had returned to Seattle, but what happened to Mr. Rideout has not been discovered.

John Edward Hawkins came to Seattle in 1890 and worked as a barber. But Hawkins had other hopes and ambitions, and from 1890 to 1895 he studied law at night with Judge Isaac M. Hall, W. A. Slater, and others. On May 18, 1895, he was admitted to practice law before the King

County Bar—the first black person to be admitted to practice in Washington without having had prior certification elsewhere.

At first, Hawkins shared an office with Conrad Rideout. They often worked on cases together, and one of the better-known ones was the defense of Willie Holmes, a Franklin, Washington, miner convicted and sentenced to death for the fatal shooting of another miner. The case became well known through Hawkins' and Rideout's efforts, but their work to save him from hanging failed.

Courts at the turn of the century were often attended by the public, and Hawkins was a popular personality among those who gathered. He was known to be eloquent and humorous, and was a favorite of many. Hawkins was one of the first practitioners of sports law, representing many people from the sporting world, especially boxers.

Hawkins became a very strong voice for civil rights during the closing years of the nineteenth century. The hostile racial environment was again reflected in the late summer of 1901, when many local citizens launched an expulsion campaign against Gypsies and when in that same year twenty white boys attacked a young Japanese boy at the foot of Beacon Hill.

Hawkins was often at the forefront of the legal fight against discrimination. Many times he defended the rights of black people to be served in restaurants, public baths, and theaters. One such suit was based on the federal civil rights law as amended in 1895. The jury awarded only one dollar in damages to the plaintiff, but Hawkins was undeterred: "It's the principle, not the damages that we are after."

William McDonald Austin entered the University of Washington law school shortly after its opening in May 1899. He was the first African-American to graduate from the university with a bachelor of laws degree. He had moved from Barbados to San Francisco while a boy and in 1899 came to Seattle to study law. He became the university's junior class treasurer and graduated in 1902, after completing a thesis entitled "The Civil Rights Act." In October of 1902 he went to the Philippines to practice law.

An interesting African-American who had an avid interest in the law but who never himself practiced it, though two of his grandsons did, was John Thomas Gayton. He came to Seattle in 1889 as a servant to a white family. By the time of his retirement in 1954, he was the federal court librarian. He was born in Benton, Mississippi, about 1866, the son of former slaves. He remained in the employ of the white family with whom he came to Seattle for a while, but eventually worked as a painter, painting contractor, bellboy, waiter, and headwaiter at the Rainier Club, where he undoubtedly served many of the prominent attorneys of the day. The Rainier Club hired him as its first black steward in 1901.

In the evenings he studied bookkeeping at Wilson's Modern Business College and studied law, though he never took the bar examination. Two of his grandsons, Thomas and Gary Gayton, practiced law in Seattle, and one of them, Gary, still does—in the Columbia Center.

In 1904, John Thomas Gayton took a cut in salary to accept appointment as a messenger, then bailiff, for the United States District Court, when that court had only existed in Washington for eighteen years. In August 1933, Gayton became the federal court librarian, and he served in that capacity, helping innumerable attorneys and law clerks, for over twenty years. He was a familiar figure at the United States Courthouse, wearing a flower in his lapel and his pince-nez attached to a black silk cord. By the time he retired, in 1954, he had served under every federal judge to preside since Washington had been admitted to statehood.

Women and the Bar and the Bar against Their Vote

Women practiced law and graduated from the University of Washington's law school long before they had firmly secured the right to vote in state or national elections. Women's suffrage in Washington did not occur in a linear fashion. The vote was given to and taken away from women many times from the 1850s to 1910, when the electorate finally granted it for good.

In 1854, Arthur Denny unsuccessfully advocated women's suffrage in the first territorial legislature. Between 1867 and 1871 a statute was occasionally interpreted to allow women the vote, but in 1871 the territorial legislature decided firmly that women could not vote except in school elections. The Constitutional Convention submitted the question to a general election, and women lost by a margin of 3 to 1. Finally, in 1883 the territorial legislature enacted a statute that granted the vote to women, and the supreme court upheld the statute in 1884. But the court overturned the statute in another case, in 1887. The legislature reinstated it that same year, and a year later the supreme court once again overturned the statute.

Following the twisted and tangled fate of women's suffrage in early Washington was enough to make one drunk. And that was one of the problems: suffrage became entangled with prohibition. Susan B. Anthony, a national leader for suffrage, preached temperance at the same time, striking even greater fear in the hearts—or at least the appetites—of many men. In Washington, one of the supreme court cases that overturned suffrage was apparently contrived by saloon-keepers in Spokane specifically out of fear that if women were allowed to vote they would vote for prohibition.[37] The court

decided that the United States Congress had intended only to enfranchise men and that the territorial legislature had no power to do more than that.[38]

The fight continued, led by May Arkwright Hutton on the east side of the Cascade Mountains and by professional organizer Emma Smith DeVoe and writer Abigail Scott Duniway on the west side. Because of the political problems with combining suffrage and prohibition, Duniway argued to the suffragists at Washington's Constitutional Convention that they should separate the two issues. The convention declined to make women's suffrage a right in the new constitution, but did place the issue before the general electorate—men—and it lost.

Over the next twenty years the battle continued as the role and image of women changed along with society in general. No doubt some of those who contributed to the changing role of women in Washington were the women attorneys who practiced here in the early years. In an address to the Seattle Bar Association in 1925, Judge C. H. Hanford recalled early members of the bar and remembered that the first woman to practice in Washington was Lelia J. Robinson. She had been refused admission to the bar in Massachusetts, so she came here in 1884, while the women's suffrage law was in force.[39]

Hanford reported that Robinson was treated with courtesy and respect. Judge Roger Greene appointed her to defend a penniless Chinese man charged with smuggling, and Hanford was the prosecutor in the case. When he lost to Robinson, he recalled, the joy of the many women spectators in the courtroom was irrepressible. Hanford reported that Robinson was also very deft in cross-examining witnesses.

A woman's right to vote first became a Seattle issue when Arthur Denny presented the idea to the first Territorial Legislature in 1854. It did not become a matter of state law until 1910.

Adele Parker was one of the first women students in the University of Washington School of Law in 1901. After graduation, she was admitted to the bar, practiced law, and later became a state legislator and teacher.

Lelia Robinson apparently soon returned to Massachu-setts to work on breaking down the rule excluding women from the legal profession in that state.

Mary Leonard also practiced in Washington in 1884, being admitted to the territorial bar on October 23 of that year after a panel of three lawyers examined her credentials and found her "sufficiently proficient."[40] Prior to coming to Washington she had spent eleven months in jail in Oregon awaiting trial for the murder of her husband. She was acquit-ted of the charge in 1878.

The first woman to practice law and leave a lasting mark on the legal community was Judge Reah Whitehead. She was admitted to the Washington bar in 1893 and in 1914 became one of the first women judges in the nation when Seattle voters elected her to the Seattle Justice Court. She served in the capacity from 1914 to 1949.

Othelia Carroll was one of two women in the first class at the University of Washington law school in 1899. Upon her graduation in 1901 she practiced law with her father and brother. She was elected a justice of the peace in Seattle after serving in that position by appointment when her brother left the job to serve in World War I. She married a classmate from law school, Walter Beals, who later served on the King County Superior Court bench and the Washington Supreme Court.

Adele Parker was Carroll's classmate in the first class at the law school and is pictured in the classes of 1901, 1902, and 1903. She had arrived in Seattle in 1886 from Whitehall, Michigan, and lived in Seattle for the next seventy years until her death on May 9, 1956.

Parker was notable even before she attended law school. She gave a speech at the laying of the cornerstone of Denny Hall on the University of Washington campus in 1894; the hall would later house for a time the university's law depart-ment. Her portrait appears on the murals at the university's student union building.

Parker married Charles Enoch Allen Bennett and they spent their honeymoon in Siberia. Before returning, however, Parker spent two years, 1922-23, as the Moscow correspon-dent for the International News Service. Upon returning to Seattle she was very active in the women's suffrage movement, serving as president of the Equal Suffrage League before enactment of the Nineteenth Amendment. After her return, she also took up the practice of law.

She remained active in the Seattle Bar Association her entire life, and in addition to practicing law she taught political economy and civil government at Broadway High School and was the executive secretary of the Seattle High School Teachers League.

From 1935 to 1936 she served a term in the state legislature from the 37th District. She had been elected on a campaign to exclude homes from taxation, to exact uniform income taxes on incomes over four thousand dollars, to establish an old-age pension, and to provide adequate educational revenues.

Nothing remains in public records of the two other women in those early law school classes that Parker and Carroll attended, B. Rosenbaum and Grace Mitchell. They are but faces in photographs of the classes of 1901 and 1902.

Finally, a Library and a New Bar Association

When John McGilvra left the presidency of the King County Bar Association in 1889 to Orange Jacobs, McGilvra had urged the members to organize and establish a law library under the auspices of the Bar Association. In 1895, finally, attorneys organized the Seattle Law Library Association, which was funded with twenty-five thousand dollars from the sale of capital stock in the association. Its trustees included the president of the King County Bar Association, Orange Jacobs, as well as T. W. Gordon, R. W. Emmons, John Arthur, and John Battle. In April 1896 the association bought the law library of Henry M. Herman of Spokane. The library had over two thousand volumes and was a firm foundation for Seattle's law library. After this initial purchase, books quickly accumulated.

In 1902 Thomas Burke retired from practicing law, giving up his retainer as western counsel for the Great Northern Railroad and dissolving the last of his several firms, Burke, Shepard & McGilvra. The McGilvra who was practicing with Burke then was Burke's brother-in-law and John McGilvra's son, Oliver McGilvra. In 1903, John J. McGilvra, the man whose law career spanned nearly the entire history of Seattle, died. By that year Orange Jacobs was seventy-five, though he would live another eleven years and preside over the King County Bar Association until his death on May 21, 1914. The old pioneer attorneys were nevertheless giving way to the new.[41]

Accordingly, in the summer of 1906 a new bar association was formed, the Seattle Bar Association. Its constitution echoed the purpose clause of the ABA's constitution when it stated that it was "established to maintain the honor and dignity of the profession of the law, to increase its usefulness in promoting the due administration of justice, and to cultivate social intercourse among its members."

One of the primary reasons for founding the new bar association, according to Seattle Bar acting chair Fred Bausman, was "to restore the traditional standard of the bar of King County." Though the King County Bar Association still existed, Bausman stated, "the old bar association had many members whose methods are peculiar."

The Seattle Bar Association elected Richard A. Ballinger as its first president, W. A. Peters as its first vice president, Walter A. McClure as its secretary, and as treasurer, George Ladd Munn. Ballinger had just finished a term as mayor of Seattle. Walter A. McClure was the brother of Henry McClure, who had written the letter to Edgar McClure regarding the Seattle fire. Edgar joined Walter and Henry in Seattle after the fire, and the three of them thereafter maintained one of the largest law offices in Seattle. Seattle had survived, and its attorneys had flourished.

The School of Law moved to the current University of Washington campus in 1903. Shown is the university's library in the rafters of Denny Hall.

GROWTH AMID TURMOIL AND WAR

The earthquake that destroyed San Francisco in 1906 was emblematic of the periodic eruptions that resulted from the social tensions that had been mounting throughout the Gilded Age of the Nineties. These recurring eruptions would mark the next several decades internationally, nationally, and locally.

Seattle: "The City of Lawyers"

It is unlikely, however, that any of the fifty attorneys who gathered at the city's Chamber of Commerce offices on June 27, 1906, to form the Seattle Bar Association (SBA) imagined that over the next several decades they would witness social eruptions that would sharply divide them against one another: massive union organizing, World War I, the Seattle General Strike, Prohibition, the Stock Market Crash, the Depression, and the eventual internment of the Japanese. But each of these events had a profound effect upon the profession, the Association, and the lawyers present at its inception.

Charter members who attended the initial meetings of the Association included some of Seattle's earliest attorneys: Thomas Burke, of course, and Judges Roger S. Greene, and C. H. Hanford. Among them too was the law school's dean, John Condon, and then there were the

Among the most hotly contested civic issues of the early 1900s was the location and construction of a new King County Courthouse, which ended with its opening on April 30, 1916. Shown is the courthouse in the early 1920s.

Shown (left to right) at the King County Superior Court Judges' retreat at Sol Duc Hot Springs in 1909, were Robert B. Albertson, 1903-17; J. T. Ronald, 1909-49; A. W. Frater, 1905-25; Mitchell Gilliam, 1905-31; Wilson R. Gay, 1909-12; Arthur E. Griffin, 1901-09; Boyd J. Tallman, 1901-25; and, George E. Morris, 1903-09.

attorneys who had founded many of the city's first and most enduring firms: Walter McClure, George Donworth, Harold Preston, W. H. Bogle, and Alfred Battle. Once or future mayors of Seattle were there, too: R. A. Ballinger and Hiram G. Gill.

A noteworthy newcomer, and one who would cause much debate and concern over the ensuing years, was George Vanderveer. A graduate of Stanford and then Columbia Law School and a refugee from a Wall Street firm, Vanderveer had arrived in 1901, working first in Thomas Burke's firm, then at the prestigious Pyles, Donworth & Howe. By 1906 he had become a deputy prosecuting attorney for King County, having turned down an offer for a lucrative retainer from the Great Northern, and in 1908 he was elected to be the King County prosecutor. Eventually, however, he would become known—and reviled—as the best legal defender of members of the International Workers of the World, nicknamed "the Wobblies," and other labor organizers throughout the West.

His fame—or infamy—was said to be second only to Clarence Darrow's, and by 1924 he would be subject to censure by the Seattle Bar Association.

In 1906, though, the new Seattle Bar Association appointed him, as a charter member, to serve on its membership committee, and at times too he served as counsel for the Association in discipline and disbarment proceedings.

The Association also elected a man who had just completed two years as mayor of Seattle to be its first president, Richard A. Ballinger. Ballinger was born in 1858. His father, Richard H. Ballinger, had been a firm abolitionist and a law student in the office of Abraham Lincoln in Springfield, Illinois.[1] He provided for his son to attend a number of colleges, including Williams College in Massachusetts, where he met James R. Garfield, secretary of the interior under Teddy Roosevelt.

Richard A. Ballinger read for the law and was admitted to the Illinois bar in 1886. In 1889 he left for far-away Port Townsend, Washington, and built an extensive practice there, eventually serving as a superior court judge for Jefferson County from 1894 to 1897. After the expiration of his term he moved to Seattle and organized the firm of Ballinger, Ronald & Battle.

Once in Seattle, he began work on a scholarly treatise, *Ballinger on Community Property*, and on an annotated statutory code for the state of Washington: *Ballinger's Annotated Codes and Statutes*. The code was a two-volume work based upon a previous code compiled by William Lair Hill. It arranged laws passed by the Washington legislature under titles of broad generic significance such as civil procedure, probate, and criminal law. Following each section was a brief historical reference to the legislation and cross-references to other related legislation. These sections were "the sole hope of the attorney who seeks to know the origins of the early statutes."[2] Ballinger's code also included notes regarding decisions of courts interpreting similar statutes in other states. The Washington Constitution was extensively annotated and indexed.

After serving as mayor of Seattle from 1904 to 1906 and president of the Seattle Bar Association, Ballinger was appointed secretary of the interior by President Taft in 1909. Seattle historian Clarence Bagley called him the "foremost lawyer of the northwest."[3]

In his inaugural address to the members of the new Seattle Bar Association, R. A. Ballinger began with "Members of the King County..." and caught himself addressing the wrong group. Those gathered laughed at his mistake, but the mood became more serious as he stated the goals of the Association and emphasized that the group "should not only be a help to the members and the judiciary, but it should also rid the bar of elements which have become a disgrace to it."[4]

For one thing, the specter of communism and socialism was haunting Europe, the United States, and the Pacific Northwest. It was also haunting the bar. And for another thing, many in Seattle thought there were too many lawyers.

A special supplement to the Sunday *Seattle Times* on February 25, 1906, noted with mixed awe and concern the growth of the bar and the legal profession in a tone similar to that of today's press:

> So heavy is the mass of litigation that passes through the courts every year, furnishing work for this small army of legal practitioners, that Seattle has become known as the "city of lawyers."[5]

The article stated that there was "no doubt" that the profession was "overcrowded." Continuing, the writer noted too the decline of comradeship and fraternity: "Few of the old-time lawyers can today recognize in a courtroom half of the faces of the attorneys present." Noting that the bar had requested another judge to help handle the large number of cases, the article sounded the now commonplace complaint: "Litigation has increased out of all proportion to the additional help that could be rendered by the additional judge."[6]

The public and the profession were concerned too with a perceived decline in respect for the legal profession. Dr. J. Allen Smith, dean of the University of Washington's political and social science department, spoke on the subject of "The Bench & Bar from the Layman's Point of View" when he addressed the Seattle Bar Association a few years after its founding.[7] He noted that he had been asked to discuss the reason "why there has been a decline...of public confidence in the court and the legal profession...." His was a scholarly conclusion:

> The criticism of lawyers and courts heard from one end of this country to the other is but the inevitable result of a system which makes it the duty of the courts to interfere with the expression of public opinion in legislation.[8]

The 1906 annual report noted that the "resources" of the bar for the 1907-1908 year were projected to be $780. In the 1907 report, the SBA's Judiciary Committee noted that the judiciary was "greatly underpaid" and recommended to the Bar Association that it urge the Washington legislature to increase the yearly income of the members of the supreme court to six thousand dollars and of the superior court judges to forty-five hundred dollars. The committee further recommended that elections for judges be held at times other than the general election. The Association later voted to recommend that superior court judges receive five thousand dollars annually, not merely forty-five hundred.

This activity of the Association regarding the administration of justice generally and the courts and judges particularly has remained a constant. Two other activities have remained constant as well: collecting dues and sponsoring social events. The papers of Thomas Burke show that on July 10, 1912, the treasurer of the bar had to write to the esteemed attorney, by now largely retired, to remind him that his account was delinquent by one year and that his five-dollar dues for 1913 were also now due.

Nevertheless, the Association continued to invite Burke to its yearly dinners: at the Seattle Commercial Club on June 16, 1912, at fifty cents a plate, at the Arctic Club on September 24, 1913, at one dollar per plate, and at the College Club at Fifth and Seneca in 1915. In 1913 the Seattle Bar Association hosted the Washington State Bar Association and planned a tour of Seattle streets. Alfred Battle and F. E. Brightman wrote to Burke that year to ask him to bring his automobile to the Alaska Building at 4:00 p.m. on August 8th so that he could help escort WSBA members on the tour.

The Seattle Bar Association's 1912 report announced that a new committee had been formed to guide the development of a law library for the proposed new county courthouse, and the 1914 report stated that "ample room" had been reserved in the proposed building for the library. These reports, though, were but a hint of what was really going on.

The big fight was not over whether to include a library or how big it should be; the real struggle was over the new courthouse's location.

Incivility over the New Courthouse

The location of a new county courthouse in Seattle became the focal point of a struggle between two groups with competing economic and aesthetic interests.[9] One group insisted that Seattle grow up—literally up—by building "skyscrapers" concentrated in the pioneer area of Seattle, near Yesler Way and east to about Fourth or Fifth. These were the southend interests, people who owned property in the area and who envisioned Seattle as another New York. They were heartened just after the turn of the century when construction began on the fourteen-story Alaska Building at Second and Cherry—their idea of where the city should be going.

The other group—property owners on the other end of town and their allied architects—thought Seattle should grow out, north toward Lake Union. To this group, skyscrapers were hideous structures that menaced health, congested streets, increased fire hazards, and destroyed the beauty of the business district.[10] These citizens envisioned a low, courtly, sprawling city—a City Beautiful—such as Paris was at the time. They championed a plan for the city developed by Virgil Bogue in 1911, and several events were on their side.

First, the leveling of Denny Hill and the creation of the Denny Regrade area, beginning around 1911, made expansion of the city to the north more plausible than it had been. Second, a two hundred-foot height limit on buildings had been imposed by the City Council around 1910, and this left the skyscraper faction a bit inhibited. Finally, the decision to locate a new federal building at Third and Union, ten blocks north of Yesler, and to locate the new public library at Fourth and Madison, six blocks north of Yesler, pointed in the northenders' direction.

Smith Tower, however, became the southenders' best stack of bargaining chips. Typewriter magnate L. C. Smith made plans in 1909 to build a skyscraper on land he had owned since 1890 at Second and Yesler. Smith planned "a building so high that there was no danger of anyone else even approaching it for many years to come."[11] In his application for the building permit, Smith made it clear that "plans for the structure...have been perfected with the understanding that Seattle's civic center will be permanently located at Third Avenue and Yesler Way."[12] Southenders had dreamed of building a new courthouse at Third and James to take the place of the old one on that damned old Profanity Hill. The block the county bought had once been occupied by the

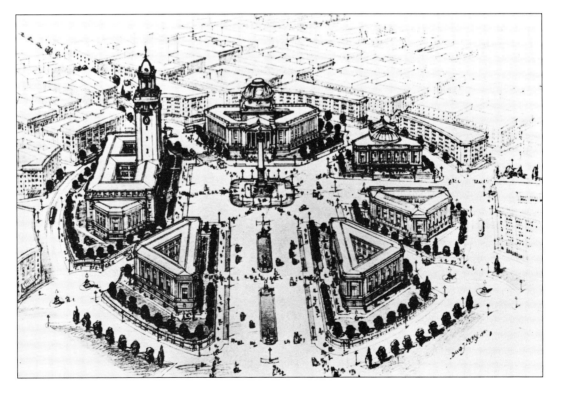

City planner Virgil Bogue in 1911 planned a Paris-inspired city of low rise buildings, including the civic building complex shown.

Yesler Mansion. The Yeslers made plans to move there shortly after the hangings of three accused felons in the Yeslers' old backyard at First and James in Pioneer Square (the present site of the Pioneer Building) in 1882. In 1883 the Yeslers began to plan their mansion: it would be three stories and have forty rooms.[13]

They finally moved into the mansion in 1886, but Henry Yesler's first wife, Sara, died the following year, and it was not until 1889 that the seventy-seven-year-old Henry reoccupied the mansion with his new wife and second cousin, Minnie Gagle, fifty-six years his junior. Henry died in 1892 and Minnie lived in the mansion until 1899, when it was finally converted into the public library. The mansion and the library burned down in 1901, and the county purchased the property in 1903.

With the space at Third and James more or less available, the southenders continued to argue that a new courthouse there, along with the new Smith skyscraper at Second and Yesler, should anchor the downtown core of Seattle. The battle raged for nearly five years. In 1912 the height restrictions were eliminated, and the voters in that same year approved a bond issue, rejecting the northend site and endorsing the new courthouse at Third and James.

The trouble was that prior to the bond election the county commissioners had allowed drawings and architectural plans to circulate among the electorate that showed that an elaborate twenty-story building could be put up on the entire block at Third and James for a mere $950,000. Evidence soon surfaced after the bond passed that the figure was suspiciously low in relation to the plans circulated to the public and that the commissioners had known it. These suspicions were reaffirmed when the actual building plans indicated a much smaller, squatter, less ostentatious structure. The northenders had one more cut at making the Denny Regrade the crown jewel of the Emerald City.

On their behalf, Fred W. Kelly sued A. L. Hamilton and others on the Board of the County Commissioners, seeking to enjoin issuance of the bonds based upon the alleged fraud of the commissioners. Kelly and friends were no doubt ecstatic when King County Superior Court Judge Everett Smith granted the injunction. The southenders, however, appealed to the Washington Supreme Court.

The Washington Supreme Court decided the fate of Seattle's downtown for many years to come when it overturned the injunction and allowed the bonds to be issued for the Third and James courthouse in *Kelly v. Hamilton*.[14] The court essentially held that the commissioners could not be liable for fraud merely because zealous southenders circulated architectural plans that were at best wishful thinking. A year later, in 1914, the electorate smothered the last gasp of the

Seattle chose to build up, not out, as Bogue had suggested. Shown under construction is the Smith Tower, which was completed in 1914.

aesthetic northenders by rejecting a proposal to return to the previous height limit of two hundred feet. The official ground-breaking for the new courthouse occurred on July 11, 1914.

Two years later and on the same day that the official opening of the courthouse was announced, April 30, 1916, the Securities Building at Third and Stewart advertised that it was "ready for occupancy."[15] That building would mark the northern extreme of "downtown" for the next fifty years. It was not until the 1970s that "downtown" finally reached the Denny Regrade.

In June of 1916 the judges moved into the new courthouse, trudging down Profanity Hill for the last time. The judges who moved in, in order of seniority on the bench, were Boyd D. Tallman, Robert B. Albertson, A. W. Frater, Mitchell Gilliam, J. T. Ronald, King Dykeman, Everett Smith, Kenneth Mackintosh, and John E. Jurey. In the election that year all of the incumbents were re-elected.

The War, the Insurgents, and the Aftermath

World War I intervened in everything, including the Seattle Bar Association. The Bar Association ceased publication of its annual report in the years 1916, 1917, and 1918. In 1919, the year of the Seattle General Strike and several months after the Armistice, the Association resumed publication of its annual report. The 1919 report noted that 117 members of the Seattle bar had given up their practices and served in the armed forces. The report stated that three people had given their lives in the battle in France. It had been, and would be, a difficult time.

Before the war there was already turmoil in the railroad and timber industries in the Pacific Northwest. Much of the population resented the economic control exacted by these two industries as well as by private producers of electric power.[16] Chief among the agitators for social and industrial reform were the Industrial Workers of the World (IWW). The IWW, or the Wobblies, as they were best known, was founded in 1905 and had been actively organizing labor and general opposition since that time in the Northwest.

Complicating matters, as the war approached, most people opposed United States involvement in what was seen as only a European concern. Gradually though, the press, commercial clubs, and professional organizations began to advocate involvement, and by the time the United States actually declared war on Germany, the sentiment for unity and conformity became a command—creating further social tension.

In Seattle, Hulet Wells—a non-practicing attorney whose socialist views and activities were long a subject of contention and litigation—began to organize opposition to the draft. He joined others doing similar work, including Anna Louise Strong, a preacher's daughter, famous Seattle activist, and school board member, and formed the Anti-Conscription League. In 1917, they published and distributed a leaflet stating, "No Conscription! No Involuntary Servitude!" and detailing the group's opposition to pending federal legislation to institute a draft.

The *Seattle Times* and the *Post-Intelligencer* both saw the fliers as treasonous and insisted the culprits be prosecuted. The federal authorities were already prosecuting many socialists across the United States, and the local United States attorney, Clay Allen, obliged the newspapers by charging Wells and others in the league with, among other crimes, conspiracy to use the mails for unlawful purposes and conspiracy to interfere with the execution of the draft law. Two charges were dropped during the course of trial, partly because the leaflets were distributed prior to enactment of the draft law, so interfering with it would have been impossible. But one charge remained.

The charge of conspiracy to obstruct by force the proclamation of war and the enactment of the national defense act stood between the defendants and freedom.[17] The attorney for the accused was Seattle Bar Association charter member and Burke firm progeny George Vanderveer. Vanderveer was the lawyer the *Seattle Times* had lionized just a few years before when he was an assistant prosecuting attorney. At that time the paper had stated the following in its special Sunday supplement on the legal profession:

> *George F. Vanderveer, who shares with the chief criminal deputy [John F.] Miller a large part of the criminal work, has convinced lawyers and the public that he is a trial lawyer of great ability. His "homespun" style of argument has sent many a criminal to the penitentiary who depended upon a marvelously well woven defense to save him from the penalty of his crime; without any attempt at oratory, without any figures of speech and attempt to pose as a logician, deputy Vanderveer has in a few chosen sentences teeming with reason afire with truth broken down defenses that it took lawyers of criminals weeks to build up.*[18]

The *Times* concluded that he was "a man to be feared in court." Now, however, it was more likely the *Times* that feared him rather than those who were charged with the crimes.

Vanderveer had secured his first law job in Seattle with the Thomas Burke firm through an introduction by Kenneth Mackintosh, a former classmate of his at both Stanford and Columbia. It was Mackintosh, elected King County prosecutor in 1904, who hired Vanderveer as a deputy prosecutor. Mackintosh went on to become a King County Superior Court judge and a Washington Supreme Court justice, the first supreme court justice born in the state of Washington.[19]

Mackintosh's mother was a teacher and his father a business developer in lumber, saw mills, real estate, and mining. Mackintosh attended local Seattle schools and at sixteen began his higher education at the University of Washington. The following year he transferred to Stanford, where he became friends with Herbert Hoover and met George Vanderveer. Mackintosh and Vanderveer then both attended Columbia Law School.

Mackintosh returned to Seattle and from 1900 to 1902 worked for the firm of Burke, Shepard & McGilvra. He worked on his own for two years and then ran successfully for the position of King County prosecutor. Once elected he hired many attorneys who would go on to make names for themselves in the legal community: John F. Miller, John H. Perry, and the county's first woman prosecutor, Reah M. Whitehead. Perhaps his most significant new attorney, however, was his old classmate George Vanderveer.

To quell the threat of violence and calm the restless Wobblies during the Seattle General Strike in 1919, U. S. Army soldiers were stationed at the Seattle Armory.

Vanderveer was elected in his own right as the King County prosecutor in 1908. He moved the prosecutor's office from the Colman Building to the Alaska Building at Second and Cherry, kitty-corner from the Hoge Building, where he would later spend many years and from which he would be banned after his defense of the Wobblies. During his tenure as prosecutor Vanderveer drafted the criminal code for the state of Washington, and it became the model for criminal codes throughout the United States. For a variety of mostly political reasons, Vanderveer did not run again for office in 1910 and instead re-entered private practice.

By 1914 he was defending some of the more famous criminal cases in the Northwest, including that of the Billingsley brothers for their violations of the local prohibition laws. In these cases Vanderveer frequently faced his former colleagues at the prosecutor's office—Al Lundin, whom he had hired to be a prosecutor—and John F. Miller and John Murphy, both of whom had preceded him in the prosecutor's office.

Vanderveer's reputation as an excellent attorney and his acquaintance with Judge Donworth, with whom he had worked after leaving the Burke firm, probably led the judge to recommend Vanderveer to the IWW to represent their members in the Northwest.

Just prior to the Wells case, Vanderveer won acquittal of seventy-four IWW members in the famous Everett Massacre case in which Wobblies had been charged with murder and conspiracy. Now, defending Wells and the others, he was described as follows:

> Little above medium height, with strong, wiry build, close-cropped thinning hair, and a mind like a steel trap… Vanderveer prowled the courtroom with panther-like tread, hammering away on the main defense line that this was a free-speech case, that citizens have the right to oppose proposed legislation and to petition for its repeal when enacted…. After seventeen hours [of deliberation], the jury split, seven to five, for conviction, and was discharged.[20]

Though Vanderveer had won a significant victory for his clients, it was not a complete acquittal and the federal government reindicted Wells and three other defendants. On retrial, with Vanderveer away defending Wobblies in Chicago and with anti-socialist and pro-war sentiment even higher than during the first trial, the four were convicted, and Judge Jeremiah Neterer sentenced them to two years at McNeil Island. They served their time until after the end of World War I.

The organizing of working people continued, however, despite hostile legislation and strong anti-Wobbly sentiment. In February 1919 labor disputes in the Puget Sound area led to the Seattle General Strike, which completely paralyzed all industry and commerce in Seattle for several days.

No doubt the shock of the strike led the Washington legislature to follow the national trend and pass criminal syndicalism statutes. These statutes ensured that even after the official end of the First World War, civil liberties would not fare any better. Criminal syndicalism, criminal anarchy, and peacetime sedition acts were passed throughout the United States, including all of the Pacific Northwest states. Criminal syndicalism laws were intended to end radical agitation by making it a crime to advocate, advise, teach, publish, or promote force as a means of bringing about social or political change.

For years, through court cases, the principal attorney who fought against the criminal syndicalism laws was George Vanderveer, along with his office partner Walter Pierce. The leading case challenging criminal syndicalism statutes in the Northwest, and one argued by Vanderveer, was *State v. Hennessy*.[21] Vanderveer lost.

As counsel in that case for a defendant charged with organizing the IWW in Clark County, Vanderveer challenged the conviction on a number of both procedural and constitutional grounds, grounds that later courts would most likely have agreed with but that were each rejected by the Washington Supreme Court in 1921. The court held that the criminal syndicalism statute did not violate personal rights, that it did not violate the right of free speech, and that the Fourth and Fifth amendments of the federal constitution did not restrict the power of the state and were not applicable to criminal prosecutions.

Vanderveer was not the only attorney concerned about the lack of civil liberties at this time. Another was a lawyer discussed in the last chapter, Adele Parker, who was admitted to the bar in 1903. She had published a prewar magazine, *The Western Woman Voter*, and she was instrumental in helping begin the Washington chapter of the American Civil Liberties Union. As noted previously, she was also a longtime member of the Seattle Bar Association.

After Vanderveer, however, the most active and often resented counsel for the downtrodden was Mark Litchman.[22] Litchman represented the entry of the working class into the legal profession, a profession that had up until around 1910 been occupied largely by the sons of the rich or at least the sons of the well-to-do entrepreneur or farmer. He left New York City in 1909 with the specific purpose of becoming "a lawyer for the hoboes...for the downtrodden."[23]

Litchman came to Seattle because the law school at the University of Washington was tuition-free, and a working-class kid could possibly afford it. He supported himself through odd jobs, combined some needed high school credits with college credits, and eventually finished law school and passed the bar exam in 1913.

For the next ten years, Litchman's legal work took place largely out of the public spotlight provided by the courtroom. He worked less conspicuously through settlements and negotiations and in large part in the quasi-legal atmosphere of deportation hearings. He defended socialists in political discrimination cases and he attacked a legislative enactment that imposed tuition on students at the University of Washington. He argued that the tuition imposed a discriminatory burden upon the poor. In denying the challenge, the Washington Supreme Court wrote the following:

> *While we may, and do, greatly sympathize with the laudable and alleged desire of the appellants to obtain a higher education at the university, and with their lack of means and inability, as stated in their complaint, to comply with the law as it now exists, we are powerless. Their arguments, cogent as they are, should be addressed to the Legislature and not to the courts.*[24]

Litchman joined the Socialist party, partly under the influence of a speech he heard by another Socialist party member, Homer T. Bone, who later joined the Democratic party and became a United States senator from Washington in 1934. Litchman and his wife, Sophie, held weekly "open house" meetings in their home where Seattle's intelligentsia gathered to discuss books and social and political ideas. He was instrumental in forming the Seattle Labor College in 1920 and saw to it that the college provided free courses for adults on a variety of subjects at the Labor Temple.

Litchman's education efforts led him to create similar educational programs for the local B'nai B'rith and for the Seattle Bar Association. After 1923 Litchman became somewhat disillusioned with the socialist and labor movements and increasingly became what he called an "average lawyer."[25] His work on unpopular or progressive causes, however, did not completely cease. Through the Depression he continued to work on cases involving the Wobblies, the state's Old Age Pension Act, and deportation cases.

Deportation had long been a tool of the majority to rid itself of an unwanted minority: in Seattle it had been used against the Native Americans in the 1850s, the Chinese in the 1880s, the Gypsies and East Indians at the turn of the century, and in the turbulent first two decades of the 1900s, against foreign-born labor organizers. Thus, on January 18, 1918, a committee representing federal officials in Seattle unanimously agreed that the deportation of alien IWW's would be the most effective technique for repressing labor agitation.[26]

Deportation hearings were more effective than courts in curtailing agitation because the hearings lacked the due-process requirements of the courts. As the local commissioner of the Immigration Bureau, Henry M. White, noted, the federal officials rejected the route through the courts "because of the multiplicity of suits and because of the procedure, in that every man must be proven guilty of a particular offense." The United States attorney at the time, Clarence Reames, joined in the effort.

Having to prove guilt beyond a reasonable doubt, in a land where an accused is presumed innocent until proven guilty, was just too bothersome. The Immigration Bureau therefore began to arrest all IWW aliens who were undesirable or pro-German, and the arrests extended to those who possessed IWW literature or who held certain beliefs or those aliens who looked like IWWs or those who had collected funds for the organization or those who had come from "points East...for the purpose of agitating and causing disturbances among the lumber workers."[27]

The local bureau inserted into all IWW files a mimeographed brief that described members of the IWW as "yegs and tramps," and as the "scum of the earth...a landless and lawless mob, who, having no property themselves, recognize no rights of property...no law, and no authority save the policeman's night stick of physical violence."[28]

In the first two weeks of the arrests, hundreds of people were detained, and they filled the federal detention facilities as well as all of the county jails in Western Washington. The arrests were a very effective way for employers to control labor agitation because agitators on the job site could be identified and arrested. In writing to Washington senator J. W. Beckham, a prominent local attorney, Clem Wittemore, claimed that "Every commercial institution and employer of labor in the lumber and shipbuilding district are vitally interested and behind the movement."[29] Eventually, so many were arrested that they had to be sent as far east as Ellensburg, Yakima, and Walla Walla to be detained.

Finally, federal officials in Washington, D.C., under President Wilson, brought a halt to the extreme zeal of immigration officials in Seattle. Over the winter, however, nearly 150 imprisoned aliens awaited hearings on deportation. The hearings were kangaroo courts at best, with everything from the alien's physical appearance or his friends to his itinerant life-style being held as sufficient evidence for deportation.

The IWW cared for its members' needs, including free soup kitchens for its strikers.

The relative success of repressing labor agitation through arrest and deportation in Seattle became a model for repression on a national scale in the 1920s, with the Palmer raids of 1920 as one of its progeny. Ironically, through the use of the extra-judicial immigration process, the repression in Seattle conveniently sidestepped the effectiveness of the attorneys in a place that had in 1906 been termed the "City of Lawyers." One commentator noted how this sidestep occurred:

> Immigration detentions blocked habeas corpus actions, avoided the puzzling problem of proving individual guilt, and by-passed the delays and technicalities of judicial process.[30]

The Bar Association Censures Its Own

In the atmosphere of prosecutions and deportations, the Seattle Bar Association showed its susceptibility to the pressures of war and conformity. Though the minutes of the Association's grievance committee are filled with the usual ethical complaints—high fees, conversion of funds, neglect—occasionally complaints were brought against attorneys for their political activities.

For instance, on January 24, 1919, the minutes of the committee indicate that Assistant United States Attorney Clarence Reames met with the committee to convey information he had about an attorney, E. H. Foster, who Reames said was "guilty of subordination of perjury in course of acting as counsel for the IWW." The committee decided it needed more evidence.

On December 14, 1921, the grievance committee responded to a letter from the attorney general of the state regarding George Vanderveer. Apparently the letter charged and contained evidence that Vanderveer had "permitted his home to be used for purpose of receiving and distributing literature prohibited by the Criminal Syndicalism Act." The committee decided there was sufficient evidence to convict him under the act, but no further action is noted in the minutes.

The minutes of the quarterly meetings of the general membership of the Seattle Bar Association reflect an equal amount of concern about lawyers' political activities—in other words the minutes are largely about the day-to-day concerns of the Bar Association—but occasionally there are other matters considered. For instance, on March 13, 1918, the Committee of War Activities of the Bar was ordered by the Association "to make a thorough canvass of the members of the Association to ascertain names of those not now engaged in some phase of patriotic service as well as those willing to do additional work." On December 10, 1919, the Association passed a resolution stating "that it is the sense of the Bar Association that every member having knowledge of alien enemies, or of IWWs, should report the same to the Department of Justice of the United States."

Perhaps the greatest outrage was leveled against George Vanderveer for his activities in 1924 in opposition to the re-election of sitting members of the Washington Supreme Court. On August 27, 1924, members of the Seattle Bar Association petitioned the Association's secretary for a special meeting regarding the "false propaganda now being spread against the State Supreme Court" and the attempt "to excite class prejudice in election of judges to that court...." The irate letter was signed by, among others, John Powell, Henry McClure, Harry Ballinger, Harold Preston, Frank Helsell, and Alfred Lundin. Vanderveer, though not mentioned in the letter by name, was the true subject of the letter nevertheless.

Vanderveer had written an open letter to members of the Letter Carriers' Union, and probably its most inflammatory lines were the following: "On the one side stand progressives of this type [three people named who were running for the Supreme Court] contending for clean government in the interest of the common people. On the other stand the reactionaries defending a record of corruption in office and the sacred rights of vested privilege." In essence, Vanderveer's letter appears to be a simple statement of why certain named candidates should be supported over other unnamed candidates.

Nevertheless, at the special meeting of the Bar Association, members passed a resolution that stated in part the following:

> WHEREAS, there has come to our attention a circular letter signed and issued by G. F. Vanderveer (known as the leading attorney of the IWW and reputed to be in sympathy with the aims of that organization) over the title of "Seattle Central Labor Council Legal Bureau," whereby false and misleading propaganda is now being circulated among the voters of the state...
>
> WHEREAS, the plain inference from such propaganda is that the supreme court of the State of Washington has with "unfailing regularity" held unconstitutional laws designed to protect those engaged in labor...
>
> NOW THEREFORE, BE IT RESOLVED that we condemn the effort to make able, honest and courageous judicial officers the victims of misleading propaganda;
>
> BE IT FURTHER RESOLVED, that while we recognize the right and propriety of all citizens to have their preferences for members of the courts, and to seek by all honorable and truthful means to procure the election of the candidates whom they prefer, nevertheless, it should be borne in mind by every voter that the courts are instituted and maintained to serve and protect all the prople [sic], and should not be subservient to any class; that "the class struggle," if it exists in the domain of economics, as so fervently believed by some, has no place in the courts...we can but most severly [sic] condemn any effort by whomsoever fathered, to make the courts or any judges the conscious representatives of any class.

The resolution was proposed by Mr. Powell and unanimously adopted by those present at the special meeting. Mr. Vanderveer did speak at the meeting but there is no record of his vote. It is unlikely that he voted for the resolution proposed and passed by many with whom he had helped found the Bar Association. The divisions in the Bar Association, and in the United States, were never more clear.

Prohibition Bellies Up to the Bar

Charter members and later members of the Seattle Bar Association confronted one another too over the issue of Prohibition. Among them were Hiram Gill, George Vanderveer, Thomas Revelle, William Whitney, and John Dore. Gill and Dore were both mayors of Seattle during critical periods of Prohibition; Vanderveer, along with Dore, defended most of the more well known rumrunners of the period; and Revelle and Whitney were both involved in the prosecution of those same rumrunners.

But members of the bar and the Bar Association had confronted the issue of alcohol long before the 1920s. The King County Bar Association's first president, John J. McGilvra, had spent nearly half his time when he was the United States attorney for Washington Territory—from 1861 to 1864—prosecuting defendants for selling liquor to the Indians.

By the turn of the century the "dry" forces were beginning to have a real influence on local politics. Hiram Gill, who sat with Vanderveer and Ballinger and Burke and the others at the first meeting of the Seattle Bar Association, figured prominently in the years preceding and including Prohibition as an on-again, off-again mayor of Seattle, sometimes favoring a "wide open" city and sometimes taking an ax to "drugstores" that were selling liquor under the counter. He also confiscated the private reserves of many prominent Seattle families, including the Boeings.

In the mayoral primary and election of 1910, the Republican Gill argued that a section of the city—notably Pioneer Square—should be "restricted" and that it should be allowed to carry on the businesses for which it had become known: gambling, drinking, and prostitution. The rest of the city would be dry. This was a "wide open" platform for the day. When Gill won the primary, a reform element in the Republican party that included the temperance lawyer Austin Griffiths shifted its support to the Democratic candidate, seeking an end to the "machine rule" it thought Gill represented.

Gill won the mayoral race but the celebration was short-lived. Right after his election, Gill, with the support of *Seattle Times* owner and publisher Alden Blethen, proceeded with his "wide open" plan for the city by first appointing as chief of police Charles Wappenstein, a suspected graft-taker from an earlier administration. The business owners in the restricted section of the city were to pay "Wappy" a percentage in return for not being harassed. This included ten dollars per month per prostitute in the legal prostitution houses. The area blossomed and attracted national attention.

A national magazine of the time described Seattle thus:

Seattle Bar Association member Hiram Gill won the mayoral election in 1910, but was recalled because of his views on vice in 1911. Gill was again elected mayor in 1914, the same year the state voted for prohibition. Shown is a Hiram Gill rally in 1911.

The city seemed to have been transformed almost magically into one great gambling hell. All kinds of games simultaneously started up, in full public view. Cigar stores and barbershops did a lively business in crap-shooting and race-track gambling…. All over the city "flat-joints," pay-off stations, and dart-shooting galleries were reaping a rapid harvest…in the thirty or forty gambling-places opened under the administration of Hi Gill.[31]

A coalition of forces converged against Gill. Religious organizations, commercial clubs, public power advocates, labor leaders, and others joined together under the umbrella of the Public Welfare League to advocate city reform. Eventually this group, along with the Clean City Organization, the Municipal League, the Seattle Federation of Women's Clubs (women had just been granted the vote in Washington), and such attorneys as James Haight, C. J. France, and Austin E. Griffiths, succeeded in ousting Hi and Wappy from office in a recall election in 1911.

"Booze barons" and "rumrunners" kept the city supplied with liquor during Prohibition. Shown is liquor that had been intercepted by police in 1916.

Soon cities throughout Washington were voting to go "dry," including nearby Everett and Bellingham. On November 3, 1914, in the largest vote in the state's history, 60 percent of the people voted in favor of a statewide prohibition initiative. The initiative prohibited the sale or distribution of liquor, but it allowed private stocks for private consumption and public sale for medicinal purposes.

The law became enforceable on January 1, 1916, and on that first day none other than Mayor Hiram Gill, re-elected in 1914 and 1916, grabbed the local headlines when he invaded, illegally and without warrant, the homes of aviation pioneer William E. Boeing, cement manufacturer John Eden, and industrialist David E. Skinner and confiscated their private reserves. Of course, private reserves were not illegal, but Gill and his "Dry Squad" were out to make a point.

Drugstores could also legally sell liquor for medicinal purposes, and between January and March of 1916, sixty-five new drugstores opened up in Seattle. Gill was soon pictured in the local press with his shirt sleeves rolled up and his ax in midair, attacking the liquor shipments arriving at these stores. The Stewart Street Pharmacy, owned by Logan and Fred

Billingsley, was one such establishment, and in May, the Dry Squad caused ten thousand dollars damage when Gill and his gang stopped a shipment of liquor and axed the inside of the store.

Gill's once and future friend and former Seattle Bar Association colleague George Vanderveer represented and later defended the Billingsley brothers. This early arrest resulted in a minor fine, but a later arrest, after a federal statute prohibited any shipments of liquor into a "dry" state, resulted in prison terms for the embattled pharmacists.

But the major prohibition court case in Washington and nationally was yet to come. The National Prohibition Act gave force to the Eighteenth Amendment. The act forbade people to manufacture, sell, possess, transport, or even think about—almost—liquor.

But one person who thought a great deal about liquor—and liquidity—was Seattle police officer Roy Olmstead. He joined the force in 1906, when the temperance lawyer Austin Griffiths was chief of police, and Griffiths recalled that he was "bright and competent." By 1910 Olmstead was a sergeant and by 1916 he was one of the youngest lieutenants ever on the force; he was also a personal friend of the reformed Hi Gill and the Dry Squad.

But within the next decade he would become known in the newspapers as the booze baron and the king of the rumrunners. In 1920 he was dismissed from the police force after prohibition agents confiscated the largest shipment of liquor ever seized in the Northwest and saw Olmstead leaving the scene. He was arrested, fined, fired, and freed to pursue his growing fortune in the liquor business.

The National Prohibition Act was enforced by the Treasury Department, headed in this area by Roy C. Lyle. He left the actual investigations and arrests up to his agents, the supervisor of whom was William M. Whitney, a Seattle lawyer, former chair of the King County Republican party, and a member of the Seattle Bar Association.

Whitney picked up on the ax-and-hammer invasion techniques of Hiram Gill, and by 1922, after having offended many prominent citizens by searching their homes and automobiles, he was extremely unpopular. Adding to his negative ratings, the treasury agents were known to be brutal, were often drunk themselves, and were too frequently found in compromising positions. They also tended to ignore the liquor at the Rainier Club, the Arctic Club, and the Elks Club, and go after the less influential imbibers. The newspapers urged that he be replaced.

By 1923, however, everyone's attention was focused on Roy Olmstead, who made little secret of his growing wealth or how he was earning it. He hired ships out of Vancouver, British Columbia, and engaged in exporting liquor from there to Mexico. But most of it never made it south of Seattle.

Olmstead's crew would drop large shipments of liquor on islands in Puget Sound and north in the dark of night, and Olmstead would then have additional swift boats take the liquor from the islands onto the mainland. He grew so bold as to occasionally bring a boat directly to the Seattle docks in broad daylight and unload them into trucks marked generically with labels such as "Meat" and "Fresh Fish." Olmstead would even supervise the unloading. Roy, you see, had a very good relationship with his former colleagues on the police force. His phone calls, frequently tapped by Whitney, were often made to members of the force in an attempt to iron out minor skirmishes some of his crew members would get into with the officers. But Olmstead knew that his phone calls were often tapped, so in addition to throwing in many profane references to Whitney in each of his phone calls, he frequently gave out false information over his phone line regarding shipments. Then he'd sit back and enjoy the thought of Whitney and his agents scrambling to a dark, lonely, wet island beach and wasting the entire night there while Olmstead's crew unloaded the liquor at another destination he had arranged on a nearby pay phone.

Yet Whitney was tenacious. He found he could charter boats that were faster than Olmstead's, and the two teams would play race on Puget Sound—each team discovering newer and faster boats between widely separated heats. But because of Olmstead's good relations with the Seattle police, and because he often outwitted the federal agents, his principal adversaries were hijackers, not officers.

Nevertheless, by 1923 liquor was abundant in Seattle, and most of it was brought in by Olmstead, who also had a reputation for selling quality products at a reasonable price. Business was so good that he soon was lavishly rich and bought a spacious colonial home in the Mount Baker district of Seattle.

On November 24, 1924, it came to an end. Whitney invaded the offices of Jerry Finch, one of Olmstead's attorneys, and seized many records. He then went on to Olmstead's home, where he seized both records and booze. In January 1925, Olmstead and ninety others, including Finch, were indicted for violating the Prohibition Act, and it became the biggest trial under the Eighteenth Amendment.

Judge Jeremiah Neterer, the same judge who had presided over the Hulet Wells trial in 1917, presided over the Olmstead trial. Twelve of the indicted retained George Vanderveer. Many of the others allowed Finch to represent them. Thomas Revelle, a Seattle Bar Association member, represented the government.

When the trial opened Revelle described Olmstead as the "unofficial chief of police" of Seattle. William Whitney, a star witness, was reported to be close to nervous collapse. And Vanderveer had again taken on his accustomed courtroom persona: pacing, pensive, and angry.

What Vanderveer was angriest about would be the principal issue in the case—all the way to the United States Supreme Court. The volumes of transcripts of the wiretapped conversations involving Olmstead and the other defendants were never introduced into evidence but were used by the prosecution's witnesses to constantly refresh their memories—and Vanderveer was never allowed to view the transcripts before, during, or after the trial. Furthermore, the "transcripts" were pages typed by Whitney's wife, who had typed them from the longhand notes of the agents who had been listening to the tapped conversations. And worse, the longhand notes had been destroyed.

Vanderveer's motions were unavailing and the trial proceeded. The courtroom was always full, usually with law professors and students from the University of Washington's law school and with others curious to watch one of the classic legal battles in Northwest history. In the end, twenty-three of the ninety-one defendants, including Olmstead and Finch, were convicted.

In a lecture similar to those delivered today to drug dealers, the judge addressed the principal defendant:

> *As to you, Roy Olmstead, I'll say this…if the same constructive force, organizing ability, which was devoted to this enterprise had been used legitimately, in harmony with the laws, the final result would have been marvelous.*[32]

Vanderveer and his friend and co-counsel John F. Dore, later a mayor of Seattle, petitioned the United States Supreme Court to hear their appeal. It was premised primarily on two grounds: one, that the wiretaps were an unconstitutional search and seizure under the Fourth Amendment, and two, that the taps were an unconstitutional compulsion of testimony against oneself under the Fifth Amendment. Wiretapping was an issue that was widely and heatedly debated throughout the country, and the attorney who had originally argued on behalf of the federal government, Mabel Willebrandt, felt so strongly opposed to the use of governmental wiretaps that she eventually withdrew from the case.

Chief Justice Taft, however, writing for a severely divided court, rejected Vanderveer's and Dore's arguments, holding that wiretaps did not violate either the Fourth or the Fifth Amendment rights of the defendants.[33] In a famous dissent that eventually became the law of the land, Justice Brandeis stated that wiretaps could violate the constitutional rights of defendants. He was joined in dissent by Justices Holmes, Butler, and Stone.

Olmstead served his four years at the federal penitentiary on McNeil Island, near Tacoma, and was released in 1931. Repeal of Prohibition by a statewide initiative came a year later in 1932 and federal repeal the next year. That same year Alfred Schweppe, longtime Seattle Bar Association leader, began drafting the liquor control law that, today in part, governs the sale of liquor in Washington.

Even before repeal, though, some key players were having regrets. United States Attorney Thomas Revelle wrote the following in a letter dated October 31, 1929:

> *I have always felt that much of the testimony that resulted in the convictions of a number of men who I tried was at least colored, if not perjured…. The thing that is concerning me today is the amount of injustice perpetrated upon these men whom I convicted…. Feeling as I do, had I my way, I would go to McNeil's penitentiary and unlock the doors and let every such man walk out…. If these men have been done a wrong, I would at least like to feel in the closing hours of my life that I have done what I could to remedy the same.*[34]

Perhaps this melancholy mood was engendered in part by another social eruption that had occurred just two days prior to the letter: the stock market crash on "Black Tuesday."

The Homeless Find a Home in Hooverville: Seattle and the Depression

When Roy Olmstead rode across the bay from McNeil Island to Steilacoom, forty miles south of Seattle, on the day he was released in 1931, he returned to a world that was very much the same and very much changed. Liquor was as plentiful—and as illegal—as it had been when he was king. But the Roaring Twenties had been silenced by the Great Depression.

In Seattle a shantytown, "Hooverville," named after the president whose term marked the collapse of the economy, arose near the railroad tracks and just south of Pioneer Square, at Railroad Avenue and Connecticut Street, today Royal Brougham and East Marginal Way, near the Kingdome.[35] This "Hooverville" was just one of many such settlements throughout the United States consisting of houses made from packing crates, scrap lumber, and pieces of metal. At its most populous, Seattle's Hooverville had twelve hundred male residents, a few women residents, and an unofficial mayor and chief of police. Hooverville was fully integrated, with Caucasians, both native and foreign-born, constituting 70 percent of the population, and black, Filipino, and Mexican people constituting the rest. Among the citizens were people from many occupations, including at least one doctor and two attorneys. The city twice deliberately burned Hooverville down, but the residents always rebuilt it until finally in May 1941, when the economy had improved, they let the city bulldoze it a final time.

Unfortunately, the Depression engendered the same sort of scapegoating that had occurred prior to and during World War I. Arrest and deportation were again the twin weapons against dissenters and the foreign-born.[36] When demonstrators and speakers appeared again in the Skid Road area of Seattle, the crowds of unemployed were urged to organize for communism, or socialism, or anarchism. The city police often arrested the speakers before they could get out a complete sentence. Incensed by such violations of free speech, a University of Washington sociology and law student organized a committee to protest the violations. His name was Edward Henry and he would later go on to become a founder of the Washington chapter of the American Civil Liberties Union, a member of the Seattle Bar Association, and many years later, a judge for the King County Superior Court. Fortunately for Henry and his friends, Seattle Bar Association member John Dore was elected mayor in 1932. Under Dore, who had occasionally been co-counsel with Mark Litchman or George Vanderveer, civil liberties survived a bit more readily in Seattle than elsewhere. But repression was more common than one would expect with Dore at the helm.

Gender Bias and the Bar[37]

Despite the early work of women attorneys such as Lelia J. Robinson, Mary Leonard, Reah Whitehead, Othelia Carroll, and Adele Parker, among others, the woman attorney was still viewed as an anomaly during the first four decades of this century. Newspaper headline writers throughout the thirties and forties could not help noting the anomaly with headlines such as these: "Girl Proves Her Mettle as a Lawyer" (1936); "Portia Picks Matrimony" (1939); "Mother Passes Bar Exam" (1941); "One Girl and 14 Young Men Are Sworn in as Attorneys" (1945).[38]

Though women still attended law school during this period and faced little more than token opposition, getting a job was extremely difficult. The dean of the University of Michigan law school told one of the early women attorneys in Seattle, Lady Willie Forbus, upon her graduating first in her class, that she would "make a good stenographer for some lawyer someday."[39]

Despite this endemic opposition of the male bar, many women adopted the same attitude that Mary Ellen Krug did. While she eventually rose to prominence in the Seattle bar, in the early years she determined that she only needed one job and was not going to stop until she found it.

Forbus decided to fool them: she would do it on her own. As out-of-state attorney, she was required to serve a year as a law clerk, which she did at Donworth & Todd. She then opened her own practice in 1919 and practiced law for the next sixty years, retiring in 1979.

During Forbus' career she worked as a Special Assistant Attorney General, served a term in the state legislature, and lobbied for women's suffrage in 1920. Years later she said she faced less discrimination than expected and that this may have been because of her attitude: "I was an advocate, not a woman and I let it be known that I asked no quarter and gave none."[40]

Krug went the firm route. After her graduation from the University of Washington in 1943, she clerked for Judge Beals, whose wife was an attorney, Othelia Carroll Beals, and then worked for Al Schweppe. Eventually, she became known as one of the premier labor lawyers in the Northwest and became a partner with Schweppe, Doolittle, Krug, Tausend & Beezer. Krug was chairperson of the American Bar Association's Labor Law Section when she died.

Roberta Kaiser chose yet a different route. She attended one year of law school in 1933, but had to quit to raise two children. Later, she became a stenographer in the offices of James Ballard and finally gained admission to the bar in 1941 through the clerkship program. In her first job she drafted contracts and assisted on briefs, though she was kept well clear of anything that might end up in court. Seeing no future for women in her law firm as men returned from World War II, she quit and later took a job with the Inheritance Tax Division in Olympia. She served, others say, "brilliantly" in that capacity from 1955 to 1979, when she retired.

Two other attorneys from the University of Washington chose a route that was novel, though not unprecedented, for the time: Muriel Mawer and Maryhelen Wigle formed their own partnership in 1935. They cleared their expenses starting in the first month, and mostly handled civil case referrals from former classmates and other attorneys in their building, whom Mawer described as "very generous." Mawer and Wigle, however, were probably not the first all-woman partnership: Grace Dailey Mifflin and Cordelia Theil were apparently practicing together during the same period.

Mifflin served as a divorce proctor at the beginning of her career in 1926, but left that position and opened the partnership with Cordelia Theil in 1935. Theil had been chief criminal deputy in the prosecutor's office and was known as "a good, hard-fighting, tough lawyer."[41] Sadly, she became seriously ill in 1941 and Mifflin left the partnership to practice with her husband and his brothers in the firm of Mifflin, Mifflin, Mifflin & Mifflin.

Practicing with family was a route occasionally taken. Bernice Jonson, who graduated from law school in 1936, joined her father's practice in Ballard that year and has practiced there with noteworthy success ever since. During the 1960s and later, she was the most feared divorce lawyer in Seattle. Tessie Schmitt, a UW graduate of 1923, practiced with her father, Nicholas Schmitt, in Seattle.

Mawer & Wigle was dissolved in 1940, and Muriel Mawer worked for a brief time for the Office of Price Administration before joining and transforming the name of Karr, Tuttle, Koch, Campbell, Mawer & Morrow.

Though Mawer recalled that most male attorneys were very generous, she did recall that occasionally governmental or Bar Association lunch meetings she attended at the Rainier Club or the Arctic Club had to be moved to more private dining rooms. The reason for the move was that women were not allowed into or through the main dining rooms of those clubs during many years of her practice. In the 1970s the Seattle-King County Bar Association passed a resolution that no SKCBA meeting of any kind could be held in the Rainier Club, the Washington Athletic Club, or the College Club, where such "male only" rules were in force.

In 1942 another fascinating attorney followed Mary Ellen Krug in clerking for Judge Beals: Esther Jane Johnson. She was a 1940 graduate of the University of Washington law school and received a master's-in-law degree from Columbia.

After clerking for Beals she clerked for a large Wall Street firm and then went overseas to prosecute war criminals at Nuremberg for three years. Eventually she returned to Seattle and opened a private practice, still open today.

Mary Alvord was a major inspiration to women attorneys from the beginning of her practice in 1921, with the firm of Hyland, Elvidge and Alvord. In a 1936 *Seattle Post-Intelligencer* article about her (quoted in Cynthia Whitaker's article on women attorneys in Washington and the basis of much of the preceding information), Alvord stated a common desire:

The law is the science of human relationships and touches everyone. It is my ambition that all women in business and the professions should be unmarked: that they work and are recognized on the same basis as men. Personally I do not want to be considered a woman lawyer, but as just a lawyer.[42]

Many of the women who began practicing law in the first three decades of this century were still practicing fifty years later. A few of their male counterparts were, too. Ralph Potts entered practice in 1925 in Seattle, after a short time in Tacoma. He had graduated from the University of Oregon law school when it was located in Portland. Consistent with the way many new attorneys began practice in those days, he began with a personal introduction from the University of Oregon law school's dean, J. Hunt Hendrickson, to members of an insurance company, London Guaranty. Potts went on to a successful career in insurance defense cases with the firm of Pearson & Potts.

Potts wrote several books chronicling the history of the law and of Seattle, including a biography of George Vanderveer entitled *Counsel for the Damned*, a book on Seattle entitled *Seattle Heritage*, and a book loosely based upon the life of Seattle Teamster leader Dave Beck entitled *Sir Boss*. Mr. Potts was listed in the *Directory of Lawyers* as late as 1990. He died in 1992.

Robert B. Porterfield graduated from Harvard Law School in 1923, and after some time in New York City as a law clerk for seventy-five dollars per month, he arrived in Seattle and began work with Chadwick, McMicken, Ramsey & Rupp. He was paid one hundred dollars per month while doing extensive research for the firm's clients, including Seattle-First National Bank and the telephone company.

Porterfield recalled that in those early days associates were expected to prepare their own documents on a typewriter and rarely were afforded a secretary. No billable hours were kept either: "Fees were not charged by the hour, but by the case, on a case by case basis."[43] A simple will cost fifteen dollars and a difficult divorce might get as high as one hundred dollars. Superior court filing fees were five dollars.

John Day practiced law for fifty years after his 1930 graduation from the University of Washington School of Law. His first law job, while he was still in law school, paid him twenty-five dollars per month. After law school he worked for Meyer & Meagher in exchange for office rent, rather than a salary. "I paid for my keep by serving process at night, and doing my own typing." Eventually he moved to Revelle, Simon & Coles, but still was doing his own typing and exchanging his work for office space. Soon he entered political life, running for several offices, and served as mayor of Mercer Island for over ten years.

Starting practice in Seattle in 1933, George H. Bovingdon, Sr., remembered fifty years later that he worked all day Saturday, usually Sunday, and that "nights were part of the job." He worked for the "large" firm of Roberts & Skeel for fifty dollars per month. About his colleagues he remembered this: "At that time, there may have been thirty-five hundred attorneys in this state, but not more than fifteen hundred lawyers in Seattle and King County. You tended to know all of them.... While there were always a few SOBs, practice was on a very open basis."

Ray Ogden went to work for his father after he graduated from the University of Washington School of Law in 1935. His pay was seventy-five dollars per month. John Rupp was only a few years behind Ray Ogden at the University of Washington and in 1937 got the "best of all jobs," working as a law clerk for the supreme court at $125 per month. The job lasted two years and established a financial basis for his later entry into law practice.

Longtime Bar Association activist and Washington Supreme Court justice Charles Horowitz began work with Preston, Thorgrimson & Turner in 1929, after graduating from the University of Washington in 1927 and spending two years as a Rhodes Scholar at Oxford. Justice Horowitz stated that the practice of law had become increasingly complex over the years, especially with the advent of many new civil procedure rules and the growth of case law from the appellate courts.

It was also in this era that the state bar became a mandatory organization, largely through the efforts of Alfred Schweppe. In 1929, Schweppe, at the time the dean of the University of Washington law school, took on the task of being the secretary of three organizations: the State Bar Association, the State Judicial Council, and the Seattle Bar Association. Out of this work grew the idea that the state bar should be an "integrated" bar, meaning that it should be not a voluntary organization but a mandatory one.

Al Schweppe, George McCush, and Roger Meakim drafted the State Bar Act, which made the mandatory bar a reality. Getting the legislature to pass the act that year was no easy task. That year's legislature has been viewed by historians as remarkably "anti-establishment," and it looked on the organized bar as the epitome of the establishment. What finally convinced the legislators to pass the Bar Act was one legislator's favorable analogy between the act's provision for mandatory membership and a labor union's desire for closed shops: "All the lawyers want is their own union and a closed shop. We ought to give it to them."[44] They did.

Subsequently, State Supreme Court Chief Justice Walter Beals appointed Schweppe and others, including Seattle attorney Charles H. Paul, to organize the mandatory association. Under the act, the supreme court had certain regulatory powers over the bar. That year, 1933, the state bar elected Charles H. Paul as its first president and took up residence in the Dexter Horton building, sharing its offices with the Judicial Council and the Seattle Bar Association.

Serving the Poor: The Legal Aid Bureau

As the 1930s came to a close, the Depression in the United States neared its end. But a decade of hard economic times had alerted the public and the bar to the plight of the poor. Further, since 1934 the legal profession had played a significant role in the social service orientation of Roosevelt's New Deal administration, and the profession increasingly turned some of its efforts toward helping those who could not afford legal services. Within this environment, the Seattle Bar Association became one of the first bar associations to establish a legal aid bureau.

As early as 1937 the Seattle Bar Association's trustees had passed a motion to appoint a committee to investigate providing free legal aid.[45] The chair of the committee was Arthur Simon. After nearly a year of work, Simon reported to the SBA's board regarding the committee, and the board passed a resolution to establish a legal aid bureau to be financed by "the Bar Association, the Community Fund or other local funds."

But the Bar Association would only go so far. When it became known that a young attorney named Ed Henry intended to introduce state legislation calling for public funding of legal aid bureaus, the Seattle Bar Association held two long and tortuous special meetings on whether the board should back such legislation. Ed Henry was then a recent graduate of the University of Washington law school and a founder of the Washington State chapter of the American Civil Liberties Union.

During the 1930s, the poor came from everywhere, and their plight became the focus of the Seattle Bar Association, the first bar association in the country to establish a Legal Aid Bureau. Shown is Hooverville—Seattle, 1932.

In the end, a majority of the sharply divided board went against the recommendations of its own legal aid committee and, while reaffirming the Association's commitment to providing free legal aid, went on record as opposing the expenditure of public funds in the effort.[46]

Later that year, however, the board took action to insure that legal aid would be provided locally. In April 1939 the new chair of the Legal Aid Committee, Frank P. Helsell, reported on the work of the committee and recommended that separate offices and separate personnel be retained to carry out the work of the Legal Aid Bureau. As a result, the board eventually passed a resolution that stated, in part, the following:

> RESOLVED, that the Legal Aid Committee of the Seattle Bar Association be and it hereby is authorized to extend its activities to include the operation and maintenance of a bureau having its own office and personnel, to be known as the Seattle Bar Association Legal Aid Bureau; to employ in the operation of such bureau a director and clerk, and to do all things necessary for the successful operations and maintenance of such bureau....[47]

According to Frank E. Holman, an attorney who would play a significant role in bar activities, in 1939 he chaired the committee to raise the necessary funds to continue and enlarge the Legal Aid Bureau. As he notes in his memoirs, "Seattle was one of the first cities in the country whose Bar Association established, at its own cost and expense, a Legal Aid Bureau staffed with a regular lawyer and a secretary."[48]

ASSUMPTIONS AND ABDICATIONS OF RESPONSIBILITY

In 1939, there was darkness and there was light. Franco was ascendant in Spain, and Washington granted diplomatic recognition to the regime. Hitler invaded Prague, Czechoslovakia, in May. The next month, the Daughters of the American Revolution refused to allow the world-renowned contralto Marian Anderson to sing at Constitution Hall in Washington, D. C., because she was an African-American. In September, Hitler invaded Poland, but the United States announced that it would remain neutral. Not long after that, the State Department refused to relax immigration laws that limited Jewish entry into the United States, and a ship carrying more than nine hundred European Jews was turned away at New York harbor.

But there was startling light as well. President Roosevelt, opening the New York World's Fair, announced that it was "open to all mankind." At the fair, too, Albert Einstein explained to the crowd how cosmic rays worked before he hit a switch that made those rays light up the exposition, with its theme "The World of Tomorrow." Benny Goodman, Gene Krupa, Lionel Hampton, and Teddy Wilson were popular in jazz, and Hollywood put out such hits as *Gone with the Wind*, *The Wizard of Oz*, *Stagecoach*, and *Mr. Smith Goes to Washington*, among many others.

At the peak of its wartime production in 1943, The Boeing Company employed 78,400 workers. Shown are Boeing employees celebrating the company's completion of its 5,000th B-17.

Contradictions and Resolutions

Disparate elements coexisted in the Seattle Bar Association as well. At the annual meeting in June 1939, probably largely because of their work with the legal aid issue, elected to the SBA Board of Trustees were Edward E. Henry and Frank E. Holman. These two attorneys came to the SBA board by widely divergent paths.

Henry had been active in city politics and civil liberties issues since well before he became an attorney. As a sociology student at the University of Washington, he had led and won free speech issues on campus and had become involved with an associate of George Vanderveer's, Marion Zioncheck, in Zioncheck's successful campaign to recall Mayor Frank Edwards in 1930.

During that period, Henry often attended mass meetings of the unemployed in the Pioneer Square area and watched as Seattle police officers on horseback, at the direction of Mayor Edwards, broke up the rallies. Henry reported seeing the officers on horseback charge into the crowd and pull the speakers from their soapbox podiums, hauling them off to jail before they had uttered a complete sentence.[1] It was this, in part, that led Henry to join the recall campaign.

Henry formed a committee to protest the free speech violations in Pioneer Square and to propose that the city set aside an area near the County-City Building to be used as a forum for such speeches. The city council proposed instead that the area be well away from the seat of government. Henry's committee continued to press for the closer site, even after Edwards was recalled and an interim mayor, Robert Harlin, was sworn in.

By 1931 Henry was working his way through the University of Washington's law school, supporting himself as a process server. Given the ongoing need for civil liberties support, he turned to a recently formed national organization, the American Civil Liberties Union. He and several other local activists, including attorneys Mary Farquharson and Irving Clark, decided to form a local chapter of the ACLU and began meetings to that end.[2] Henry became the executive secretary.

The organization hit a slump in 1933, when Henry transferred to the law school at George Washington University in Washington, D. C. He went there to work with Marion Zioncheck, who had been elected to Congress the year before. By the late 1930s, however, Henry was back and active in projects to provide legal help to those who could not afford it or to whom it was not offered because of their beliefs.

Frank E. Holman, on the other hand, arrived on the Seattle scene in a more traditional manner. Born, raised, and educated in Utah, he became a Rhodes Scholar at Oxford after his graduation from the University of Utah at Salt Lake in 1908. After obtaining a law degree at Oxford he came to Seattle.

He arrived by train in 1911 at the King Street Station, and by that afternoon he had already interviewed for his first law job in the tower of the Great Northern Railway Station, across the street from the King Street Station. He met with Frederick Brown, the western counsel for the Great Northern. Brown suggested he speak with Charles P. Spooner, counsel for the Union Pacific, who had just left the Bogle, Merritt & Spooner firm to form his own practice.

Spooner hired Holman for fifty dollars a month until he passed his October bar exam. On passing, he received seventy-five dollars per month. In January 1912 Holman was forced to return to Salt Lake to take care of his parents, who were in ill health. He practiced and taught law there, but longed to return to the Northwest. Twelve years after his forced exit, Holman returned with his wife and three children to Seattle.

The Holmans found a suitable home in the Madrona district, and the Rhodes Scholar with thirteen years of experience began job-hunting. While many firms received him cordially, none of them offered him a job. He finally opened his own office: on the tenth floor of the Hoge Building, next door to Donworth, Todd & Higgins. Judge George Donworth had been the first federal district judge to preside in Tacoma, from 1909 to 1912, and had formed his firm in 1912 after he resigned the bench. Donworth and former U.S. attorney Elmer Todd were both charter members of the Seattle Bar Association.

It had been the Donworth firm that employed the feisty George Vanderveer after his stint with Thomas Burke, and it was the same Hoge Building that refused to rent to Vanderveer after his Wobbly work. Holman found his new offices serviceable, and was content knowing that the members of the Donworth firm, who had turned down his request for a job, would see his name on the door every day as they went to work.

Mr. Higgins dropped by one day and told Holman that he doubted that a stranger to Seattle could succeed in law practice in the city. When Higgins learned, though, that Holman had several prestigious clients from his days in Salt Lake City, he told Holman that he should have mentioned the clients in his job interview with the firm because then he would have received "more serious consideration." At any rate, Higgins said, Holman could at least use the Donworth library.

Eventually, both the Bogle firm and the Donworth firm sought Holman as a partner. Though he initially went to Bogle, Holman left for Donworth, with Bogle's blessing, when Higgins made a better offer. The senior Bogle, however, quietly advised him that Judge Donworth, whom Holman had met only once, was not an easy man to work for. Within a few

War for the United States began on December 7, 1941, at Pearl Harbor. Shown are navy personnel and planes assembled below deck in an aircraft carrier during World War II.

days of working with the new firm, Holman found out just how difficult he could be. Donworth took him aside and lectured him as follows:

> Mr. Holman, I do not know what assurances either Mr. Higgins or Mr. Todd may have given you as to the permanency of your place here in our firm, but I thought I should tell you that as far as I am concerned, you are here on trial and if for any reason your work should seem unsatisfactory, or your personality not all we had expected, your partnership with us may be terminated at any time.[3]

The warning was not necessary. In 1926, Higgins left the firm for a partnership in New York, and his old firm changed to Donworth, Todd & Holman.

One of the junior partners of the Donworth firm at that time was William M. Allen, who would head the Boeing Company into prosperity at the end of the 1940s.

Donworth, Todd & Holman was not long-lived. Donworth resigned from the partnership over differences with Elmer Todd and the firm became Todd, Holman & Sprague, with Allen as an unnamed partner. The firm did not change again until Mr. Todd left in 1942 to become the publisher of the *Seattle Times*.

After his resignation, Donworth opened a practice with his son, Charles T. Donworth, also in the Hoge Building. Charles Donworth soon thereafter served as vice president of the Washington State Bar Association and in 1934 served as president of the Seattle Bar Association. Charles was subsequently appointed to the Washington Supreme Court in 1949, where he remained until his retirement in 1967.

Holman originally became active with the Seattle Bar Association in the latter years of the 1930s. At the annual meeting in June 1941, Holman was elected president of the Association.[4]

World War II and the Internment of the Japanese

Most members of the bar, like most citizens, had been acutely aware of the war in Europe. It was far away from United States soil though, and in 1938 the bar could still make light of it. The program committee at the annual meeting presented "a short skit" entitled "The Trial of Santa Claus by the Totalitarian Powers."

At the 1941 annual meeting, the signs of war's inevitability were patent: the board passed a resolution allowing that the dues of any SBA member on active duty in the military would be waived. George H. Revelle, Jr., who had been officially elected that same day as secretary of the Association, resigned when he was called to military service. The trustees replaced him with the first woman officer of the Seattle Bar Association: Mary H. Alvord.[5]

War finally arrived on December 7, 1941, when Japanese pilots bombed the United States military base at Pearl Harbor. Frank Holman's recollections of the first moments of the war were both typical and political:

> I was in our Windermere home reading and listening to the radio when the news of Pearl Harbor came. Naturally it was a tremendous shock.... [Roosevelt's] treatment of the Japanese Ambassador and his other attitudes toward Japan were such as to force the Japs into action or lose face.[6]

Three days into the war, Holman presided over a meeting of the SBA at which the trustees passed a resolution regarding the forced relocation of the King County Law Library:

> WHEREAS, due to the War Emergency, a number of the Public Offices now located in the County-City Building have been given notice to move, including the King County Law Library, and
> WHEREAS, the removal of the King County Law Library to any quarters outside the County-City Building would very seriously affect and handicap the functioning of the courts, the attorneys practicing before the courts, and the citizens of said county....
> NOW, THEREFORE, BE IT RESOLVED...that the President...of the Association...appoint a committee...to confer immediately with [several governmental officials]...to the end that satisfactory and suitable arrangements may be promptly made to acquire suitable quarters for the library in the County-City Building....[7]

When war was declared, action was swift. Many attorneys contributed to the war effort through direct service in the military—some giving their lives—while others performed civilian duties related to the war. During the week following Pearl Harbor, Frank Holman left Seattle by train for Kansas City to spend Christmas with his family. When he reached Portland, he was given a telegram forwarded by his office to the train depot there stating that he had been appointed to chair the Alien Enemy Hearing Board of the Western District of Washington.

He intended to decline the appointment, but his wife insisted it was his patriotic duty. By the time the train reached Shoshone, Idaho, the argument was over. Holman bid his family good-bye and got on the next train west. Ironically,

Shoshone, Idaho, was only a few miles from where, less than a year later, thousands of Seattle's Japanese citizens would be interned at the Minidoka Internment Camp.

When President Roosevelt signed the expulsion order in 1942, 14,400 Japanese and Japanese-Americans lived in Washington State—9,600 in King County and 7,000 of those in Seattle. In Seattle the largest number lived where people of color always had: south of Yesler and Jackson from Fourth to Twenty-third.

Holman's family celebrated Christmas in Kansas City, and stayed there in the relative safety of America's Midwest. Holman returned to Seattle, closed up their Windermere home, and moved to the Olympic Hotel to be closer to the city during the hard winter. He served two years as chair of the Alien Enemy Hearing Board and another year as a member of the National Panel of Alien Enemy Hearing Boards. The alien boards tried Japanese, Germans, and Italians, and committed them "when necessary to internment camps."[8] Holman, though, was determined that due process be afforded those who came before him.

He was therefore outraged when, a few months after his hearings had begun, the Commander of the Armed Forces for the Western Area of the United States, General DeWitt, issued a blanket order for the seizure and internment, without hearing or trial, of all people of Japanese ancestry, including those who were United States citizens. Holman remembered the general's order this way:

> Under the DeWitt order, Japanese who were American citizens, were taken from their homes and farms, loaded into buses, and moved with such personal belongings as they could hurriedly assemble, to distant internment camps. Filipinos and others were put into possession of their property without due process of law. There were not then and there never have been two classes of American citizens—one class of persons whose personal rights and property rights can be arbitrarily forfeited without trial or hearing, and another class with these rights entitled to the protection of the Constitution.[9]

His legal conclusions were equally adamant:

> This was an illegal, unnecessary, and a ruthless order and was so held by certain courageous Federal judges, like Judge Alger Fee of Portland. Nothing like it was attempted elsewhere in the country, not even in the Hawaiian Islands where there was a very large Japanese population. The Alien Enemy Hearing Boards were carefully screening and interning, after a hearing, all Japanese who could in any way be dangerous and there was never one single instance of Japanese sabotage.[10]

Gordon Hirabayashi was a student at the University of Washington, a Quaker, and a conscientious objector. Like many others, he was outraged by the Pearl Harbor attack. He was, however, equally indignant when President Roosevelt signed Executive Order 9066 on February 19, 1942, and ordered the expulsion and detention of over 110,000 people of Japanese ancestry on the West Coast.[11] Hirabayashi refused to register for internment and in March 1942 refused to obey a curfew order established for Japanese people. With his attorney, Arthur Barnett, Hirabayashi turned himself over to the FBI in May 1942, and eventually spent two years in jail for these crimes, but not before a fight.

Hirabayashi's family were farmers in the Green River valley. As a student, Hirabayashi lived in a YMCA dormitory on the university campus in Seattle. His friends there would always help him keep track of the time so that he would not violate the curfew. Finally one evening he tired of running for the dorm from the library or the coffee shop, and he stopped and walked. From that day on he consciously refused to obey the curfew and kept a diary. He decided to go public with his stand against registration and the curfew, and contacted a fellow Quaker who was a local attorney, Arthur Barnett. Barnett was in contact with another local attorney, Mary Farquharson, who happened to be the state senator from the University District and a founding member of the ACLU.

Over several days Hirabayashi met with both Farquharson and Barnett. They decided to make his a test case, and they set up a committee to support the challenge. On May 16 they went to the FBI office and gave the FBI a four-page statement of the reasons for his refusal.

The FBI confiscated Hirabayashi's briefcase and found in it the diary where he had recorded his three curfew violations. Hirabayashi was given an opportunity to register, but he refused and eventually he was jailed in the King County Jail. He was offered temporary internment at the Puyallup fairgrounds, where the Japanese people were being held pending their shipment to the camps, but he refused this as well. He awaited trial in the King County Jail.

The notices that the Japanese were to depart Seattle had been posted on Tuesday, April 21, 1942, about one month prior to Hirabayashi's stand. The notices stated that the forced evacuation was to occur in one week. Japanese on Bainbridge Island had already been shipped east. Seattle's Japanese gathered at Eighth Avenue South and South Lane Street and other departure points throughout the city on the appointed day. They could bring only what they could carry: suitcases and duffel bags, tagged with preassigned numbers. In a scene reminiscent of the forced expulsion of the Duwamish in the 1850s and the Chinese in the 1880s, nearly the entire Japanese population was expelled over three days.

NOTICE

Headquarters
Western Defense Command
and Fourth Army

Presidio of San Francisco, California
May 15, 1942

Civilian Exclusion Order No. 79

1. Pursuant to the provisions of Public Proclamations Nos. 1 and 2, this Headquarters, dated March 2, 1942, and March 16, 1942, respectively, it is hereby ordered that from and after 12 o'clock noon, P. W. T., of Friday, May 22, 1942, all persons of Japanese ancestry, both alien and non-alien, be excluded from that portion of Military Area No. 1 described as follows:

All that portion of the County of King, State of Washington, within that boundary beginning at a point about midway between the Cities of Tacoma and Seattle (east of Des Moines) at which U. S. Highway No. 99 intersects Washington State Highway No. 5A; thence easterly along said Highway No. 5A to Green River; thence easterly and following Green River to the King-Kittitas County line; thence southerly and following the King-Kittitas County line to the King-Pierce County line; thence westerly and following the King-Pierce County line to U. S. Highway No. 99; thence northerly along U. S. Highway No. 99 to the point of beginning.

2. A responsible member of each family, and each individual living alone, in the above described area will report between the hours of 8:00 A. M. and 5:00 P. M., Saturday, May 16, 1942, or during the same hours on Sunday, May 17, 1942, to the Civil Control Station located at:

Auburn High School Gymnasium,
711 East Main Street,
Auburn, Washington.

3. Any person subject to this order who fails to comply with any of its provisions or with the provisions of published instructions pertaining hereto or who is found in the above area after 12 o'clock noon, P. W. T., of Friday, May 22, 1942, will be liable to the criminal penalties provided by Public Law No. 503, 77th Congress, approved March 21, 1942, entitled "An Act to Provide a Penalty for Violation of Restrictions or Orders with Respect to Persons Entering, Remaining in, Leaving or Committing Any Act in Military Areas or Zones," and alien Japanese will be subject to immediate apprehension and internment.

4. All persons within the bounds of an established Assembly Center pursuant to instructions from this Headquarters are excepted from the provisions of this order while those persons are in such Assembly Center.

J. L. DeWITT
Lieutenant General, U. S. Army
Commanding

The 1942 notice of internment of "all persons of Japanese ancestry" who lived or worked in "Military Area No 1." Shown is the General Dewitt order.

Hirabayashi stayed behind, behind bars. His was not the first challenge to the registration and curfew requirements heard in King County courts. On April 13, 1942, attorney Austin Griffiths filed a habeas corpus petition in the federal district court on behalf of Mary Asaba Ventura, a native-born Japanese-American, alleging that the curfew order unlawfully restrained her liberty. Griffiths was mentioned in the previous chapter as the "temperance lawyer" who had served as a King County Superior Court judge from 1921 to 1929 and for a brief time as Seattle's chief of police.

Griffiths filed the petition on Monday morning and it was argued that evening before Federal District Judge Lloyd L. Black, an army reserve officer, former American Legion post commander, and a "law and order" prosecutor in Snohomish County who had sided with the lumber mill owners against the Wobblies from 1917 to 1919.

University of Washington student Gordon K. Hirabayashi became the Japanese-American symbol of resistance against curfew laws and registration for internment in 1942. He was defended by Seattle Bar Association members Arthur Barnett, Mary Farquharson, and later, Frank Walters.

Two days after argument, Griffiths was taken aback by the vitriol of Black's oral opinion from the bench. In turning aside the petition on the legal grounds that it was improper because Ventura was not in custody, Black nevertheless felt compelled to rule on the legality of the curfew order. He said that any profession of loyalty on the part of Ventura or other Japanese could merely be pretense and that they could easily "become enemy soldiers over night."[12] Further, he intoned, he was certain that the enemy "in Tokyo" considered all Japanese everywhere to be loyal subjects of the Japanese Imperial Government:

How many believe that if our enemies should manage to send a suicide squadron of parachutists to Puget Sound that the Enemy High Command would not hope for assistance from many such American-born Japanese?[13]

Gordon Hirabayashi would face the same Judge Black in his challenge to the curfew and registration requirements. By the time trial arrived on October 20, 1942, Hirabayashi was represented by Frank Walters. Arthur Barnett had felt too inexperienced to handle such an unprecedented constitutional case. It was difficult to find another attorney willing to represent such a controversial client. Even George Vanderveer and a young associate in his office, John Geisness, turned down the case.

Barnett and Farquharson speculated that the refusal was because of the Vanderveer firm's representation of local Teamster leader Dave Beck, who wholeheartedly supported the internment. Finally, Barnett convinced a respected corporate lawyer, Frank L. Walters, to take the case. Walters was, like Black, a member of the American Legion; Walters too was a longtime member of the Seattle Bar Association.

Walters first moved to dismiss the charges of curfew and registration violations on the grounds that these requirements violated the due process and equal protection clauses of the Fifth and Fourteenth amendments. Both amendments provide that a citizen cannot be deprived of life, liberty, or property without due process of law. In addition, the Fourteenth Amendment provides that no citizen shall be denied the equal protection of the law, prohibiting laws that treat one group more favorably or less favorably than another. In his written opinion denying the motion to dismiss, Black cast aside the "mass of citations" in Walters' brief. Considering the citations, the judge felt, would result in "tediously extending" his opinion. He turned, instead, to thinly veiled racial stereotypes and his own sense of justice:

Of vital importance in considering this question is the fact that the parachutists and saboteurs, as well as the soldiers, of Japan make diabolically clever use of infiltration tactics. They are shrewd masters of tricky concealment among any who resemble them. With the aid of any artifice or treachery they seek such human camouflage and with uncanny skill discover and take advantage of any disloyalty among their kind.[14]

Black dismissed the constitutional challenge, claiming that such a "technical interpretation" of the due process clause would "endanger all of the constitutional rights of the whole citizenry...."[15] Faced with this written opinion, Walters prepared for trial by making sure he would perfect the record for appeal: he insisted on a jury trial and posed numerous objections to Black's rulings.

The court virtually instructed the jury to return a guilty verdict, and despite Walters' hinting that the jury should exercise its historical role in nullifying unjust laws, the jury returned in ten minutes with a guilty verdict on both counts.

The arrival of people of Japanese ancestry for internment on the Puyallup fairgrounds in 1942.

The next day, having already served five months in jail, Hirabayashi was sentenced to an additional ninety days on each count, which were to be served concurrently.

One year after Roosevelt signed Executive Order 9066, the federal court of appeals heard several consolidated appeals challenging the legality of the curfew and registration requirements, including the case of Gordon Hirabayashi. In an unusual move, the court, without deciding the issue, certified the consolidated cases directly to the United States Supreme Court.

Argument at the United States Supreme Court began on May 10, 1943. Seattle attorneys Arthur Barnett and Frank Walters, along with several others, stepped before the bench to be sworn in as members of the Supreme Court bar. The court heard two other cases, one argued by the ACLU's general counsel, Arthur Garfield Hays, and one argued by the National Association for the Advancement of Colored People's (NAACP) lawyer Thurgood Marshall, also an ACLU board member.

After the prior cases were concluded, Frank Walters approached the bench on behalf of Gordon Hirabayashi and presented the facts in the cases. Further argument ensued, and at the end of two days of arguments, none of the defense attorneys held any hope of a decision in their favor.

On June 21, 1943, Chief Justice Harlan Stone announced the unanimous decision of the court upholding Hirabayashi's convictions. The majority included esteemed justices Hugo Black, Felix Frankfurter, and William O. Douglas.

There was little organized opposition from the Seattle Bar Association regarding the treatment of the Japanese during World War II. Individuals in the Bar Association have since indicated that while not excusable, the curfew and registration requirements were fully in keeping with the tenor of the times. Such professed "progressive" organizations as the National Lawyers Guild actually supported the internment.[16] The national board of the American Civil Liberties Union, though several of its members were active in representing Japanese defendants, insisted that the defense not forthrightly challenge the constitutionality of the internment and curfew.[17]

Even the Japanese American Citizens League (JACL), faced with no other choice, urged patriotism and cooperation. In one proclamation the JACL stated that "therefore be it resolved that the Japanese American Citizens League of

Seattle go on record as indorsing [sic] cheerful and willful cooperation by the community with the government agencies in carrying out the evacuation proceedings...."[18]

After the defeat at the Supreme Court, Gordon Hirabayashi was returned to prison. It would be another four decades before he achieved, with the help of Seattle attorneys, principally Arthur Barnett and Rodney Kawakami, the justice he sought in 1942. Other Seattle attorneys who helped win justice for Hirabayashi four decades later were Camden Hall, Michael Leong, Daniel J. Ichinaga, Craig Kobayashi, and Benson D. Wong.

Postwar Boom and Bust

William Boeing founded the Boeing Airplane Company on Lake Union in 1916, but following a bitter fight with the Roosevelt administration, which forced the breakup of his company, he was disassociated from the company that would retain his name.[19]

The law firm of Todd, Holman & Sprague in its various incarnations represented the Boeing Company through most

Seattle attorney William M. Allen joined The Boeing Company as its president in 1945 just after a one-month, 78 percent cut in the company's employment. Shown is President Allen boarding a B-47 for a test flight in 1947.

of the company's existence. It was full-time work involving government contracts, acquisitions, and associations. Boeing Airplane & Transport Corporation stock went public in November 1928 and its full subscription was swift.

Then came the formation of United Aircraft & Transport Corporation in 1929, which became the largest air transport company in the country. Soon after, it merged with Boeing, Pratt & Whitney, Hamilton Propeller Company, Boeing Air Transport, and Pacific Air Transport, and William Boeing became chair of the huge new enterprise.

Boeing began to withdraw from active participation in the company in 1933 and began to divest himself of United Aircraft & Transport stock because he had promised himself that he would retire at age fifty. His withdrawal was short-lived. He felt compelled to return in 1934 to defend the company against governmental charges that the company had acquired airmail routes through unfair competition. President Roosevelt canceled all governmental airmail contracts with Boeing and ordered the army to fly the mail. It did, and during the next two months it lost a dozen of its pilots.

Roosevelt was undeterred, however, and the United Aircraft & Transport Corporation was split up by the government. William Boeing sold the rest of his stock and left the airplane business for keeps.

By 1939 the Boeing Airplane Company was a separate entity, having lost its founder and having moved next to the river that bore the name of the city's first residents: the Duwamish. It was still represented by Todd, Holman & Sprague, and the company's sole customer was the federal government. From that time until the United States officially entered World War II, the company moved from employing four thousand people to employing over thirty thousand. And that was just the beginning.

At the peak of war production in 1943, Boeing employed 78,400 people and grossed $600 million. (Five years earlier, total sales for the entire city of Seattle had only been $70 million.) It was the beginning of "so goes Boeing, so goes Seattle."

The war ended in 1945, and so did the Boeing boom. In one year, the company's employment plummeted from 69,884 down to 8,917 at the end of 1946. Sales dropped to $14 million. During that period, too, the president of Boeing, Philip Johnson, died. He was replaced by Boeing's attorney: William Allen.

Allen faced difficult times. Boeing's concessions to labor and labor's concessions to Boeing helped even out the hard times between 1946 and the beginning of the Korean War. It helped too that the company developed two new planes, the B-47 and the B-52, which both improved Boeing's fortunes.

But Allen knew that Boeing could not continue to stand or fall on the basis of war or threats of war, and in 1952 he directed the company's move into the commercial airplane business and the "Jet Age." The financial security of Boeing wavered until Pan American World Airways took delivery of its first 707-120 in 1958. On the strength of military contracts, including one for KC-135 tankers, from which the 707 design had been adapted, Boeing's employment was near one hundred thousand at the end of the fifties.

When the first 707, bearing the marks of Pan American World Airways, thundered off the runway in 1959, Boeing's commercial airline success was assured. Even greater successes, and risks, followed with the 727, the 737, and the 747. The startling success of the company was tied inextricably to one person, a lawyer: William Allen. Seattle historian Roger Sale concluded this about the Allen years:

> When one looks at Boeing from the point of view of the aerospace industry or of the national manufacturing economy, the Allen years are remarkable. The company has consistently recognized that its strengths lay in its unsurpassed engineering excellence and it has, with a combination of daring and determination, worked from its strengths to develop a rightfully proud industrial giant.... Its people are almost all extremely low-keyed and hard-working and, among the older major figures in the company, touchingly loyal to William Allen.[20]

The Canwell Committee: McCarthyism's Local Precursor

Given the rising specter of fascism in Europe in the late 1930s, the majority of the local legal profession seemed relatively unafraid of communism as World War II approached. The Seattle Bar Association had even welcomed an address in 1939 entitled "The Lawyer and Public Relations" by a controversial Marxist economist, Professor Harold Laski of London University.[21]

Laski was controversial in Seattle. His appointment as the Walker-Ames Lecturer at the University of Washington for the winter quarter of 1939 had been protested by the Daughters of the American Revolution, the American Legion, the *Seattle Times*, and the *Seattle Post-Intelligencer*. A member of the British Labor Party, Laski had been linked with the unionization of teachers and other public employees, with the United Front of the Communist Party, and locally with the Washington Commonwealth Federation.

Within the Seattle bar, there was no unanimity with regard to Laski, though Thomas Balmer, a Seattle attorney and president of the University of Washington Board of

Regents, had a definite opinion. He wrote to university president Lee Paul Sieg regarding the "friends the University has lost through having Laski here, and how much more difficult it has made our efforts to obtain an adequate legislative appropriation for the forthcoming biennium."[22] Sieg prevailed and the Laski controversy died amid the terrible events of World War II, but it portended much strife ahead.

Strife did not seem inevitable. Communist leaders in the United States, who in the late 1930s had been sent to jail for their beliefs, often were pardoned in the early 1940s in the interest of unity with our wartime ally the Soviet Union. The Communist party helped out, too. The members renamed the party the Communist Political Association in 1944 and the party's leader, Earl Browder, declared that the association was "ready to cooperate in making capitalism work effectively in the post-war period."[23]

In 1943, President Roosevelt spoke of Stalin and the Soviet Union, stating his belief that "we are going to get along very well with him and the Russian people—very well indeed."[24] That same year, *Life* magazine informed its readers that the Russians were "one hell of a people" who "look like Americans, dress like Americans and think like Americans," and added that the Russian secret police were simply a "national police similar to the FBI."[25]

In 1945 the ACLU reported that its caseload was down and that it looked forward to fewer court challenges to civil liberties and more institutional protections for those liberties.

Somewhere between 1945 and 1947, all that changed. Leading the vigilant was state representative Albert F. Canwell. He chaired the state's Joint Fact-Finding Committee on Un-American Activities, established by the state legislature in 1947. Various explanations have been offered for the resurgence of rabid anti-communism in the late 1940s: an unprecedented wave of labor strikes occurred throughout the nation; the postwar cooperation between the Soviet Union and the United States failed; a renewed obsession with internal espionage rose, fueled by several notable spy cases; the Communist party abandoned its Communist Political Association ideas and policies; and the Truman administration adopted an increasingly hard line against foreign and domestic communists, epitomized by the Truman Doctrine and a new government loyalty program.

With this background, Truman wrote ominously in his diary in September 1946: "[T]he Reds, phonies and 'parlor pinks' seem to be banded together and are becoming a national danger. I am afraid they are a sabotage front for Uncle Joe Stalin."[26] Less than a year later, on March 21, 1947, Truman signed an executive order on government loyalty.

Following its establishment in 1947, the state's Joint Fact-Finding Committee on Un-American Activities was chaired by State Representative Albert F. Canwell. It became a communist-hunting group with little regard for civil rights or the Constitution in general. Shown is one of many Seattle protests in 1948.

Under the Truman loyalty program, all present or prospective government employees were to undergo a loyalty investigation. The investigation would include gathering any information that the FBI, military intelligence, the House Un-American Activities Committee, or local law enforcement might have about an individual. Negative or "derogatory" information would result in a further and fuller investigation and often in a hearing. Adverse decisions in the hearing would be appealed to a Loyalty Review Board. It was to this loyalty program that historians generally attribute the beginning of what became known as "McCarthyism."

In February 1947, many people in the Northwest organized the Progressive Citizens of America (PCA) in order to denounce Truman's loyalty program, as well as his announced military aid for Greece and Turkey. Members of the University of Washington faculty, including Albert Franzke, Melvin Rader, Ralph Gundlach, and R. G. Tyler, joined the PCA. Each one of them became a target of the newly formed Canwell Committee, which held two sets of hearings in Seattle in 1948, one focusing on the Washington Pension Union, the other on the University of Washington faculty.

The Canwell hearings were held in the Seattle Field Artillery Armory, on the grounds of what became Seattle Center. During the sessions involving the University of Washington faculty, many were accused of communist affiliations and were subpoenaed to testify: Herbert Phillips, Joseph Butterworth, Ralph Gundlach, Garland Ethel, Harold Eby, Maude Beal, Angelo Pellegrini, Melville Jacobs, and Melvin Rader. The first three refused to answer any questions. The rest, except for Rader, admitted past membership in the Communist party, but they refused to testify against others. Rader denied any communist affiliation.

Rader, whose denials were later proved to be absolutely accurate, recalled several incidents from the hearings:

> It seemed appropriate that the hearing should be held in the massive stone structure of the 146th Field Artillery, with armed guards stationed at various points. In the packed hearing room Chairman Canwell gaveled the committee and

the crowd to order with military dispatch. One could easily imagine that the scene was that of a court-martial, with the uniformed members of the state patrol ready to suppress any strong dissent. At a long elevated table facing the audience sat Canwell, flanked on both sides by members of his committee.... Immediately in front of Canwell, in the center of the room, was a large table around which were grouped committee counsel William J. Houston, his chief assistant John Whipple, and a court reporter.[27]

Despite the decorum, the committee did not seem overly concerned with due process. Rader recalls an often-recounted incident:

The...witness...was my colleague in the Philosophy Department, Professor Herbert Phillips.... Being duly sworn he asked that his testimony be postponed until he had time to consult his attorney John Caughlan. When I saw that he was being pressured to testify without benefit of counsel, I felt that I had a duty to protest. So I rose to my feet and asked, "May I say a word?"

"No...," snapped the chairman. "We are not going to disrupt the hearing from the rear of the room." I was not in the rear of the room, but the remark was directed at me.

After Phillips again requested legal advice, Canwell ordered him to testify before noon or no later than two o'clock whether or not he could reach his attorney.

When he did return before the noon recess he was accompanied by Caughlan.

As Phillips mounted the stand, Caughlan asked permission to state a legal objection. He was told that no objections would be permitted. He then asked if Mr. Phillips would be allowed to state any objections.

"No, he will not," said Canwell. "We are not going to debate the issue of the legality of this Committee or its processes."

"I have a third question to ask," responded Caughlan.

"You will ask no more questions," ordered Canwell. "We are not going to go on with any ridiculous procedure here. You will either comply with the instructions of the Committee or you will be removed. Now, let's understand that for good. Are you going to comply? You are going to comply with the procedure here, or you are not going to be here."[28]

It is little wonder then that when Rader and his attorney, Ed Henry, were called, Rader's heart began to pound. Henry was given equal treatment. When he asked to enter a statement countering an accuser's remark, Henry began cautiously: "I don't want to be thrown out of here but I—." The chairman

cut him off, telling him that it would be fine if his client wanted to cooperate, but "I don't think we will carry this discussion any further."[29] Rader was excused after a few more words.

After the Canwell hearings had concluded, the university held tenure and disciplinary hearings regarding several of the faculty members who had been called before the Canwell Committee. Final tenure decisions were left to the university's Board of Regents. The 1949 tenure matters were fought out between members of the Seattle Bar Association.

Bar member Tracy Griffin represented the administration before the board, a board that included bar member Thomas Balmer. Also before the board were attorneys John Caughlan, C. T. Hatten, and Seattle Bar Association member Edward Henry. These latter three continued their representation of several of the faculty members that had begun with the original Canwell hearings. Griffin urged the board to immediately dismiss the six faculty members: Phillips, Gundlach, Butterworth, Eby, Ethel, and Jacobs. He accused Caughlan and Phillips of using Communist party tactics in propagandizing against President Allen of the university.

The board fired Gundlach, Butterworth, and Phillips and put Eby, Ethel, and Jacobs on a two-year probationary period. None of the three dismissed members were ever rehired, nor did they receive any offers for other faculty positions. Butterworth subsisted on odd jobs and, eventually, public assistance. Phillips knew many influential academics, but never received any job offer, and he eventually worked as a building laborer and retired in San Francisco. Gundlach moved to New York and became a clinical psychologist, doing individual, family, and group therapy.

The Canwell episode had ended round one.

The Founding of the Young Lawyers Division: 1949

The 1946 entering class for the University of Washington's School of Law was the largest ever. Many of the new students were veterans of the war, and the Washington legislature granted them two quarters of law school credit for their military service. As a consequence the veterans could finish a four-year program in two and a half years, and many did.[30]

The bar welcomed the newcomers and in 1948 insisted that the bar examiners grade the bar exams as quickly as possible. With the need for lawyers so high, the graduates got their bar results a week and a half after finishing the three-day exam. Many of them immediately sought membership in the Seattle Bar Association, and they put that membership to work by forming a committee to help find seasoned attorneys

During World War II, the number and diversity of new lawyers reflected the reduced number of law school graduates. Shown is the 1942 King County Court swearing in ceremony for new lawyers.

to teach the new attorneys the day-to-day skills needed for law practice. By 1949, they were calling the new committee the Young Lawyers Committee.

Jack Veblen, the committee's first chair, recalled the way the committee got seasoned attorneys to teach the newcomers: the new attorneys volunteered for the senior bar's Speaker's Bureau. While some bar members worked to educate their junior colleagues in the nuts and bolts of practicing law, a number of junior attorneys developed an interest in the Legal Aid Committee and the Legal Aid Bureau of the Seattle Bar Association. The new attorneys revitalized the bar's interest in these matters and in the final years of the forties found new sources for funding the programs, including a fund drive aimed at the more established attorneys.

Under the supervision of University of Washington law professor Cornelius Peck, members of the Legal Aid Committee were soon representing actual clients. Judge Jack Schofield, at the time a new attorney, remembered his first opportunity to represent clients as "very gratifying, if nerve wracking." At one time the bar almost agreed to a proposal to move the Legal Aid Bureau to the university campus, where law students could be more directly involved, but the board was finally persuaded to keep the bureau downtown, where most of the clients and attorneys were found.

The energetic new attorneys organized other events as well: luncheons, where practicing attorneys would speak about practice and procedure matters, and less formal brown bag lunches, where young attorneys could talk about their cases and concerns. When William Helsell chaired the committee,

he began the tradition of "nitty gritty" tours of the courthouse, showing new attorneys where to find the library and the clerk's office.

Not to be outdone during the energetic postwar period, the "senior" bar also kept up a good pace. In addition to helping revitalize the Legal Aid Bureau, the Seattle Bar's board began weekly meetings, rather than the quarterly or monthly meetings that had once been the norm. Among other activities, the board began polling attorneys in order to rate candidates for the King County Superior Court and the Washington Supreme Court.

The bar had not played a significant role in recommending or condemning judicial candidates prior to this time. The only previous episode involved the "Vanderveer slate" in 1924 and 1926, when the established bar who opposed Vanderveer gathered some four hundred signatures in opposition to his slate and ended up publicly condemning Vanderveer's electioneering tactics. By the 1940s, the organized bar apparently wanted to be more organized about its judicial preferences. As a consequence, prior to the 1948 election, the Seattle Bar Association conducted the first bar preferential poll for supreme court candidates.[31]

The impetus for the poll was undoubtedly the controversy involving Washington Supreme Court Judge William Millard. Millard had grown increasingly unpopular with certain sectors of the bar, having established himself as a liberal activist working against the conservative majority on the court. Worse, it was rumored at the time, though never proved despite several investigations, that he might have received money from individuals whose cases were pending before the court.

In 1947, the Seattle Bar Association's board passed a resolution recommending that the state bar investigate any charges of judicial impropriety by "any" member of the state supreme court. By 1948, the board was more specific, passing a resolution that stated that the attorney general had found that Millard had "solicited and received loans from various parties who were then interested in litigation then pending before the court." Based upon this "finding," the Bar Association's resolution "condemned the conduct of Judge Millard" and urged his defeat at the coming election.

The Association polled its members twice, and both times the majority urged defeat of Millard. As Charles Sheldon, today's chief historian of the court, notes, "With the Seattle Bar Association leading the attack, followed by most of the other county bars and the state Grange, Tom Grady defeated Millard by a substantial majority in the November balloting."[32]

The Seattle Bar Association had taken a bold step in polling its members regarding judicial candidates. No other bar association in the state had taken such steps, and for the next forty years such polls would decide the fate of most supreme court judicial candidates and many superior court candidates. Court historian Sheldon noted the great importance these polls have played since the 1940s:

> For the next forty years the Seattle and state bars shared responsibility for polling lawyers before each contested election and publicizing the results. With few exceptions, voters heeded the profession's advice.[33]

The Fifties and the Right Resurgent

Witch hunting has remained an unfortunate, but popular, pastime in the legal and extra-legal history of the United States. The Canwell Committee was no longer active in Washington in the early 1950s, but the federal government had taken up the slack. The federal Un-American Activities Committee was at its peak from 1950 to 1954, under the leadership of Senator Joseph R. McCarthy. In January 1954, the Gallup Poll found that McCarthy was still quite popular and favorably regarded by 50 percent of the American people. But soon it seemed that the American people and President Eisenhower and moderate Republicans were tired of McCarthy—especially the Army-McCarthy hearings in the spring of 1954.

In June of that year, a resolution was introduced in the United States Senate to censure McCarthy, and by December 1, 1954, the censure passed by a vote of 67 - 22, with all Democrats voting against McCarthy and the Republicans splitting, 22 -22. During the spring of 1954, the House Un-American Activities Committee (HUAC) decided to pay a visit to Seattle to investigate communist infiltration in the Pacific Northwest.

The HUAC was then chaired by Harold Velde and became known as the Velde Committee. One particular target of the committee was that portion of the law community that had defended accused people before the various HUAC and HUAC-type committees during the late 1940s and early 1950s.

The Seattle Bar Association responded to the Velde Committee's attack. Of particular concern to the bar was a sentiment among many citizens that attorneys who represented people before the committees, and who advised their clients to claim a Fifth Amendment privilege against self-incrimination, should be disciplined or disbarred. The SBA passed a resolution that spoke to these issues, stating the following:

> BE IT RESOLVED by the Board of Trustees of the Seattle Bar Association on this 11th day of June, 1954:
> That certain of the fundamental principles underlying the representation by lawyers of unpopular persons and causes

Following Canwell was Harold Velde, who chaired the House Un-American Activities Committee in 1954. The Seattle Bar Association responded to the committee's call for discipline and disbarment of attorneys who advised their clients to claim protection under the Fifth Amendment before the Velde committee. Shown (from the left) are unknown, Frank B. Tavenner, Gordon Scherer, Kit Clardy, Donald Jackson, Clyde Doyle, James B. Frasier, Thomas Beal, William Wheeler, and Robert L. Kunzig. Tavenner, Wheeler, and Kunzig were attorneys, and Beal was the committee's chief clerk.

> should be set forth at this time for the information and assistance of the public and the bar and that, therefore, the following statement should be issued and made public:
> Throughout the course of history lawyers have been frequently called upon to represent and defend persons and causes known to be unpopular. This has been particularly true in criminal matters, but it has been and is also true in other fields, including investigations and hearings conducted by the legislative department of the government.
> The right of an accused person, or of a person called as a witness in a legislative investigation, to have legal counsel carries with it the right of the lawyer to represent and defend him in accordance with the ethical standards of the bar.
> Having undertaken any such representation, the lawyer has a duty to assert for his client every remedy or defense authorized by the law of the land. The duty of the lawyer is to be performed, however, only within the bounds of the law and his office does not permit or demand of him, for any client, any violation of the law nor any manner or fraud nor improper conduct.
> The public and the bar should recognize the duties and responsibilities of the lawyer in such cases and should keep in mind that such representation, when performed in accordance with the applicable ethical standards, is lawful and proper and that it does not impute to the lawyer his client's views, character, deeds or reputation.[34]

The bar made certain that this resolution was publicly expressed by sending it to the major newspapers in the city. During these years many attorneys stepped forward to represent those subpoenaed before the Velde or similar committees. Some of these attorneys were members of the Seattle Bar Association, some were members of the local ACLU, some members of both. They included Benjamin Asia, Phil Burton, John Caughlan, Jack Harlow, C. T. Hatten, Ed Henry, Ken MacDonald, and Solie Ringold.

In keeping with his association's resolution in 1954, Mike Copass, then president of the Seattle Bar Association, agreed to represent for no charge an "accused Communist," Stanley Hendrickson, who had been subpoenaed to appear before Velde. Al Schweppe, a longtime Washington State Bar activist and at the time the former dean of the University of Washington's School of Law, agreed to represent a fellow attorney: John Caughlan.

It was not the first time Caughlan had faced adversity for his legal work. Shortly after he was sworn in as a Washington attorney in 1937, he was fired from his first job for his refusal to withdraw from a case contesting the city's revocation of a permit to the Communist party to hold a meeting at the Civic Auditorium. In 1948, he was accused of perjury in federal court based on his denial of membership in the Communist party. In the perjury trial he was represented by Irv Goodman of Portland, Richard Gladstein of San Francisco, and Seattle attorney Stan Soderland.

Caughlan was acquitted of perjury, but he was again a target when Velde came to town in 1954. Caughlan and his partner at the time, C. T. Hatten, represented others before Velde, and Caughlan persuaded the committee to put off his appearance until after his clients had appeared, to protect their right to counsel.

When finally before the committee, he was faced once again with the question that still echoes in the minds of those who remember the fifties: Are you now, or have you ever been, a member of the Communist party? Caughlan refused to answer the question, blasting the committee for its disregard of the Bill of Rights and stating that a federal jury had already been satisfied that he was not a member of the Communist party; that, he felt, should be sufficient.

The HUAC returned again in 1956 and 1959, but to an increasingly hostile atmosphere. Retired Court of Appeals Judge Solie Ringold remembers the era:

By and large, I think the bar respected what we were doing in defending people before the committees. By the time the last HUAC hearings were held, the Thomas Committee, we were able to get the Seattle-King County Bar Association to pass a resolution guaranteeing that the bar would furnish attorneys for anyone called before the committees.[35]

The New Seattle-King County Bar Association

In 1957, the Young Lawyers had a powerful ally in the Seattle Bar Association's new president, Charles Horowitz. Horowitz significantly changed the organization of the Bar Association, first by forming sections that were aimed toward serving the specialized interests of attorneys in specific legal fields, and second by reorganizing most of the standing committees.

William Wesselhoeft recalled that Horowitz was especially enthusiastic about the formation of the section for young lawyers. The section had an increasing number of members to serve. In 1957 new lawyers were sworn in to the federal bar in one large group rather than individually, and a huge number of people had just passed the bar: forty-five. Horowitz convinced Wesselhoeft to chair the section, urging him to continue the work of providing practical skills training and other assistance to new lawyers.

Charles Horowitz was a longtime bar activist and not one who fit the often inaccurate stereotype. He spent his first eight years "in the tenement district of lower east side Manhattan."[36] When his family moved to Seattle in 1913, Horowitz attended public schools, sold newspapers, delivered magazines after class, and in the evening, sold candy in a Seattle movie theater. In the summer he worked at fruit and vegetable stands and mowed lawns. His savings allowed him to go to the University of Washington at seventeen and to later attend the university's School of Law.

Once at the School of Law, Horowitz began to compile a more typical resume. He graduated summa cum laude in 1927, served as editor-in-chief of the *Washington Law Review*, and wrote several of the review's first law notes. He was awarded a three-year Rhodes Scholarship at Oxford University, where in two years he earned a B.A. degree in jurisprudence with first-class honors in 1929.

He joined Preston, Thorgrimson & Turner in 1929 and began a prestigious career in the law and in law-related activities in numerous bar organizations, including the Seattle Bar Association. When the voters approved a constitutional amendment in 1968, creating an intermediate court of appeals in Washington, Horowitz was one of the twelve judges appointed to that bench by Governor Dan Evans. He was elected to the Washington Supreme Court in 1974, receiving the top rating in the state bar's preferential poll in both the primary and the general election.

In the 1950s, Horowitz was deeply involved with the Seattle Bar Association. In 1953 he served on the SBA's Civil Rights Committee and by 1955 he was chair. In 1956, in the tradition of former SBA president Mike Copass, he joined with the SBA president for that year, John Rupp, as well as members Chester Adair, Arthur Barnett, David Hamlin, and David Williams, in volunteering to represent people called before yet another version of the House Un-American Activities Committee.

Horowitz was elected president of the Association in 1957. He was joined on the board that year by many who would lead the bar and the judiciary into the sixties: George H. Bovingdon, Frank J. Eberharter, Kenneth A. MacDonald, Walter T. McGovern, Muriel Mawer, and Stanley C. Soderland. In the very first meeting Horowitz presided over, he proposed a massive reorganization of committees and the creation of specific law sections. Various board members were appointed to act as liaisons to the new committees and to act as vice chairpersons to the new sections.

The board approved the creation or continuation of the following committees: Continuing Legal Education, Uniform Jury Instructions, Selection of Judges, Public Service and Public Relations, Lawyer Referral Service, Civil Rights, Legal Aid, and Peace and Law through United Nations. The eighteen proposed sections included the following: Administrative Law, Criminal Law, Labor Relations Law, and Family Law. The Board then set about finding chairpeople for all of the committees and the sections.

In early 1958, the board moved to ensure the continuing existence of the Legal Aid Bureau by incorporating it as a separate entity and turning over all funds the bar had collected for its operation to the new corporation. Among the many items the board considered during Horowitz's tenure, a notable one was the KIRO TV proposal for a weekly television show featuring local attorneys. The Bar Association also kept up its concern with the administration of the courts and providing appointed counsel for indigent defendants who wanted to appeal their convictions.

Finally, at the last SBA meeting over which Charles Horowitz presided, on June 4, 1958, the board approved amending its articles of incorporation to change the organization's name from the Seattle Bar Association to the Seattle-King County Bar Association.

Thus, as the Boeing plant on the Duwamish River prepared in 1959 to deliver the plane that would dominate the aerospace industry for the next decade, the 707, the Seattle-King County Bar Association in downtown Duwamps prepared to roar into the second half of the twentieth century.

Shown in 1951 is Seattle-Tacoma International Airport, which opened in 1947.

PROTEST AND THE PROFESSION

Perhaps more than any other period of time, the decade of the 1960s was a watershed for new ideals and responsibilities, shaping the nation's social, political, intellectual, artistic, financial, and natural environment.

For many, the 1960s began in Seattle in the same spirit that was afoot throughout the United States: with enthusiasm and with what would later appear to be innocence and naiveté. The newly elected president of the United States embodied that spirit for many: John Kennedy was young, charismatic, and handsome, and he espoused a life of vigor and engagement. The dark days of the Second World War, the Korean War, and the McCarthy era were disappearing in the rearview mirror of the big-finned automobile. In this atmosphere, Seattle built and produced a futuristic world's fair to celebrate the ascendancy of optimism: Century 21.

The New Seattle-King County Bar Association

The Seattle-King County Bar Association (SKCBA) reflected this vigor: it had a new hyphenated name, a new organizational structure, and a new publication, the *Seattle-King County Bar Bulletin*. Though one volume of the *Seattle Bar Bulletin* had been published in 1957 - 58, under the

Civil disobedience tested constitutional rights of free speech and assembly during the 1960s and 1970s, as public demonstrations against U.S. involvement in Vietnam grew in frequency and intensity. Shown is the 1970 anti-war demonstration that blocked the I-5 freeway between the University of Washington campus and downtown Seattle.

In direct contrast to the end of the decade, Century 21, which opened in 1962, was a celebration of the ascension of optimism. Shown is the Space Needle's foundation, which required seven hundred truckloads of concrete—twenty-eight hundred cubic yards poured continuously for sixteen hours.

presidency of Charles Horowitz and the editorship of Betty Fletcher and Louis Pepper,[1] it was not until December 1960 that the publication began to publish regularly. For the next three decades, up until the present, the *Bar Bulletin* has published the news of the Association and the bar generally.[2]

The Bar Association soon became involved in new, more commercial arenas. Its board appointed a committee to participate in the World's Fair, the "Century 21" exposition.[3] Several Seattle attorneys, including many Bar Association members, were already involved. William Goodloe was one of the first. In the early 1950s he began to promote the fair, and as a state senator in the mid-fifties he wrote and co-sponsored legislation authorizing the Seattle World's Fair. As the fair became more of a reality, he was appointed to chair the planning commission.

A major question arose regarding the exact location of the World's Fair, and Goodloe appointed several people to a subcommittee on sites, but that group had difficulty reaching a decision. The thorny issue was not resolved until the Seattle City Council created the Civic Center Advisory Committee. That committee was to develop ideas about acquiring land for and building a civic center around the Civic Auditorium on Denny, and that site became the site of the World's Fair as

well. The committee's chair was a longtime Seattle Bar Association member, Harold S. Shefelman, "a stocky little attorney of much ingenuity and experience," as Murray Morgan described him in his book on the fair.[4]

The group of prominent citizens could find no other time to meet except 7:00 a.m. breakfast meetings, and these drowsy affairs became known as "Sleeping Time with Shefelman." The group finally recommended building the civic center around the Civic Auditorium, and using the same site for the World's Fair was a logical development of that decision. The city council submitted the matter of funding the civic center to a bond issue, which the people passed by a 3 to 1 margin.

But this was not the end of the matter. Remember that the dispute over the county courthouse at the turn of the century was a fight between northend business interests and southend business interests, both of whom advocated building a civic center around the courthouse in their end of town. The fight over the civic center in the 1960s was a similar struggle. Just as in the earlier contest, the bond issue that the voters originally approved fell well short of the costs of the ambitious politicians' plans.

By the time the land was acquired with the money from the bond issue, there was little money left for the building plans, and of course the estimates on the original building plans were found to be far too low. The city council therefore enacted an ordinance revising the original plans. The council recommended building a concert-convention hall within the shell of the then-existing Civic Auditorium structure, instead of building a separate hall as promised under the first bond issue.

Rising from the midst of some disgruntled citizens, long-time Seattle Bar Association member Al Schweppe objected. Historian Murray Morgan has described Schweppe in this manner:

> In every American city there is somebody deeply suspicious of City Hall and its works, convinced that elected officials must be kept under close surveillance lest they circumvent the Constitution and the prescribed processes of law and order. They are given to emitting hallos of outrage and distress in public meetings and the public press. In most communities the practitioners of sustained dissent are ineffectual persons whose opinions may be taken at discount. It is Seattle's particular fate that one of its citizens most subject to feelings of question about proposed public action is a distinguished and able corporation lawyer; a past president of the Washington State Bar Association; a former dean of the University of Washington Law School... in short, a formidable foe.[5]

Characteristically, after the city council altered the original plan, Schweppe is said to have muttered, "By God, they think at City Hall they can get away with anything.... I just gently called their attention to the fact that they couldn't do what they were talking about doing because it wouldn't be legal."[6] Consequently, Schweppe and his client, William H. Davis, sued the city, Mayor Clinton, and the City Council, winning an injunction against the council's alteration of the original plan. Schweppe, you see, was an opera fan and wanted a separate opera house as originally planned. He had campaigned for the original bond issue on that basis. But the city submitted the matter to the voters and the electorate approved the altered plan.

Undeterred, Schweppe and Davis filed a second suit seeking an injunction against the altered plan by claiming that the percentage of voters approving the plan was not the percentage that the Washington Constitution mandated for such elections. Schweppe claimed that he was reluctant to sue: "I never was against the civic center or an Opera House. But I damn well am against the wrong way of doing things."[7] Both suits were appealed to the Washington Supreme Court, and a narrow majority, 5-4, held the election valid and lifted the injunctions.[8]

Alfred J. Schweppe was dedicated to the practice of law. During his career he was dean of the University of Washington law school, president of the Washington State Bar Association, a political activist, and a respected corporate lawyer.

Schweppe had practiced law in Seattle since 1922, when he arrived here from the University of Minnesota law school. After four years of private practice he became the dean of the University of Washington law school at age thirty-one, one of the youngest law school deans anywhere. In 1930 he left the law school and joined McMicken, Ramsey, Rupp & Schweppe, one of the oldest firms in the city, with roots in the Struve & Leary firm. He was still a member of the firm at its dissolution fifty-nine years later, in 1989. His name has been raised often in this history, in reference to the redrafting of the state's liquor laws after prohibition, and in reference to being the secretary of three organizations at the same time, the Washington State Bar Association, the State Judicial Council, and the Seattle Bar Association. His longtime partner John Rupp noted that Al in the 1960s became famous in Seattle as the keeper of the public conscience, involved in many public concerns such as the opera house dispute, a controversial expressway, and the declaration of the Northlake area as a "blighted area" by the university.[9] Rupp noted, however, that most of these controversies were taken on by Schweppe because he was representing clients, not himself. "Inevitably, however, because of the force of Al's personality and because of the wisdom and imagination that he brings to bear on a case in which he is counsel, it is not long before the public loses sight of the client and thinks of the cases as 'Schweppe's case.' "[10]

The Goldmark Case[11]

Despite much that was positive in the early years of the 1960s, anti-communist hysteria was still widespread. Its poison led to a tragic series of events, beginning with several defamatory newspaper articles regarding John Goldmark. Goldmark, a state representative from Okanogan County in Eastern Washington, had just begun his campaign for re-election. He brought suit against several individuals who had accused him of being a communist, accusations that proved both socially and politically costly for Goldmark.

The suit drew state- and nationwide attention. Representing Goldmark was Seattle attorney William Dwyer, who would go on to the presidency of the Seattle-King County Bar Association and eventually to serve as a federal district court judge.

John Goldmark was a respected three-term Democratic state legislator and ran for re-election in 1962. One of the county's weekly newspapers attacked him as a communist sympathizer. Proof of this, the article claimed, was threefold: First, he advocated repeal of the McCarran Act, a statute that required all Communist party members to register with the government. Second, his son Charles was attending Reed College, "the only school in the Northwest" that had invited Gus Hall, the secretary of the Communist party, to speak. Third, Goldmark was a member of the American Civil Liberties Union, "an organization closely affiliated with the Communist movement in the United States."[12]

The article proved to be only the opening salvo in a barrage of terrible rumors and meetings attacking Goldmark. He eventually lost the election.

John Goldmark and his wife, Sally, had moved to Okanogan County from Brooklyn, where both had grown up. John, whose father was of Austrian Jewish descent, attended Quaker schools and eventually went to Harvard Law School, where he graduated with honors. He subsequently served in World War II. Goldmark met Sally Ringe in Washington, D. C., in 1941; by 1942, they planned to marry.

Sally told John that she had become a member of the Communist party in 1935, at a time when the party was large and relatively popular. Though John disagreed with the communist objectives and Sally's party association, the two married in 1943. He continued to object to communism, but he did not ask Sally to end her membership. Charles, their first child, was born in 1944. When John was finally discharged from the service, the family moved west in search of an unspoiled landscape.

They eventually bought a large ranch in a remote part of Okanogan County and set about becoming ranchers. Eventually though, in 1950, Goldmark took the bar exam in Seattle, and soon afterward he began attending Democratic party political events. In 1956 he ran successfully for the state house of representatives. Sally's political past, however, continued to haunt them. In 1949 two FBI agents had visited the Goldmark ranch to ask Sally about her former activities in the Communist party. In 1953, John, in order to pass a security clearance required as part of his navy reserve service, had to discuss his wife's political history with naval intelligence officers.

In 1956, at the height of the national paranoia, Sally was called to Seattle to appear before the federal House Un-American Activities Committee. The committee members questioned her in a private executive session, but nothing came of her testimony.

But in 1962, members of the John Birch Society, the *Tonasket Tribune*'s editor, Ashley Holden, and the never-say-die witch-hunter Albert Canwell, who had been the chair of the local Un-American Activities Committee in the forties, launched a public campaign against Goldmark that was successful. Goldmark was defeated in his bid for re-election by a 3-1 margin.

Goldmark sued Canwell, Holden, and others for libel. The case went to trial in 1963 and lasted ten weeks. In January 1964, the jury found the defendants liable and awarded the Goldmarks forty thousand dollars in damages. The verdict was eventually set aside because the United States Supreme Court held, in another case, that a public figure such as Goldmark had to prove "actual malice" in order to succeed in a defamation suit. Nevertheless, Goldmark was thoroughly vindicated when the trial judge, Theodore S. Turner of Seattle, noted that Goldmark was neither a communist nor a pro-communist.

An even darker era awaited the Goldmark family, over twenty years later. In the early morning hours of Christmas Eve in 1985 a terrible tragedy struck. Charles Goldmark, the son of John and Sally Goldmark, and Charles' wife, Annie, and their two children, Colin and Derek, were brutally murdered in their Seattle home by a deranged young man named David Lewis Rice.

John Goldmark was a naval reserve intelligence officer, a cattle rancher, and a lawyer. In 1962, during his bid for re-election to the state house of representatives, he was accused by the local newspaper of being a communist sympathizer.

Rice admitted that although robbery was one of his motives, he chose the Goldmarks under the completely mistaken belief that Charles Goldmark belonged to the Communist party; he thought that he could get Goldmark to tell him about a worldwide communist conspiracy. Rice also mistakenly thought the Goldmarks were Jewish. Charles Goldmark had been very active in the local bar and was a well-respected lawyer.[13] He had attended Reed College and Yale Law School and was admitted to the bar in Washington in 1973. He worked briefly for Davis, Wright, Todd, Riese & Jones before starting his own firm in 1975: Wickwire, Lewis, Goldmark & Schorr.

His practice emphasized what he described as "public law," representing municipally chartered public authorities throughout the state that undertook projects such as historic preservation, low-income housing development, and rehabilitating Seattle's Pike Place Public Market.

Goldmark was intensely involved in bar activities as well as other civic work. He served on numerous committees of the Washington State Bar Association and the Seattle-King County Bar Association. He served as a member of the board of trustees and eventually as chair of the Young Lawyers Section of the Seattle-King County Bar Association.

At the time of his death, Goldmark was president of the Legal Foundation of Washington, a foundation that channels interest on lawyer trust accounts to benefit legal services for the indigent. Goldmark had been a driving force behind establishing the foundation and had helped secure the Washington Supreme Court's approval of the plan. Today, the memory of the Goldmark family is preserved by the foundation in its yearly Charles Goldmark Pro Bono Service Award.

James Wickwire, Goldmark's longtime law partner, gave the following statement on behalf of the firm:

Chuck Goldmark was one of this state's most brilliant and outstanding attorneys, a wise counselor, our partner and friend. He was one of Seattle's finest, hardest-working and most generous and public-spirited citizens. He loved his wife Annie, and together they raised two wonderful children in a happy home. He was the best of all of us. His death is a tragedy for everyone of good will in the Seattle community. We will never understand or accept this.[14]

The Lasting Effects of a Tumultuous Decade

Despite the bar's attention in the early sixties to the World's Fair and other commercial controversies, the Association remained concerned with the plight of those who were under-represented by the law. In March 1961, the Bar Association opened its Lawyer Referral Service to meet the many requests for referrals to attorneys in the area. This was maintained alongside the Legal Aid Bureau, which was specifically to provide assistance to people unable to pay for legal services.

The Association directed its energy toward the community too by its use of the media. *The Daily Journal of Commerce* began publishing a weekly article on the activities of the Seattle-King County Bar Association and, for a short while, named a "Lawyer of the Week." The first two recipients were Sam Levinson and Frank P. Helsell. In 1960, the Bar Association began sponsoring radio and television programs on KING regarding various aspects of the law. Another television series started in 1969 on KCTS, jointly sponsored by SKCBA and the Washington State Bar Association. The first show was entitled "The Limits of Protest."[15] The reinvigorated Young Lawyers Section (YLS) took advantage of the new social spirit as well. In the same month that the new *Bar Bulletin* was born, the YLS began a tradition of meeting with the Canadian Bar Association of British Columbia, and for the next fifteen years the two groups traded off hosting one another.

The YLS also continued to sponsor seminars that were designed to teach new lawyers the "nuts and bolts" of law practice. The seminars were often taught by people such as future Washington Supreme Court Justice Robert Utter and other local luminaries such as Ken MacDonald and John

What began as a Martin Luther King boycott of public transportation in Alabama in 1955 spread to Seattle, and following Dr. King's death in 1968 the voices for equality for all came from streets across America. Shown is a public equal rights demonstration in Seattle in 1965.

Mucklestone. Those who attended were not always "new," either.

YLS actively supported pro bono legal work and other community interests. In 1966, the YLS formed the High School Lawyer Liaison Committee to provide an attorney for every high school in the city in order to help teach students about the law and to distribute various booklets on legal topics of concern to high school students. Booklet subjects included the draft and the right to protest, which directly reflected national tension over the Vietnam conflict.

In that same year, 1966, YLS formed the Law and Poverty Committee. YLS's chair, Tom Zilly (a future SKCBA president and today, a federal district court judge), assured the senior bar members that YLS would fulfill the senior bar's commitment to organize 1,250 hours of volunteer attorney time to help deliver legal services to those who could not afford an attorney.

The young attorneys worked their volunteer hours at the three newly opened Legal Services Centers. The offices opened in November and December of 1965. The main office was in the Central Area of Seattle, at 1700 East Cherry Street, where among other issues, racial discrimination was a matter of growing concern to the legal community. The other offices were at the High Point Housing Project in West Seattle and at Pioneer Square. The offices were partly funded by the Office of Economic Opportunity (OEO) and were forerunners of today's federal legal services program.

The Seattle-King County Bar Association led the initiative for these offices. In 1965, it employed Lawrence L. Shafer as a consultant to plan and develop a legal services program that would meet the OEO specifications for such programs nationwide. Shafer subsequently became the associate director of the services centers and Robert D. Ashley was named the executive director of the program.

The new legal services centers eclipsed, but stood as a testament to, the bar's Legal Aid Bureau. The *Bar Bulletin* noted the continuity:

> Legal aid has a long and honorable history in King County. It all started in 1939 with the establishment of the Legal Aid Bureau, which was supported entirely by the local bar. Mrs. Esther V. Healy, who has served as director of the Bureau since 1953, will continue as a staff member under the new program. Her dedication to the legal aid program has earned the respect and gratitude of the bench and bar.[16]

In the year before the legal services centers opened, the Legal Aid Bureau had processed some four thousand applications on a budget of $30,000. In the first year of operation, the new centers operated on a budget of $220,000. The OEO granted $180,000 of the budget and the remaining $40,000 came from donations of money and services by local attorneys, their spouses, law students, and law school faculty.

In addition to Ashley and Shafer, the full-time paid staff included six attorneys. George T. Mattson, today a King County Superior Court judge, was one of the six. The governing board of trustees for the program included Judge Charles Z. Smith, who has since become the first African-American on the Washington Supreme Court.

Throughout the 1960s the Bar Association continued its support of legal services to the poor. It incorporated its own legal aid bureau, it instituted a lawyer referral panel, it supported legislation to create the legal services corporation as a means of meeting community needs for legal services, and it opposed legislation that would have seriously underfunded the corporation.

In 1963 the Bar Association began to develop a list of attorneys who were willing to represent indigents in federal court and to represent conscientious objectors, whose numbers were growing in proportion to the nation's expansion of its military activities in the Far East.[17] After the founding of the legal services centers, the Association turned its attention to indigents accused of crimes.

In 1968, the Bar Association approved sponsorship of a one-year pilot program for a public defender office, and in April, University of Washington School of Law Professor John Junker, Bertram L. Metzger of the SKCBA-initiated Legal Services Centers, and Robert G. Moch, who represented the Seattle-King County Bar Association, presented a plan to the Seattle City Council's finance committee regarding funding for the public defender office. The office was to be organized along the lines of the Legal Services Center but it would also provide legal counsel for people in criminal cases. (In the first year of its existence as a pilot program, the defender office had only represented individuals charged with misdemeanors in municipal court.)

With the program's success and the demonstrated need for its continuation, the Public Defender Corporation was formed one year later. The corporation was jointly sponsored by the city of Seattle, the Seattle Model Cities Program, and the Seattle-King County Bar Association. The *Bar Bulletin*'s July 1969 issue carried a front page article announcing the new program and its search for a director. In 1970, with a newly hired staff of attorneys, the Public Defender Corporation opened for business.

But just as representation for criminal defendants became surer, representation for indigent people in civil matters became less assured. In 1969, after the election of President Nixon, an appropriation bill in Congress threatened the operation of the anti-poverty legal services programs upon which SKCBA's Legal Services Centers had been founded. In reaction, SKCBA's president that year, William H. Gates, Jr., announced the trustees' unanimous disapproval of the Murphy amendment to the appropriation bill, which singled out Legal Services from other anti-poverty programs by making its work subject to the veto of any state governor and denying the OEO director the authority to override such a veto.

The American Bar Association also opposed the bill, stating that, if it passed, it would effectively end the Legal Services program. Joining in the opposition were many others, including the National Legal Aid and Defender Association, OEO director Donald Rumsfield, and the dean of the University of Washington law school, Luvern V. Rieke, as well as eighteen faculty members and two hundred of its law students.

In the final year of the decade, the YLS committee on Contemporary Legal Problems coordinated and monitored the Bar Association's implementation of recommendations in the Kramer Report, which had been developed by a statewide commission on the Causes and Prevention of Civil Disorder, headed by Washington Secretary of State A. Ludlow Kramer. The report, entitled "Race and Violence in the State of Washington," was an outgrowth of the civil turmoil that had occurred in Seattle and elsewhere in the United States in the preceding years. Specifically with regard to the law, the Kramer Report in part recommended the following: reorganize the state board against discrimination, prohibit fraternal organizations and private clubs from denying membership because of race or religion, appropriate money to state agencies to facilitate employing and training of disadvantaged job seekers, create a state housing agency, and make every effort to preserve the federal financial support of the OEO Legal Services program.

Eventually the Murphy Amendment was defeated and many of the Kramer Report recommendations were implemented. What had begun as the Legal Aid Bureau in 1939, had grown into the Legal Services Centers in 1965, with the help of federal funding. Shortly after that, the Pierce County Bar, with OEO funds, opened a legal services office in Tacoma, then one opened in Spokane, and finally a fourth office opened to serve Snohomish, Whatcom, Skagit, and Island counties.

By 1972 the need for statewide organization of the legal service centers became apparent, and the Washington State Bar's board of governors approved a $3,700,000 program for creating and funding a statewide legal services network.

At a luncheon in 1973 SKCBA honored one of the individuals who had kept the concept of representing the indigent a reality for many years, Esther V. Healy. Healy had served as director of the Seattle-King County Legal Aid Bureau from 1953 to 1966, when she became a staff member of the new Legal Services Center. She was a University of Washington law school graduate and was admitted to practice in 1920. Between 1920 and 1923, she was in the King County prosecuting attorney's office. After marrying another attorney, Tim Healy, a member of the Washington State Legislature, she raised four children and continued to practice law. In the final twenty years of that practice, she exclusively provided representation for the poor.

Local courts also changed considerably in the late sixties. First, King County Superior Court Local Rules went into effect in September 1968. Then the electorate approved a constitutional amendment creating a new intermediate court of appeals. Governor Dan Evans appointed several well-known Seattle attorneys and judges to the division of the court with jurisdiction over Seattle and the counties north of Seattle. The judges were Frank D. James and Robert F. Utter, as well as attorneys Jerome Farris and Charles Horowitz.

Also in 1968, President Nixon appointed longtime Seattle attorney Eugene A. Wright to the Court of Appeals for the Ninth Circuit. Eugene's father, Elias, was a longtime member of the Association and a recognized figure in the legal community for nearly the entire century.

The new Washington Court of Appeals opened in October 1969.

Anti-War Sentiment and Impeachment

The optimism of the early 1960s finally came completely apart at the end of the decade. Lyndon Johnson declined to run for the presidency in 1968, citing the need to devote all of his efforts to ending the Vietnam War. In that same year, Martin Luther King, Jr., and Robert Kennedy were both assassinated. Richard Nixon was elected president, and SKCBA board member John Ehrlichman resigned to serve in the Nixon administration. The war did not end, it escalated, and opposition grew even within the often conservative legal profession. The opposition within the Bar Association was polite. In January 1970, the World Peace through Law Committee of the Young Lawyers' Section of SKCBA presented a panel discussion entitled "The United States and Vietnam in the 1970s." It was not a wild group: the most radical proposal came from Judge Frank Hale of the Washington Supreme Court, who recommended withdrawal from Vietnam by the fall of 1970 in order to avoid a land war with China. University of Washington School of Law Professor Roy

Prosterman thought such a speedy withdrawal would be disastrous, and he supported Nixon's planned rate of withdrawal. United States Army captain Bernard Lockrem, a Seattle University military science instructor, agreed with Prosterman. Seattle attorney James Munn urged the audience to be more skeptical of the views of those who dissented against the war and urged maintaining military strength. Professor Derek Mills, active in War-Peace Studies, challenged the view that military power was the prerequisite to participating in international affairs, but he warned of the dangers of an isolationist policy.

In the streets and on college campuses, however, opposition was more defined. By 1970, protests at the University of Washington, and on the streets of Seattle, were nearly a daily occurrence. In Chicago, seven defendants faced criminal charges arising from their participation in demonstrations at the Democratic party convention in the summer of 1968. They became known as the Chicago Seven. In February, when those seven defendants were charged with contempt in the Chicago courtroom where one of them had been shackled and gagged, protests erupted everywhere, including Seattle. Protesters closed down the freeway as they marched from the University of Washington to downtown Seattle, where they surrounded both the federal courthouse and the Federal Building. The slogan for the demonstration was "Stop the Courts!" At the courthouse, the police were not to be seen, concealed as they were in the public library across the street.

When some people engaged in minor trashing, the police launched a tear-gas grenade and then poured out of the library. Chaos ensued and doors and windows in the courthouse were smashed. As a result, eight members of the Seattle Liberation Front were charged with conspiracy to damage the courthouse. When one of them could not be found, the group became known as the "Seattle Seven." Judge George Boldt was assigned to the resulting federal conspiracy trial. Because Boldt sat both in Seattle and Tacoma, he moved the trial to Tacoma in consideration of public safety. Spokane attorney Carl Maxey and Seattle attorney Jeff Steinborn were joined by Michael Tigar and other out-of-state attorneys in defending the Seattle Seven. Over the course of several months, Boldt charged several in the group with contempt and jailed them without bail. The Ninth Circuit overturned his decision to deny bail, and those in jail were released.

Trial began in November of 1970, and it was intensely followed by the public and the press. Eventually the defendants were convicted and sentenced to serve time in federal prison.

The Bar Association, while adopting a cautious approach to the question of the war, was nevertheless conscious of protecting the civil liberties of those who protested against it. When in the spring of 1970 the tactical squad of the Seattle police attacked an encampment of people on the University of Washington campus, an encampment consisting largely of undercover university police officers, the conduct of the police generally with regard to policing protesters became the subject of public debate. Members of the Bar Association, including its president, William Gates, Jr., met with Mayor Uhlman regarding the conduct of the police. The Association continued to urge and to monitor changes in the police force that would ensure that such incidents did not occur again.

Watergate was the next national concern to attract the attention of the organized bar. In October 1973, the Young Lawyers Section passed a resolution regarding Watergate, urging that a special prosecutor be funded in the wake of Nixon's firing of Special Prosecutor Archibald Cox. In January 1974, the Bar Association had a general meeting regarding its public position on "the subject of the conduct of President Nixon." Fred Tausend, Lem Howell, Don Schmechel, and Simon Wampold argued for a resolution favoring impeachment, while Ken Eikenberry, Frank Kitchell, and Bob Beezer argued against it.

In a follow-up meeting at the end of January, attorneys filled the presiding judge's courtroom for the special meeting of the bar on the Watergate matter. By the end of that long and acrimonious debate, the members there had passed the following resolution:

> *Now, therefore, be it resolved that this Association urge the House Judiciary Committee to send to the House of Representatives a resolution and Articles of Impeachment specifying the charges against the President as may be determined by the committee urging the House to vote to impeach the President so that a full public hearing on the facts may be had in conformity with the procedures established by the Constitution....*[18]

The Bar Association had never before taken such a position.

Indian Fishing Rights

Judge George Boldt and his decision regarding Indian fishing rights are threads that weave together much Pacific Northwest history. George Boldt was born in Chicago in 1903, the son of a Swedish immigrant. The family soon moved to Montana, where Boldt grew up. After receiving his law degree from the University of Montana in 1926, he headed for Seattle with another attorney, Archie Blair.[19]

It was the summer of 1927, and when they reached the summit of Blewett Pass in their open-top Ford, purchased a few days earlier for thirty-five dollars, they began to realize

Judge George Boldt was appointed by President Eisenhower to the federal district bench in Tacoma in 1953.

that their car's brakes were failing. They were lawyers, not engineers, and their attempt to slow their car's headlong descent by dragging a tree behind them did not work. Both of them had to leap from the car just before it went over an embankment and ended up in pieces off the side of the steep highway pass.

Moments later, though, fate came rolling along behind them. A dynamite truck drove up and offered them a ride in exchange for the salvageable parts of their Ford. Thus, in 1927, Boldt and Blair rode into Seattle in a dynamite truck.

Boldt began practicing law with Ballinger, Hutson & Boldt. As one of his colleagues on the federal bench, Judge Eugene A. Wright of the United States Ninth Circuit Court of Appeals recalled of Boldt, "When I was admitted to practice in 1937, he was a Seattle lawyer and a partner in a very fine firm and already well known as a great lawyer."[20]

During World War II, Boldt served as a paratrooper in the army and an intelligence officer in the Office of Strategic Services, the forerunner of the Central Intelligence Agency.

Indian fishing rights were hotly contested in the 1970s before and after the Boldt decision, based on George Gibbs' words in the Medicine Creek and Point Elliott treaties, which stated that native people had the right of "taking fish at all usual and accustomed grounds and stations...in common with all citizens." Shown are Governor Albert D. Rosellini and Chief Robert Satiacum at an Indian rights demonstration in 1965.

When he returned to Washington he began a new practice in Tacoma, and occasionally served as a special assistant attorney general. In that capacity he represented the state in litigation over the collapse of the Tacoma Narrows Bridge, which became known as "Galloping Gerty." In 1953 his judicial career began when President Eisenhower, whose brother David was a respected Tacoma attorney, appointed Boldt to the federal district bench. Boldt became a well-known speaker, and he was the honored speaker at the Seattle Bar Association's fiftieth-anniversary celebration in 1956. From the bench, he became known as the judge who, in 1959, sentenced International Teamster president Dave Beck to five years in prison for income tax evasion. His reputation spread further when he heard the case of the Seattle Seven, mentioned above.

But Boldt will be remembered by most for the 1974 fishing rights case that has come to bear his name, the "Boldt decision." Even though the treaties of 1854 and 1855 had promised the native people the "right of taking fish at all usual and accustomed grounds and stations...in common with all citizens," both the places and the fish soon began disappearing.

As early as 1866 big canneries were established on the Columbia and, by 1883, fifty-five canneries dotted the banks of the river and its tributaries. Cannery-owned fish wheels and traps netted hundreds of tons of fish, and the use of gill nets hastened depletion of the state's fishery. The habitat then

began to change when the rivers were dammed and when some water was diverted for irrigation. For fish, the environment had deteriorated.

Soon a series of federal and state court cases, as well as state regulations, limited to some degree the off-reservation fishing rights of natives. The Puyallup River was an example of how the limitation on fishing progressed. In 1925, the state declared the steelhead a game fish and prohibited capture of the fish by net except by natives. By 1927 the state had extended the net ban to natives as well. In the early 1950s, members of the Puyallup Tribe, living alongside the river, decided to challenge these laws: they laid nets into the river at their traditional fishing places.

For several years nothing happened, but in 1964 the state arrested Chief Robert Satiacum and James Young of the Puyallup tribe for fishing in the river with nets. Though their convictions were eventually overturned, the state authorities continued to challenge native off-reservation net fishing.

For the next decade the controversy spread to other rivers and other tribes, and it eventually led to the famous fish-ins of the 1960s. These fish-ins, in the days of widespread protest and dissent, involved tribal activists such as Janet McCloud, Hank Adams, and Bill Frank, Jr., as well as many others who were joined by national figures such as Marlon Brando and comedian Dick Gregory.

In deliberately challenging the fishing laws, Indians and Indian supporters were being arrested and tried. The era culminated in an encampment by natives on the Puyallup River, which was eventually broken up by federal authorities with tear gas and arrests. Finally, the federal government decided to intervene by suing the state of Washington to determine the fishing rights of all the people in the area. That case, called *United States v. Washington*, came to be heard by Judge George Boldt and became the Boldt decision.

Boldt decided that the tribes under the original 1854 and 1855 treaties had a right to fish at their usual and accustomed grounds and stations off the reservation and in common with the other citizens. He interpreted this to mean that the tribes had a right to 50 percent of the fish catch.

The decision, announced on February 12, 1974, was immediately controversial, causing many non-Indian fishermen to bitterly attack the judge and eventually to call for his impeachment. In the footsteps of the anti-war protesters of a few years before, seven hundred sport-fishing citizens marched around the federal courthouse in Tacoma, protesting the ruling. In September of that same year, non-Indian gill netters and their supporters showed up to protest at the courthouse, too. But within a year the Ninth Circuit Court of Appeals upheld the decision and, in 1979, Boldt was finally vindicated when the United States Supreme Court affirmed his original 1974 decision.

Boldt, as a federal judge, had decided in much the same way as John J. McGilvra, as United States attorney in the 1860s, had decided, that the treaties were enforceable contracts and that as a consequence the native people deserved a portion of the bargain they had struck with the government when they surrendered millions of acres of their land.

The Diversification of the Bar Begins

In the 1970s many people went to law school, and law school student-bodies became more diverse. Dean Richard S. L. Roddis of the University of Washington School of Law observed that between the years 1965 and 1969, law school admissions had been level, but that "sharp increases" occurred after 1969. In 1969 there were 523 students enrolled in law school. After Gonzaga in Spokane and the University of Puget Sound in Tacoma opened law schools, the number increased by nearly a thousand in 1972, when the total number of students in Washington's law schools reached 1,472.[21] The nation as a whole experienced a similar increase in the number of law students.

Roddis listed a variety of reasons commonly given for the increase: more students generally, due to the baby boom; a constriction in other professional fields; returning Vietnam veterans entering law school; and the perception that the law was an effective arena for social change.

The increase in law students was gradually reflected in state bar admissions figures as well. Though the number had been gradually rising in the 1960s, there were sharp increases beginning in 1971 and 1972. Regarding diversity among law students, Roddis noted: "Proportionately, at least, the numbers of women and of members of minority groups seeking legal education have increased, though in absolute terms neither is a large factor in the total numbers."[22] To increase the number of minority admissions, the University of Washington instituted an alternative admissions program.

Out of that program arose one of the first test cases of "reverse discrimination" in affirmative action programs, over the application of Marco DeFunis to attend the University of Washington law school. When he was not admitted, he claimed reverse discrimination because of the law school's program for admitting minority students. King County Superior Court Judge Lloyd Shorett ruled in his favor, referring in part to the *Litchman v. Shannon* [23] case, discussed in chapter three in regard to Mark Litchman's case against the state for charging tuition at state schools. Shorett ordered the school to admit DeFunis, who began classes shortly afterward.

The case was angrily debated in the Seattle legal community, as well as nationwide. The Bar Association considered the issue at its December 8, 1971, quarterly

meeting. Afterward, by a vote of 110 to 32, the members passed a resolution in favor of the board seeking permission to file an amicus curiae brief. Though the brief was not to be filed on behalf of either party, it was to support the "implementation and continuance of SKCBA's minority scholarship program." Through this program, instituted under William Gates, Jr.'s presidency in 1969, SKCBA contributed ten thousand dollars to a scholarship specifically earmarked for minority law students.

When the DeFunis case was eventually appealed to the United States Supreme Court, it was the first time that court faced a "reverse discrimination" issue. The Court ultimately declined to decide the issue, finding the case "moot" because, by the time the Court would have decided the issue, DeFunis would have already graduated from law school. Today, Marco DeFunis practices law in Seattle.

The issue of law school admissions and minorities in the legal field did not end with DeFunis. In 1975, two state bar committees issued reports on areas of concern to minority and women law students and attorneys. One, called the Zilly Report after its chairman, Tom Zilly, focused on the Special Admissions Program at the University of Washington law school. The other, called the Grim Report after the committee's chair, G. Keith Grim, addressed proposals for making the state bar exam more fair.

At a state bar board meeting after the reports were issued, representatives of the Washington Women Lawyers (WWL), Anne Ellington, today a superior court judge, and Jane Noland, today a member of the Seattle City Council, criticized the reports. WWL's position was that the Grim and Zilly reports "do not provide the Board or the bar association with the answer to the question raised: why do a disproportionate number of minority applicants fail to pass the Washington bar examination?"[24]

Several other groups joined the WWL in the criticism, including the Loren Miller Law Club, the Coalition for Justice in the Legal System, the Asian Law Association, and the Young Lawyers Section of the Seattle-King County Bar Association. Lish Whitson, representing the SKCBA Young Lawyers Board, reported to the state bar meeting that his board endorsed the WWL's recommendation that further study be undertaken to identify the reasons for minority applicants failing the bar.

The under-representation of minorities in the practicing bar continued to be a bar concern. The actual number of minority attorneys practicing in the state is often difficult to ascertain. In a 1983 article in the *Washington State Bar News*, Hwa-Tsun Feng reported his findings on the issue. Hwa-Tsun Feng chaired the Seattle-King County Bar Association's Minority Representation in the Law Committee, one of the Young Lawyers Section's committees.

The article, with what evidence was available, made the following assertions: that there were too few minority lawyers, that minorities were generally under-served by the legal profession, that minorities were under-represented in the legal profession generally, and that a higher percentage of minority lawyers practiced as government attorneys and too few practiced in private firms, especially the larger firms. Finally, the article noted the statistics showing a leveling off of minority admissions at the University of Washington School of Law. These assertions were confirmed several years later, when the Washington Legislature established the Washington State Minority and Justice Task Force to investigate many of the same concerns that Hwa-Tsun Feng's article touched upon. Charles Z. Smith, who was soon to be a supreme court justice, chaired the task force beginning in 1987.

Judge Betty Fletcher became the first woman president of the Seattle-King County Bar Association in 1972, and in 1979 she was appointed to the federal appellate bench by President Carter.

In 1990, the task force released its report, which, among many findings, offered hard statistics showing that minority attorneys were a small percentage of the bar, were likely to earn far less than non-minority attorneys, and were more likely to work in government agencies than were non-minority attorneys.

The report also noted that of the 371 judges in the state, on all levels, only 16, or 4.3 percent, were identified as racial and ethnic minorities, slightly less than the percentage of minority lawyers. All of these judges, except for Justice Smith at the supreme court and another judge in Pierce County, served on the bench in Seattle and King County.

To remedy this under-representation, the task force had many recommendations, among them increasing the number of minority law school students, increasing financial assistance to minority law school students, and instructing in the schools on the effects of racial and ethnic bias. The task force recommended that bar associations publish information regarding bar membership, support legislation to enlarge the jury source list, increase minority representation on judicial screening committees, and ensure that judicial screening committees screen candidates for cross-cultural awareness and sensitivity.[25]

The Washington Women Lawyers organization was just two years old when it shook up the state bar with its attack on the Grim and Zilly reports, and the WWL continued throughout the era to be an advocate for women and minorities in the profession. In 1970 there were only seventeen first-year women law students in Washington, three women judges, and a handful of women attorneys.[26] A small group of Seattle attorneys formed WWL in 1970 for the purpose of promoting equal rights for women and advancing women to positions of leadership in the legal profession.

The legal profession, and its professional organizations, had long been dominated by males. Accordingly, with rare exceptions, the board of trustees of SKCBA had long been all-male. In the latter decades of this century, occasionally a woman's name would appear in the minutes, inevitably as secretary of the board. The name most often appearing—Betty Fletcher—gradually emerged from that status and became an officer other than secretary.

It was not the first time she had been first. She had been the first editor of the *Seattle Bar Bulletin*. She had been first in her class at the University of Washington law school, and was the first woman to become a partner with Preston, Thorgrimson.

Judge Fletcher's father, John H. Binns, was an attorney, and her daughter Susan Fletcher French became a professor of law, as did one son, William Fletcher. Judge Fletcher married

Robert L. Fletcher, a professor of law at the University of Washington law school, in 1942. Then in 1972, Betty Fletcher became the first woman president of the Seattle-King County Bar Association. Under her presidency the Bar Association created a Long-Range Planning Committee, chaired by William Dwyer, established a plan for moving from the Arctic Building to new offices in the Central Building, and continued its support for legal services and the lawyer referral service. In 1979 President Carter appointed her to the federal appellate bench—not the first woman there, but among the first—where she continues to serve today.

Progress in affirmative action occurred elsewhere. Ten years after the founding of Washington Women Lawyers, 30 to 40 percent of the students at the University of Washington law school were women. Women sat at all levels of the state bench as well as the federal district court and Ninth Circuit Court of Appeals. And by 1990, WWL estimated, 250 to 300 women were practicing law in the state.

In 1981 Governor Dixie Lee Ray appointed Carolyn Dimmick to the Washington Supreme Court, the first woman on the high court in Washington. Dimmick had served on both the court of appeals and the King County Superior Court benches. She resigned the state's high bench in 1984 and was appointed to the United States District Court in Seattle.

Following Judge Dimmick to the high court was Judge Barbara Durham. In 1980, Durham had been the first woman in Washington to sit on the court of appeals.

Though women eventually were routinely elected to SKCBA's board of trustees, including its presidency, it was some time later before any number of minority members became trustees of the board, and the presidency has yet to be filled by a minority member. Fortunately, the same is not still true of the state's supreme court. In 1988 a longtime Seattle judge, lawyer, and bar activist, Judge Charles Smith, was appointed to the Washington Supreme Court.

Smith became the first African-American and first member of any ethnic minority to serve in that position. Smith had begun his career in Seattle in the early 1950s, when the unspoken rule was that firms did not hire black attorneys. As a consequence, he applied for a judicial clerkship with the state supreme court and accepted an appointment from Justice Matthew Hill. This experience left a permanent impression upon Smith, who has often said that nine months working for Hill were far better than the three years he had spent in law school.

After clerking, Smith worked in the King County prosecutor's office before leaving for the Justice Department at the request of United States Attorney General Robert Kennedy. He worked there on the team investigating the Teamsters' Union pension fund. It was Smith who eventually brought an indictment against the union's president, Jimmy Hoffa.

Upon returning to Seattle, Smith served on the municipal court bench, then the superior court bench from 1966 to 1973, when he resigned to teach at the University of Washington School of Law. Eventually, Smith returned to private practice with the firm of Rosenblum & Smith, where he was a partner until his appointment to the supreme court.

Political Assassination and Justice on Main Street

When a young Filipino man, Silme Domingo, crawled outside onto the sidewalk in front of a union hall one afternoon in June 1981, a cook from the restaurant across the street thought at first that the downed man was just another drunk on South Main Street. The inebriated stumbled through the area all day and night and had been doing so for nearly a century. Main Street runs parallel to Yesler Way, and since the city's founding, Yesler has been a dividing line: north of it lived the wealthy and the white, south of it, those who were neither well off nor white.

Where Domingo and the cook faced one another was two blocks south of Yesler, on the edge of Seattle's tenderloin, Pioneer Square. Just a few blocks west of the spot, a logger had been shot during the anti-Chinese riots in 1886, and just a few blocks east, in the 1940s, two Filipino unionists had been killed by a cannery employer's son. Sprawled on the sidewalk in front of the cannery workers' blue and grey union hall, with his long black hair and tan skin, Domingo looked like what many local whites would call "just another drunken Indian." At least he did until the cook saw all the blood. Inside the union hall, Gene Viernes lay, mortally wounded, a letter he was typing still rolled into the typewriter.

The area south of Yesler was the dark part of Seattle's psyche. It had always been the scene of vice, most notably and silently the vice of segregation. The Chinese, who had lived on Third and Fourth between Yesler and Main prior to the federal Chinese Exclusion Act and their wholesale expulsion from Seattle in 1886, had gradually returned, but were moved again to make way for the King Street Station and the tunnel leading to it. The new "Chinatown," as it became known, was along King Street, with Fifth Avenue the western boundary, Dearborn on the south, Yesler, the northern boundary, and Rainier on the east.

Among the most respected attorneys of the 1990s, Joanne Maida, Assistant U. S. Attorney, successfully prosecuted Ferdinand Marcos, then president of the Philippines, and his wife, Imelda, proving their liability for the murders of union activists Silme Domingo and Gene Viernes.

The Japanese, especially between 1890 and 1900, originally settled on lower Main Street after the Chinese had been expelled. Gradually this settlement moved east on Main Street toward Sixth and Seventh avenues. After the Japanese Exclusionary Act of 1924, however, the number of Japanese dropped, and Filipino immigration filled the need for cheap labor in the area and in the Alaska salmon canneries. These people largely settled in the new Chinatown, too, and the area, more and more an International District, remained a relatively isolated and self-sufficient community.

In the 1960s, however, a freeway split the community and the raised concrete strip came to mark the eastern edge of the district. When Seattle wanted to become a contender for major league sports, the area just south of the district became a target for another removal: the county planned a large covered stadium and its attendant parking lots for the area south of the train depots, and once again the people south of Yesler were

asked to accommodate. Many people in the International District protested throughout 1972, but in November of that year county officials broke ground for the dome amid a noisy protest. For some businesses, the stadium's location would prove advantageous, while others suffered.

Having lost the battle over the stadium, community opposition leaders turned their attention to marshaling energies toward ensuring that the government would provide low-income housing in the area. One of the leaders of the opposition was Silme Domingo, a young University of Washington student of Filipino ancestry. Domingo became the editor of a newspaper in the International District, the *Asian Family Affair*, and the paper covered not only the battle over the dome but also many international, national, and other community concerns, including organizing against the regime of Ferdinand Marcos in the Philippines.

During this time Domingo and another young activist, Gene Viernes, as well as others in the Filipino community, became involved in organizing for better working conditions for the mostly Filipino work force that was shipped out yearly from Seattle to the Alaska canneries. They organized the Alaska Cannery Workers' Association and successfully filed suit against the Alaska cannery owners for discrimination and for deplorable working conditions.

Domingo and Viernes, like many political activists of the sixties, increasingly turned in the late seventies toward the "long march through the institutions." The union that represented the Alaska cannery workers, the Cannery Workers Local 37 of the International Longshoremen's & Warehousemen's Union, had long been suspected of corruption in its practices in dispatching workers to Alaska.

In 1978 Domingo and Viernes and others organized the Rank and File Committee to advocate change in the union, and in 1980 the committee ran a reform slate of candidates for office in the union. Domingo was elected secretary-treasurer and Viernes dispatcher. However, the local's president, Tony Baruso, was re-elected. Shortly thereafter Domingo and Viernes traveled to the union's international convention in Hawaii and advocated from the floor that the international union go on record opposing Marcos.

May and June are the primary months when workers are sent to the Alaska canneries out of Seattle, and Domingo and Viernes were busy reforming the dispatch practices of the union on June 1, 1981, when two young Filipino men entered the union hall and shot the union officers at point-blank range.

Viernes died instantly, but Domingo was able to get out onto Main Street and summon help from the cook across the street. When medics and firemen arrived, from just a half a block away on Main, Domingo was able to tell a fireman the names of the assailants—Pompeyo Benito Guloy and Jimmy Bulosan Ramil—who had driven away with a third person in a black Pontiac Trans Am, with an American Eagle decal on the hood.

By the time Domingo died, less than twenty-four hours later, the police had determined that the murders were related to criminal gang activity and the gang's involvement in gambling and union dispatch practices. The two assailants, Guloy and Ramil, were said to be members of the Tulisan street gang, which controlled certain enterprises in the International District.

But the families of the slain men, as well as many of their friends in the community, insisted from the first day that the guilt went much higher than two young thugs. Family members and members of the community formed the Committee for Justice for Domingo and Viernes and would fight for nearly ten years before their theories were finally proved in the state and federal courts in Seattle.

When the gun that killed the two twenty-nine-year-old men was discovered in a trash can in West Seattle, and when it turned out to be registered to the local union's president, Tony Baruso, a few more links in the chain of guilt were added to the committee's theory. Shortly after this discovery, the police arrested Baruso, but he was released due to insufficient evidence. He contended that the gun had been stolen from his car in the International District several months earlier. The police traced the Trans Am to the reputed head of the Tulisan gang, Tony Dictado, and he was arrested shortly after Baruso. Eventually, Ramil, Guloy, and Dictado were convicted and sentenced to life in prison without possibility of parole.

A year and a half after the slayings, the police arrested a fourth man, Teodoro Domingues, also known as Boy Pilay and a member of Tulisan. He was viewed as at least a key witness, if not a participant, who could lead the authorities to others involved in the killings. But the prosecutors had to release him shortly after his arrest due to insufficient evidence, and barely two months later he was dead, two bullets in his head, his body thrown into the brush near a school in South Park.

The Committee for Justice had lost a key witness but continued to insist that Baruso was guilty, too. More stunning, though, was the committee's contention that the Philippine president, Ferdinand Marcos, and the Philippine intelligence network had paid for the killings because of the anti-Marcos organizing done by Domingo and Viernes. Nearly everyone dismissed the contention as absurd.

Absurd, that is, until the committee filed suit in federal court against Marcos, his wife, Imelda Marcos, and the Philippine government, and through discovery began to find documents making the links ever more apparent. Finally, the attorneys found a document linking a friend of the Marcoses', a wealthy San Francisco banker, Leonilo Malabed, to the

murders. The local's president, Tony Baruso, had traveled to San Francisco a few days before the killings, and it appeared as though Malabed had paid him for the assassinations of Domingo and Viernes. The sum involved matched the amount determined to have been paid to the Tulisan gang for the killings.

When Marcos was finally run out of the Philippines for his family's pillage of the country, the Committee for Justice's attorneys were able to take his deposition in Hawaii. In a videotaped deposition, Marcos admitted that he used four agencies to gather intelligence in the United States against people organizing against him here. He described Malabed as a friend, but invoked his Fifth Amendment right against self-incrimination when asked about any intelligence agency connections with Malabed. After many years of legal work, the civil suit, which was argued for by Assistant U. S. Attorney, Joanne Y. Maida, was tried before a six-member jury in the courtroom of United States District Court Judge Barbara Rothstein. Eight years after the murders, the jury found Ferdinand Marcos and his wife, Imelda, liable for the murders of Domingo and Viernes and ordered Marcos' estate to pay the families of the slain men $15 million. In 1990, based upon the information gathered from the civil trial, Tony Baruso was again arrested and tried for the murders of his two fellow union officers. This time he was convicted, and today is serving a life sentence for the murders.

Few other cases in Seattle legal history have involved as large an army of attorneys and judges over such an extended period of time as did the various criminal and civil trials that resulted from the murders of two young union activists on Main Street. During the nearly ten years the case had continued, the bar had undergone many changes.

The Legal Profession in Transition

The legal profession at Seattle's inception was populated by characters such as the humorous and "absorbing" Ike Hall, the dapper and fastidious James McNaught, and the oddly named Orange Jacobs. The names and deeds of Burke and McGilvra and Greene and Hanford were well known among the general population, and often the entertainment of the day was to attend court proceedings. But as lawyers grew in number, the unique ones became harder to see. Further, the growing number of corporate attorneys appeared less and less often in the public forum of the courtroom.

A few striking personalities remained though, even into the second half of this century. Elias Wright was among the few. In C. H. Hanford's history of Seattle, *Seattle & Environs*, he reports that Elias Wright arrived in Seattle in 1905 to begin the practice of law. What first struck people about

Wright was his dress: he wore high-top shoes, a Prince Albert-style frock coat, and a high, stiff collar, and carried in one hand a well-worn briefcase and in the other a cane—with which he occasionally struck people. On his head he often wore a hat, and he always wore a ponderous frown.

In a short, informal history of some early bar figures, Seattle attorney Roger Shidler tells of one time when an opposing attorney, Spencer Gray, obtained an order from the court allowing him to inspect a car in the possession of one of Elias Wright's clients. Mr. Wright informed Gray that the car would be in front of Wright's office, probably in the Burke Building at Second and Marion, at a date and time certain.[27]

When Gray arrived on the appointed day, he gave the car a cursory inspection and then began to open the hood. Mr. Wright loudly objected, telling Gray "You can't do that, the order didn't allow you to inspect inside the car." When Gray persisted, Wright began swinging his cane and chasing Gray around the car. Out of the gathering crowd another well-known attorney emerged, Tracy Griffin. Griffin knew both attorneys well and realized he should intervene before harm came to one or all of them. Griffin mediated an agreement on the spot: Gray could look under the hood, but he could not crawl inside and he had to keep both feet on the ground.

John Rupp states that his father, Otto Rupp, who practiced with McMicken, Ramsey, Rupp & Schweppe his entire life, held the opinion that Elias Wright "knew more things that just weren't so than anybody else" he knew.[28] When John Rupp joined his father's firm they would often lunch together with other members of the firm at Jack Peters' Restaurant, across the street from their offices in the Colman Building.

Rupp relates the story of one lunch when Elias Wright joined them and told them all that horses had a "blind tooth" at the back of their jaws that would cause the horse to go blind if it were not removed. Mr. Wright related how he had removed hundreds of such teeth from horses in his life. The skeptical group chewed on the story for a while until John finally asked Elias, "If what you say is true, Elias, why aren't all wild horses blind?" Elias thought a bit and then replied with what should have been obvious to all: "Wild horses don't have a blind tooth."

Describing Wright, who at eighty-six still refused to retire, a local newspaper columnist, John Reddin, said that he was as much a part of the downtown scene as the Smith Tower and looked as if he had stepped directly from the pages of the *Saturday Evening Post*. Despite his often gruff and bellicose manner, Reddin related, that members of the bar and judiciary had a fondness and deep affection for their "bushy-browed and scowling adversary," Elias Wright. Wright's son,

Eugene, became a prominent attorney in Seattle. In 1968 Eugene was appointed to the Ninth Circuit Court of Appeals.

Another living connection with Seattle's legal history is Lady Willie Forbus. She turned one hundred on August 24, 1992, after having practiced law in Seattle for nearly sixty-five years, from 1918 until at least 1985, when she was ninety-three and still doing some limited legal work for longtime loyal clients. Born to a poor rural family with six children in Mississippi, she aimed early for a legal career.

In 1915, Harvard, Yale, Columbia, and Cornell law schools all turned her down because of her gender. She went to one of the few "open schools" at the time, the University of Michigan, and finished first in her class. She moved to Seattle immediately afterward when a friend advised her that Seattle was hospitable to women attorneys.

After a mandatory year's clerkship with the Donworth firm in 1918, she opened her own practice and for the next ten years was probably the only woman attorney practicing in Seattle. She became the first woman to run for King County prosecutor and the first to run for the King County Superior Court bench, and though she lost she had broken new ground for future women attorneys. In 1942 she successfully ran for the state senate and served one full term of three legislative sessions.

Over her many years of practice, Forbus was a well-known figure walking in and out of the county's courthouse. She was a highly regarded lawyer whom Judge Donald Voorhees found "always warm, enthusiastic and positive." Ken MacDonald remarked, "She has always been a forthright and articulate civil libertarian, with an intelligent and perceptive mind." Judge John Riley described her as "an old-fashioned liberal populist with a marvelous commitment to social justice, but without cynicism. No furrowed brow for Lady Willie."[29]

As the 1980s began though, there were many furrowed brows among lawyers. The long-term practitioners were becoming lost amid an apparent crush of new attorneys. The number of active lawyers increased from 3,100 in 1965 to 10,700 in 1982.[30] The Washington State Bar Association grew more between 1972 and 1977 alone than it had in the preceding forty-five years of its existence. The increase in attorneys seemed to increase litigation, too. Civil filings increased in Washington 42 percent between 1971 and 1981.[31] Worse, articles in *Money* magazine and *Student Lawyer*[32] in 1980 and *Washington State Bar News* in 1983 all seemed to indicate that job prospects for lawyers, journalists, and teachers were the worst of all the professions.[33]

Corresponding to the rise in lawyers, the early 1980s became an era of mergers throughout the corporate world, and professional firms serving those corporations mirrored the national urge to merge. By the mid-1980s Seattle's three largest firms became characterized as "mega-firms": Perkins

Coie had 180 attorneys, Bogle & Gates, 146, and Davis, Wright & Jones, 125.

Attorneys working in these firms increasingly specialized, and new lawyers coming into the firms spent most of their time writing and researching, with little or no client contact and even less contact with the inside of a courtroom. As one of the refugees from those firms, Terry Tang, noted in an article on the legal profession, things had changed: "In the old-fashioned image, the lawyer was a wise and trusted friend. The new reality of law practice is one where teams of specialized lawyers crank out countless documents for incredibly complex transactions of corporations."[34]

She noted, too, that the "old luxury of learning more than one area of law is losing out to the need to create better money-making legal technicians."[35] Increasingly in large firms, it took six to seven years to become a partner, with an expected average during those years of eighteen hundred to two thousand billable hours. This sum translated easily into fifty- to fifty-five-hour weeks.

The term "billable hours" itself was relatively new. Longtime practitioner John Rupp recalled that in the "early days" of practice, "we hadn't heard of 'billable hours' or monthly billings. Sometimes you got a fee 'up front,' but usually you rendered your bill when the matter was concluded.

You sort of looked up at the ceiling and thought of life and time and the cosmos and of work and results and ability to pay and similar factors and came up with an amount to bill."[36] In earlier times fees were generally based on the service to be rendered rather than how long it took to convey that service.

But attorneys in the 1980s who were willing and able to put in fifty to fifty-five billable hours a week were well paid for their efforts: a starting salary in the bigger firms in the mid-eighties was around $44,000. A longtime professor of law at the University of Washington noted the change from the seventies to the eighties: "Back in the early 1970s, many students thought they wanted to wrench the system. Students nowadays are much more accepting of the way things are. Back then, it was also very unpopular to admit that a substantial income was a motivation to enter the law. Now, there's absolutely no disapproval of that idea."[37]

But the result of the long hours, the pressure, the competition, the disappointed expectations, Tang noted, was often anxiety, discontent, paranoia.

Throughout the decade of the eighties, however, the merger trend and specialization continued, and billable hour expectations rose along with the salaries. It all blew up, symbolically at least, in 1989, when the Schweppe firm and the Karr, Tuttle firm rocked the legal community.

Lady Willie Forbus was a prominent woman attorney who practiced law in Seattle from 1918 through 1985. To some women she was a curiosity and to others a hero, and women often sat in court to watch Ms. Forbus. Shown is Lady WIllie Forbus in court in 1937.

The firm of Karr, Tuttle & Campbell had been around since the turn of the century. It was, and today remains, a well-respected firm, but the day after Independence Day in 1989, the firm gave one-sixth of its attorneys their sudden and irrevocable independence. Eight partners and six of thirty-seven associates were expelled from the firm. Among those dismissed were a state senator who had served as chair of the state senate's judiciary committee, a longtime bar activist, and a grandson of one of the firm's founders.

The firings shook up the legal community and made headlines for weeks afterward. A principal in the firm, F. Lee Campbell, while serving as the state bar president, had only a few years earlier bemoaned some current aspects of the profession: "Unfortunately, many lawyers now think and conduct their affairs as business people. Courtesy and cooperation between lawyers does not exist as it did just a few years ago."[38]

Campbell retired prior to the firings, and it was left to the managing partner, Craig Campbell, unrelated to F. Lee Campbell, to explain the incident. The explanation most often given by many was that the economics of law practice had changed. First, a shift had occurred in the legal profession from the decades-old practice of billing for services to billing by the hour. Second, the traditional "leverage" ratio between partners and associates had changed in most firms, too. While the ratio had been one partner to eight or ten or twenty associates in many firms, allowing the firm to make large profits by billing out the associate's work at a higher rate than the associate was paid, the firms were changing to a lower ratio. The new ratio was often more like one partner to two or one and a half associates. Finally, more firms were hiring attorneys to work for a salary, but not to be on the partner track at all.

The only other well-publicized expulsion of attorneys in Seattle's law firms occurred in 1969. Fran Holman and Bill Holman, the sons of Frank Holman (extensively discussed in the last chapter), were expelled from the Perkins Coie firm. The brothers unsuccessfully sued Perkins and the Boeing Company, alleging that the expulsions had occurred because Fran and Bill had offended the Boeing Company by taking positions hostile to its interests.[39]

Regarding the Holman firings, prominent Seattle attorney William Gates recently remarked that the event was "a real turning point in terms of public attention to the Bar. Prior to that case, the general public had no idea whatsoever about the names of law firms, who represented Boeing, the internal workings of law firms, hourly rates, or sweetheart deals. And there it was, all of a sudden in a very short period of time, exposed in full, off and on the front page of the daily press. This was very startling to those of us who had been

around a while."[40] Undoubtedly, the firing of one-sixth of the firm at Karr will be remembered longer than the expulsion of the Holmans.

The other major event among law firms that occurred in 1989 was the surprising dissolution of one of Seattle's oldest and most prestigious firms, Schweppe, Krug & Tausend. The firm had begun as Struve & Leary in 1879. In all, the end of the 1980s, with the popular perception that there were too many lawyers and too much litigation, could have been discouraging for unemployed attorneys and for the public alike. But some remembered that the public had historically complained about too many lawyers and too much litigation. In Seattle's own past, as noted in a previous chapter, the local newspapers made much the same complaint in 1906.

But more importantly, it was Al Schweppe who reminded the profession of why many lawyers were a natural result of a government based on the rule of law. Schweppe, a former dean of the University of Washington law school, wrote the following in 1956:

> A "government of laws" without lawyers is an impossibility…. In any government of laws lawyers have an indispensable place. Whenever anyone says that there are too many lawyers, I comment by saying that there are not enough; that a government of laws can survive only if the affairs of the people and of the government are at all times conducted according to law under the guidance of lawyers either by way of advice or through adjudication by courts.[41]

The Seattle-King County Bar Association kept pace with the growing profession and the changes in it, but in order to do so, further structural changes were needed. A major event in the Association in the past three decades was the institution of the executive director's position in 1966.

The first executive director of SKCBA was Helen Moulton Geisness, at the time a living connection to the Bar Association's historic past. Seattle born, she was a graduate of the University of Washington law school, served as a legal assistant and then assistant director of the Association's Legal Aid Bureau from 1956 to 1966, and served as the head of the Association's Lawyer Referral Service from its inception in 1960. She was married to another attorney, John Geisness, who had been an attorney in the firm of Vanderveer, Bassett & Geisness. Helen Geisness took the top post in the Bar Association at the same time that SKCBA moved to new offices in the Central Building and ended its long-term office-sharing arrangement with the Washington State Bar Association.

Geisness served until October 1980, when she retired and Helen Pulsifer, the assistant executive director, took over. Pulsifer had been with SKCBA for two years at the time, and had prior experience guiding volunteer organizations with the Municipal League and the Seattle YWCA. Pulsifer ably guided SKCBA through most of the profession's high-growth years of the eighties.

The present executive director is Alice C. Paine, who became director in April 1989. Before coming to SKCBA, Paine had done extensive management work with nonprofit organizations. She served as the executive director of the Northwest regional office of the American Friends Service Committee and was a director of the Cooperative Affairs Department of Group Health Cooperative of Seattle. Paine had also been active with the local chapter of the American Civil Liberties Union and the Puget Sound Cooperative Federation.

The Delay Reduction Task Force
Adding to the negative perceptions of the bar in the last half of this century has been an increase in the delay between filing a case and its final resolution. In trying to solve this problem, the major event at the close of the eighties, which involved the Bar Association, the bar generally, and the public, was the wholesale revision of the court rules for King County Superior Court. The motivating reason was a massive backlog of litigation in the courts, resulting in almost a three-year delay between the filing of a civil suit and the trial of that suit.

Members of the bar and the judiciary decided that the only way to begin to eliminate the problem was to devise both a plan to take care of the backlog and a plan to revise local court rules to ensure that such backlogs would not accumulate again in the future. The major force behind the revision was the Delay Reduction Task Force. The task force was a joint effort of the Seattle-King County Bar Association, the King County Superior Court Judges' Association, the King County Court Administrator, and the King County Council.

The whole project began when in February 1987 attorneys from King County, including SKCBA First Vice President Wayne Blair and King County Superior Court Judge Charles Johnson, traveled to a conference at the National Center for State Courts in Arizona to consider the problem of court congestion. By October of that year the Washington attorneys had organized a regional conference on court congestion, and the task force arose out of that conference. Judge Charles Johnson and that year's first vice president of SKCBA, Fred Butterworth, became the co-chairs of the task force.

The task force divided into eleven working committees, including a rules committee and a backlog reduction committee. After nearly fifteen months of hard work and intense activity, in January 1989 the task force issued proposed rules

and procedures for reducing court congestion in King County. After collecting comments from the bar by a variety of means, through written comments and public meetings, the task force put in place procedures to expedite the backlog.

Further, a whole new set of local court rules were enacted so that all the processes of a lawsuit, from filing the case to gathering information in discovery to the final preparation for trial, were supervised by the court. Those litigants and their attorneys who did not comply with the rules were out the door.

The success of the effort, only a few years later, is still to be determined.

The King County Bar Association Reborn
In the 1850s, Seattle's one-story wooden courthouse, huddled as it was between the endless dark forest to the east and the endless cold sea to the west, stood no doubt for many settlers as a symbol of protection against the wilderness, a refuge where order would be imposed and promises enforced despite the outside world of disorder, disappointment, and unexpected danger. Today, what remains of that wilderness has itself come inside the courthouse for protection against the logic of exploitation, the mathematics of growth, the laws of making a living.

The spotted owl, the eagle, the last stands of old-growth forest, the seashore, and the sea have all been placed before our courts in recent years. In the most recent and far-reaching of these cases, involving the protection of the spotted owl and its habitat in the old-growth forest, it fell to two former presidents of the Seattle-King County Bar Association, Thomas Zilly and William Dwyer, to decide what interests would prevail. Dwyer and Zilly decided the issues in their capacities as United States District Court judges for the Western District of Washington.

Prior to his appointment to the federal bench, Dwyer had been a Seattle attorney for many years, co-founding the firm of Culp, Dwyer, Guterson & Grader. In 1979-80 he was president of the Seattle-King County Bar Association, and had served both SKCBA and the Washington State Bar Association with distinction for many years. During his career as a "very contented trial lawyer" he had compiled an impressive number of legal victories, including the Goldmark defamation suit, about which he wrote a book, *The Goldmark Case*. He liked to travel, play tennis, and perhaps more tellingly, to fish and hike in the mountains that surround Seattle.

Thomas Zilly, before his appointment to the federal bench, practiced with one of the oldest firms in town, Lane, Powell, for most of his legal career. Zilly was very active in the Bar Association's pro bono work, and in 1969 was elected to the Central Area School Council, where he was instrumental in setting up the Seattle School District's voluntary busing program. He served as the president of SKCBA's Young Lawyers Section in 1966, and twenty years later he served as SKCBA president in 1986-87. Zilly too was a hiker, a very healthy one. Usually leading a pack of scouts, he traversed both the Olympic mountain range and the Cascades range several times.

By comparison, the relatively sedentary northern spotted owl was a bird of a different feather. The spotted owl uses predominantly a "sitting and waiting" tactic in foraging for food while perched in the dense canopy of the Cascade or Olympic forests. Secretive, monogamous, territorial, and nocturnal, the owl is dark to chestnut brown in color, has dark eyes, a white spotted head and neck, and white mottling on its

The Endangered Species Act, which was initially drafted to protect the dwindling number of bald eagles in the United States, was applied to the little-known northern spotted owl in the case *Northern Spotted Owl v. Lujan* in 1991. Shown are loggers protesting decisions favoring federal protection for the owl.

abdomen and breast. It is a medium-sized bird, approximately sixteen to nineteen inches tall, and has an average life span of 17.25 years, a long life for a bird.

Most studies demonstrate a close association between old-growth forests and the spotted owl, and the owl is therefore listed as an "indicator species." This means that the relative health of the northern spotted owl indicates the relative health of the old-growth forests, and vice versa.

When logging practices threatened to eliminate the remaining Pacific Northwest old-growth forests upon which the vanishing spotted owl depended, lawyers and their clients concerned with forest and owl preservation filed suit. In a series of decisions, Zilly and Dwyer have angered timber interests and heartened protectors of the owl and the wilderness.

In the case *Northern Spotted Owl v. Lujan*,[42] Judge Zilly held that Washington's Fish and Wildlife Service had abused its discretion in failing to designate a critical habitat for the northern spotted owl when the service had listed the owl as a threatened species. He ordered the service to provide a written plan for completing its review of the critical habitat for the owl.

In a series of decisions entitled *Seattle Audubon Society v. Evans*,[43] Judge Dwyer enjoined the U.S. Forest Service from selling logging rights in northern spotted owl habitat until the Forest Service complied with statutes that would help ensure the survival of the owl in old-growth forests in the Northwest.

The continuing controversy regarding the Washington wilderness and the role that members of the Bar Association have played in that controversy—as lawyers and judges—is characteristic of the King County Bar and its Bar Association over the past 106 years. Lawyers, lawsuits, and the courts—like it or not—have played a significant role in nearly every major event in Seattle history.

Nearly all the old buildings that still stand downtown—including the two train depots, Smith Tower, the Burke Building arches outside the Federal Building, the Rainier Club, as well as the Space Needle, the Opera House, and of course the King County Courthouse—have some legal history at their foundations or some noteworthy legal ghost haunting the halls.

Nearly every major social event in the city, for better or worse, has included the active involvement of members of the bar and the Bar Association. The expulsion of the Duwamish, the growth of early industry, the expulsion of the Chinese, the arrival of the intercontinental railroad, the extradition of radical labor organizers, the jailing of rumrunners, the growth of Boeing, the expulsion of the Japanese, the building of the World's Fair: all these events, and others, involved the bar.

The bar has both helped and helped harm the environment, helped and helped harm the poor person, the immigrant, the native, helped and helped harm, though less often, the entrepreneur.

Further, the Association has concerned itself with the bar's own backyard: revamping the statutory codes and local court rules innumerable times so that they would better serve the public; launching the Legal Aid Bureau; helping launch statewide the legal services system and the public defender system; ensuring that those accused of subversive activities would have representation; promoting a new court of appeals; defending both the right to protest and the orderly administration of the courts. These have been just a few of the bar's efforts specifically directed to the legal arena.

The Bar Association's recent mission statement reflects many of the concerns the bar has become involved with over the years, including the bar's goal to improve the administration of justice, to make legal services available to all regardless of their financial ability, to promote professional competence, and to increase the public's understanding of the law. These concerns, expressed or not, have often been at the core of the Association's work.

In March 1993, the Bar Association embraced its history and returned to its original name, the King County Bar Association.

The view from Profanity Hill in 1993.

Over the years, the press in Seattle has muttered about too many lawyers and too much litigation in this "City of Lawyers," while at the same time either reviling or revering attorneys such as Thomas Burke, George Venable Smith, Orange Jacobs, Isaac Hall, C. H. Hanford, George Vanderveer, or Alfred Schweppe. People have often found in these same attorneys admirable models to follow or evil models to eschew. Others have found even better role models in attorneys such as Lady Willie Forbus or Charles Z. Smith.

The attorneys discussed in these pages were neither purely saints nor purely sinners, and rarely were their motives either purely self-effacing or purely self-serving. But in looking back on their human enterprise, it seems that these attorneys and their bar association probably in the aggregate benefited the city and its people—both rich and poor—more than they harmed them.

ENDNOTES

Many who are familiar with the history of Seattle will recognize the stories and historical vignettes retold in this volume. The attempt here was to tell some familiar history with an emphasis on the role of the legal profession. Because this work was intended to be a popular rather than a scholarly history, the resources relied upon have been largely secondary, not primary or original, sources. The notes generally follow the format suggested by the standard established in the legal field by *The Bluebook: A Uniform System of Citation* (15th ed., 1991).

The principal secondary sources used were the following: Clarence Bagley, *History of Seattle* (1916) and *History of King County* (1929); Richard C. Berner, *Seattle 1900 - 1920: From Boomtown, Urban Turbulence, to Restoration* (1991); Norman Clark, *The Dry Years: Prohibition & Social Change in Washington* (rev. ed., 1988); Ivan Doig, *John J. McGilvra: The Life and Times of an Urban Frontiersman, 1827 - 1903* (Ph. D. Dissertation, Univ. of Washington); Lawrence M. Friedman, *A History of American Law* (1973); Morton J. Horwitz, *The Transformation of American Law, 1780 - 1860* (1977); Murray Morgan, *Skid Road: Seattle—Her First Hundred Years* (rev. ed. Ballantine Books, 1971); Robert C. Nesbit, *"He Built Seattle": A Biography of Judge Thomas Burke* (1961); Roger Sale, *Seattle: Past to Present* (1976); and Charles H. Sheldon, *A Century of Judging: A Political History of the Washington Supreme Court* (1988) and *The Washington High Bench: A Biographical History of the State Supreme Court, 1889 - 1991* (1992).

CHAPTER ONE

1. *United States v. Washington*, 384 F. Supp. 312, 356 (1974), aff'd 520 F.2d 676 (9th Cir. 1975), *cert. denied* 423 U.S. 1086 2(1976).

2. Steven Beckham, *George Gibbs, 1815 - 1873: Historian and Ethnologist* (Ph. D. Dissertation, UCLA, 1970).

3. *Ibid.*

4. *Ibid.* 186.

5. Quoted in Roger Sale, *Seattle: Past to Present*, 27 - 28 (1976).

6. Quoted in Ivan Doig, *John J. McGilvra: The Life and Times of an Urban Frontiersman, 1827 - 1903*, 67 (Ph. D. Dissertation, Univ. of Washington, 1969).

7. Hon. John J. McGilvra, "Pioneer Judges and Lawyers of Washington," *Proceedings of the Washington State Bar 1895* 91.

8. Norman Clark, *The Dry Years: Prohibition & Social Change in Washington*, 23 (rev. ed. 1988).

9. Orange Jacobs, "Reminiscences of the Bench & Bar," *Proceedings of the Washington State Bar 1902*, 112 and 113.

10. *Ibid.* 113.

11. McGilvra, "Pioneer Judges," 94.

12. *Ibid.*

13. John J. McGilvra, "The First Courts and Attorneys in Seattle," *Exercises in Commemoration of the Founding of the City of Seattle*, as quoted in Doig, *McGilvra*, 112.

14. Jacobs, "Reminiscences," 112.

15. *Ibid.*

16. Paul Dorpat, *Seattle Now and Then* (1984).

17. The familiar story of this lynching is compiled largely from the works cited above by Clarence Bagley, Murray Morgan, and Roger Sale.

18. In addition to the more familiar accounts of the expulsion of the Chinese discussed in the works cited above by Morgan, Nesbit, and Sale, the account here of the settlement and expulsion of the Chinese also borrows from Doug and Art Chin, *Up Hill: The Settlement and Diffusion of the Chinese in Seattle, Washington* (N.P. 1973); Art Chin, *Golden Tassels: A History of the Chinese in Washington, 1857 - 1977* (1978); George Kinnear, *Anti-Chinese Riots at Seattle, Wn., February 8th, 1886* (1911); and Robert Edward Wynne, *Reaction to the Chinese in the Pacific Northwest and British Columbia 1850 to 1910* (Ph. D. Dissertation, University of Washington, 1964).

19. Discovering that the King County Bar was founded in 1886, and not the presumed date of 1906, was a revelation, but is confirmed by one of Seattle's chief historians, Clarence Bagley, in his *History of Seattle*.

CHAPTER TWO

1. Arnold M. Paul, *Conservative Crisis and the Rule of Law: Attitudes of Bar and Bench, 1887 - 1895* (1960).

2. W. H. White to Acting Governor Charles B. Laughton, March 10, 1891; Governors' Papers, Washington State Archives, Olympia, as quoted in Nesbit, *"He Built Seattle": A Biography of Judge Thomas Burke*, 208 (1961).

3. *Ibid.* 206.

4. Marna S. Tucker, "Pro Bono ABA?" in Ralph Nader and Mark Green, eds. *Verdicts on Lawyers* (1976).

5. Lawrence M. Friedman, *A History of American Law*, 561 (1973).

6. *Ibid.* 563.

7. Alfred Z. Reed, *Training for the Public Profession of the Law* (1921) and Edson R. Sunderland, *History of the American Bar Association* (1953) as cited in Friedman, *History of American Law*, 563.

8. Other material for this section regarding the legal profession has been taken from the books cited above by Morton J. Horwitz and Lawrence M. Friedman as well as from the following sources: Perry Miller, *The Life of the Mind in America from the Revolution to the Civil War: Books One through Three* (1965); and Robert Stevens, *Law School: Legal Education in America from the 1850s to the 1980s* (1983); and Jerold S. Auerbach *Unequal Justice: Lawyers and Social Change in Modern America* (1976).

9. Bagley, vol. 1, *History of Seattle*.

10. Information on the history of the Washington State Bar Association is taken from two articles, Alfred J. Schweppe, "A Short History of the Washington Bar," *Washington State Bar News*, December 1974, 10, and John N. Rupp, "An Essay in History," *Washington State Bar News*, June 1983, 27-29.

11. Alexis de Tocqueville, *Democracy in America*, vol. I, 288 (1945).

12. *Ibid.*

13. Friedman, 549.

14. Friedman, 550.

15. Nesbit, 18.

16. Miller, *Life of the Mind* , 99, quoting The Prairie.

17. James R. Warren, *The Day Seattle Burned*, 25-26.

18. This account of the fire in relation to the courthouse is taken from Murray Morgan, *Skid Road*, 106 - 111.

19. Warren, 68.

20. *Ibid.*

21. Frederic James Grant, *History of Seattle*, 268-277.

22. As quoted in Bagley, *History of King County*, vol. 1, 585 - 587.

23. Much of the information on the firms contained here is derived from Charles H. Paul, *Origin of Some Present Day Seattle Law Firms: 1854 to Now*, an address given by King County Superior Court Judge Paul to the Lawyers' and Judges' Luncheon at the Arctic Club on February 19, 1968. Some material is taken too from *The Spectator* article cited by Bagley, 19, above.

24. Charles H. Paul, *Origins*, 11-12

25. See generally Robert Stevens, *Law School*, 20.

26. Material on legal education generally was taken primarily from two books, Lawrence Friedman, *History of American Law*, chapters XI and XII (1973) and Robert Stevens, *Law School: Legal Education in America from the 1850s to the 1980s* (1983).

27. Stevens, *Law School*, 96.

28. Quote in Jack Nortrup, "The Education of a Western Lawyer," 12 *Am. J. Leg. Hist.*, 294 (1968), as quoted in Friedman, 25.

29. Friedman, 525 - 27.

30. The section on the law school is derived almost entirely from a pamphlet prepared for the Diamond Jubilee of the University of Washington by a professor of law then at the law school, J. Grattan O'Bryan, entitled *History of University of Washington School of Law* (Seattle, 1938).

31. See e.g., Harry First, "Competition in the Legal Education Industry," 53, *New York University Law Review* 311 (1978); Jerold S. Auerbach, *Unequal Justice*.

32. Auerbach, 99.

33. Auerbach, 107.

34. I am indebted almost entirely for the material on black attorneys to Chapter 4 of *Seattle's Black Victorians, A History of Afro-Americans in Seattle* (1980) by Ester Hall Mumford.

35. As quoted in Lerone Bennett, Jr., *Before the Mayflower: A History of the Negro in America 1619 - 1964*, 221 (rev. ed. Penquin, 1968).

36. *Ibid.* 221-222.

37. Carlos A. Schwantes, *The Pacific Northwest, An Interpretive History*, 131-134.

38. *Ibid.*

39. Charles K. Wiggins, (John P. Hoyt and Women's Suffrage) *Washington State Bar News*, January 1989, 16-17.

40. Cynthia Whitaker, (The First Wave of Women Lawyers) *Washington State Bar News*, May 1981, 8.

41. From bench and bar clippings at the University of Washington law school library on the memorial to Jacobs.

CHAPTER THREE

1. Material on R. A. Ballinger is taken from C. H. Hanford, *Seattle and Environs*, vol. II, 56 - 60, (1924) and from Bagley, *History of Seattle*, vol. 3, 619 - 621, as well as from an unpublished manuscript at the University of Washington law school library by Arthur S. Beardsley on the early history of the Washington bar as noted below.

2. Arthur S. Beardsley, *Codes and Code-Makers of Washington, 1889 - 1937*, reprinted from 30 *Pacific Northwest Quarterly*, no. 1, 37 - 39 (1939).

3. Bagley, *Seattle*, 620.

4. Information on the initial meetings of the Seattle Bar Association is taken from Bagley, *Ibid.*, as well as *Seattle Times*, June 28, 1906, 5, *Seattle PI*, June 28, 1906, 7, *Seattle PI*, July 19, 1906, 16.

5. *Seattle Times*, Feb. 25, 1906, 3.

6. *Ibid.*

7. Seattle Bar Association Yearly Report, 1911.

8. *Ibid.*

9. The material for this section on the location of the courthouse was derived primarily from J. M. Neil, "Paris or New York? The Shaping of Downtown Seattle, 1903 - 14," *Pacific Northwest Quarterly*, January 1984, 22 - 33.

10. *Ibid.* 24.

11. *Ibid.* 22.

12. *Ibid.*

13. Material regarding the Yesler Mansion is taken from Paul Dorpat, *Seattle Now and Then* (vol. 1) Entry 5 (1984).

14. *Kelly v. Hamilton*, 76 Wash. 576, 136 P.1148 (1913).

15. Neil, "Paris or New York? "32.

16. Much of this discussion is indebted to Albert F. Gunns, *Civil Liberties and Crisis: The Status of Civil Liberties in the Pacific Northwest, 1917 - 40* (UW Doctoral Dissertation in History, 1971).

17. Harvey O'Connor, *Revolution in Seattle*, 89 (1964).

18. *Seattle Times*, February 25, 1906, 4.

19. Most of the biographical information on Kenneth Mackintosh is taken from Charles H. Sheldon, *The Washington High Bench: A Biographical History of the State Supreme Court, 1889 - 1991* (1992).

20. O'Connor, 88 - 9.

21. *State v. Hennessy*, 114 Wash. 351, 195 P.211 (1921).

22. The material on Mark Litchman is drawn primarily from Albert F. Gunns, *Civil Liberties in Crisis: The Pacific Northwest, 1917 - 1940*, 99 - 103 (1983).

23. *Ibid.* 100.

24. *Litchman v. Shannon*, 90 Wash. 186, 155 P.783, 785 (1916).

25. Gunns, *Civil Liberties*, 102 (1983).

26. Information on deportation during this period in Seattle is drawn largely from William Preston, Jr., *Aliens and Dissenters: Federal Suppression of Radicals, 1903 - 1933*, 152 - 180 (1963).

27. *Ibid.* 164, 166.

28. *Ibid.* 165, quoting Immigration and Naturalization Service files.

29. As quoted in Preston, 167.

30. *Ibid.* 180.

31. As quoted in Richard C. Berner, *Seattle 1900 - 1920: From Boomtown, Urban Turbulence, to Restoration*, 119 (1991).

32. As quoted in Clark, *Dry Years*, 174.

33. *Olmstead v. United States*, 277 U.S. 438 (1928).

34. As quoted in Clark, *Dry Years*, 217.

35. Information on Seattle's Hooverville was taken largely from three works: Donald Francis Roy, *Hooverville: A Study of a Community of Homeless Men in Seattle* (Master's Thesis, University of Washington, 1935); Don Duncan, *Washington: The First One Hundred Years: 1889 - 1989: An Anecdotal History*, 64 (1989); and Paul Dorpat, *Seattle Now and Then*, vol. I, section 104 (1984).

36. The following section is again indebted to Albert Francis Gunns' dissertation *Civil Liberties and Crisis: The Status of Civil Liberties in the Pacific Northwest, 1917 - 1940* (Univ. of Washington Dissertation, 1971), especially the pages following 122.

37. Material on women attorneys for this section was drawn almost entirely from Cynthia Whitaker, "The First Wave of Women Lawyers," *Washington State Bar News* (May 1981), and some independent research by the author at the University of Washington law school in its Bench & Bar Clippings. Material on others in the bar in this section was drawn largely from two articles: Ted Therriault, "Lawyers Recall 50 Years of Practice," *Bar Bulletin*, (January 1983); Marc Lampson & Fred Diamondstone, "Profile: John Caughlan," *Bar Bulletin* (January 1987).

38. For these headlines and others and other material on the subject of early women attorneys, see Cynthia Whitaker, "The First Wave of Women Lawyers," *Washington State Bar News* (May 1981).

39. Quoted in Whitaker, 8.

40. Quoted in Whitaker, 10.

41. Quoted in Whitaker, 11.

42. Quoted in Whitaker, 13.

43. Therriault, "Lawyers Recall."

44. Information on the history of the Washington State Bar Association is taken from three articles, Alfred J. Schweppe, "A Short History of the Washington Bar," 10 *Washington State Bar News* (December 1974); John N. Rupp, "An Essay in History," 27 *Washington State Bar News* (June 1983); Joseph H. Gordon, "The Washington State Bar Association," 71 *ABA Journal* (January 1962). The quote in the text is from Rupp, 37.

45. Seattle Bar Association Minutes, April 13, 1937.

46. Seattle Bar Association Board Minutes, January 3 & 4, 1939.

47. SBA Minutes, April 12, 1939, 4.

48. Frank E. Holman, *The Life and Career of a Western Lawyer 1886 - 1961*, 316 (1963).

CHAPTER FOUR

1.   Interview with Edward Henry by Albert Gunns, as reported in Albert Gunns, *Civil Liberties in Crisis: The Pacific Northwest, 1917 - 1940*, 118 - 19 (1983).

2.   Douglas Honig and Laura Brenner, *On Freedom's Frontier: The First Fifty Years of the American Civil Liberties Union in Washington State*, ACLU (1987).

3.   Holman, *The Life and Career*, 220.

4.   Seattle Bar Association, Minutes, June 25, 1941.

5.   An unfortunate absence in the record causes this statement to be equivocal. The officers of 1940 are not noted in the minutes, though the minutes from several meetings in 1940 indicate that Grace O. Dailey was the secretary then, so perhaps she was the first woman officer of the SBA.

6.   Holman, *The Life and Career*, 316-17.

7.   Seattle Bar Association, Minutes, December 10, 1941.

8.   Holman, *The Life and Career*, 318.

9.   *Ibid.*

10. *Ibid.*

11. Material regarding Mr. Hirabayashi was taken from two sources: David Takami, *Executive Order 9066: A History of Japanese Americans in Seattle* (1992); and Peter Irons, *Justice at War: The Story of the Japanese American Internment Cases* (1983).

12. Irons, 113.

13. *Ibid.*

14. As quoted in Irons, 155.

15. *Ibid.*

16. *Ibid.* 180 - 81.

17. *Ibid.* 163 - 85.

18. As quoted in David Takami, *Executive Order 9066* (1992).

19. Roger Sale, *Seattle: Past to Present*, 180 - 85.

20. *Ibid.* 184.

21. Seattle Bar Association, Minutes, March 9, 1939.

22. As quoted in Jane Sanders, *Cold War on Campus: Academic Freedom at the University of Washington, 1946 - 64*, 10 - 11 (1979).

23. As quoted in Robert Justin Goldstein, *Political Repression in Modern America: 1870 to the Present*, 288 (1978).

24. *Ibid.*

25. *Ibid.*

26. *Ibid.* 298.

27. Melvin Rader, *False Witness*, 47 (1969).

28. *Ibid.* 52 - 53.

29. *Ibid.* 80.

30. Most of the material regarding the Young Lawyers Section was taken from Mary Alice Theiler, "History of Young Lawyers Section," *Bar Bulletin*, June 1986.

31. Material for this section on Bar Association judicial recommendations was taken from Charles Sheldon, *The Washington High Bench: A Biographical History of the Washington Supreme Court* (1988).

32. *Ibid.* 25.

33. *Ibid.* 37.

34. Seattle Bar Association, Minutes, June 11, 1954.

35. As quoted in Marc Lampson and Fred Diamondstone, "Profile: John Caughlan," *Bar Bulletin*, 22, January 1987.

36. Sheldon, *The Washington High Bench*, 213.

CHAPTER FIVE

1. *Seattle Bar Bulletin*, vol. I, no. 1 (1957), and *Seattle-King County Bar Bulletin*, vol II, no. 1 (1960).

2. *The Daily Journal of Commerce* also began weekly coverage of the Seattle-King County Bar Association's activities during 1961.

3. Seattle-King County Bar Association, Board Minutes, August 2, 1960.

4. Murray Morgan, *Century 21: The Story of the Seattle World's Fair, 1962*, 51 (1963).

5. *Ibid.* 93.
6. *Ibid.*

7. *Ibid.*

8. *Davis v. Seattle*, 56 Wn. 2d 785.

9. John N. Rupp, "Alfred J. Schweppe, " *Washington State Bar News*, 2 (January 1971).

10. *Ibid.*

11. Most of the material regarding the Goldmark case was taken from William L. Dwyer, *The Goldmark Case: An American Libel Trial* (1984).

12. *Ibid.* 4.

13. Material on Charles Goldmark is taken from a tribute to him by Gerald B. Johnson, *Washington Bar News*, 19 (March 1986).

14. *Ibid.*

15. *The Daily Journal of Commerce*, January 15, 1969.

16. *Bar Bulletin*, 1, December 1966.

17. Seattle-King County Bar Association, Board Minutes, July and August, 1963.

18. *Bar Bulletin*, February 1974.

19. Don Hannula, *The Seattle Times*, February 12, 1984, A16.

20. *Seattle Post-Intelligencer*, March 20, 1984, A4.

21. S. L. Roddis, "Supply and Demand for Lawyers," *Washington State Bar News*, 4 (March 1973).

22. *Ibid.* 5.

23. 90 Wash. 186, 155 P783 (1916).

24. Jay V. White, "Women Lawyers Challenge Bar Exam Reports," *Washington State Bar News*, 17 (May 1978).

25. Minority and Justice Task Force, Final Report.

26. Melanie Rowland, Melanie and Sharon Armstrong, "Washington Women Lawyers," *Washington State Bar News*, 27 (May 1981).

27. Roger Shidler, "Reminiscences of 54 Years of Law Practice," (unpublished, University of Washington, Bench and Bar Clippings collection).

28. Comments from John Rupp on Wright are from a December 4, 1992, interview by the author.

29. Anne Ellington, "Profile: Lady Willie Forbus," *The Bar Bulletin*, 5 (November 1985). James R. Warren, "The Seventy-Five Years Behind Perkins Coie," *Portage*, vol. 9, no. 1, Spring 1988.

30. William S. Bailey, "Lawyer Glut: Myth or Reality," *Washington State Bar News*, 8 (April 1983).

31. *Ibid.*

32. *Ibid.*

33. Mary H. McIntosh, "The Darker Side of Supply & Demand," *Washington State Bar News*, 15 (April 1983).

34. Terry Tang, "Law Firm Blues," *The Weekly*, 37 (September 24, 1986).

35. *Ibid.*

36. John Rupp, "Lawyer Recalls SKCBA's Early Days," *The Bar Bulletin*, 22 - 23 (February 1983).

37. Tang, 40.

38. Eric Scigliano, "Karr Tuttle Carnage," *The Weekly*, 29 (August 16, 1989).

39. *Holman v. Coie*, 11 Wn. App. 195, 522 P.2d 515 (1974).

40. William Gates, 1993 letter to King County Bar Association.

41. Frederic C. Tausend and David Boerner, "Too Many Lawyers?" *Washington State Bar News*, 19 - 20 (April 1983).

42. 758 F. Supp. 621 (W.D. Wash. 1991).

43. *See e.g.*, 771 F. Supp. 1081 (W.D. Wash. 1991).

PAST PRESIDENTS

John J. McGilvra	1886-1889	King County Bar Association
Orange Jacobs	1889-1914	King County Bar Association
R. A. Ballinger	1906-1907	Seattle Bar Association
W. A. Peters	1907-1908	Seattle Bar Association
L. C. Gilman	1908-1909	Seattle Bar Association
Harold Preston	1909-1910	Seattle Bar Association
H. H. A. Hastings	1910-1911	Seattle Bar Association
William H. Gorham	1911-1912	Seattle Bar Association
George H. Walker	1912-1913	Seattle Bar Association
George E. Wright	1913-1914	Seattle Bar Association
L. B. Stedman	1914-1915	Seattle Bar Association
Hiram E. Hadley	1915-1916	Seattle Bar Association
William Tucker	1916-1917	Seattle Bar Association
W. B. Stratton	1917-1918	Seattle Bar Association
Marion Edwards	1918-1919	Seattle Bar Association
Charles H. Winders	1919-1920	Seattle Bar Association
W. G. McLaren	1920-1921	Seattle Bar Association
Bruce C. Shorts	1921-1922	Seattle Bar Association
O. B. Thorgrimson	1922-1923	Seattle Bar Association
Henry F. McClure	1923-1924	Seattle Bar Association
Elmer E. Todd	1924-1925	Seattle Bar Association
Alfred H. Lundin	1925-1926	Seattle Bar Association
J. H. Kane	1926-1927	Seattle Bar Association
Ira Bronson	1927-1928	Seattle Bar Association
Alfred Battle	1928-1929	Seattle Bar Association
C. R. Hovey	1929-1930	Seattle Bar Association
F. T. Merritt	1930-1931	Seattle Bar Association
C. K. Poe	1931-1932	Seattle Bar Association
Otto B. Rupp	1932-1933	Seattle Bar Association
Thomas R. Lyons	1933-1934	Seattle Bar Association
Charles T. Donworth	1934-1935	Seattle Bar Association
John S. Robinson	1935-1936	Seattle Bar Association
Gerald H. Bucey	1936-1937	Seattle Bar Association
S. Harold Shefelman	1937-1938	Seattle Bar Association
Walter A. McClure	1938-1939	Seattle Bar Association
Tracy E. Griffin	1939-1940	Seattle Bar Association
Ford Q. Elvidge	1940-1941	Seattle Bar Association
Frank E. Holman	1941-1942	Seattle Bar Association
Clinton H. Hartson	1942-1943	Seattle Bar Association
Paul P. Ashley	1943-1944	Seattle Bar Association
John Ambler	1944-1945	Seattle Bar Association
Edward R. Taylor	1945-1946	Seattle Bar Association
R. J. Venables	1946-1947	Seattle Bar Association
Charles F. Riddell	1947-1948	Seattle Bar Association
Roy C. Miller	1948-1949	Seattle Bar Association
Joseph A. Barto	1949-1950	Seattle Bar Association
J. Orrin Vining	1949-1950	Seattle Bar Association
Wilbur Zundel	1950-1951	Seattle Bar Association
DeWitt Williams	1951-1952	Seattle Bar Association
Henry W. Cramer	1952-1953	Seattle Bar Association
W. Paul Uhlmann	1953-1954	Seattle Bar Association
Michael K. Copass	1954-1955	Seattle Bar Association
Wayne C. Booth	1955-1956	Seattle Bar Association
John N. Rupp	1956-1957	Seattle Bar Association
Charles Horowitz	1957-1958	Seattle Bar Association
Victor D. Lawrence	1958-1959	Seattle-King County Bar Association
Frank J. Eberharter	1959-1960	Seattle-King County Bar Association
John M. Davis	1960-1961	Seattle-King County Bar Association
Stanley C. Soderland	1961-1962	Seattle-King County Bar Association
Chester C. Adair	1962-1963	Seattle-King County Bar Association
Richard H. Riddell	1963-1964	Seattle-King County Bar Association
Russell V. Hokanson	1964-1965	Seattle-King County Bar Association
Kenneth P. Short	1965-1966	Seattle-King County Bar Association
Willard J. Wright	1966-1967	Seattle-King County Bar Association
J. Paul Coie	1967-1968	Seattle-King County Bar Association
Pinckney M. Rohrback	1968-1969	Seattle-King County Bar Association
William H. Gates, Jr.	1969-1970	Seattle-King County Bar Association
Bradley T. Jones	1970-1971	Seattle-King County Bar Association
Jack P. Scholfield	1971-1972	Seattle-King County Bar Association
Betty B. Fletcher	1972-1973	Seattle-King County Bar Association
Burroughs B. Anderson	1973-1974	Seattle-King County Bar Association
William Wesselhoeft	1974-1975	Seattle-King County Bar Association
Robert R. Beezer	1975-1976	Seattle-King County Bar Association
Murray B. Guterson	1976-1977	Seattle-King County Bar Association
F. Lee Campbell	1977-1978	Seattle-King County Bar Association
William Helsell	1978-1979	Seattle-King County Bar Association
William L. Dwyer	1979-1980	Seattle-King County Bar Association
Paul C. Gibbs	1980-1981	Seattle-King County Bar Association
Stephen E. DeForest	1981-1982	Seattle-King County Bar Association
Harold F. Vhugen	1982-1983	Seattle-King County Bar Association
James S. Turner	1983-1984	Seattle-King County Bar Association
Bruce M. Pym	1984-1985	Seattle-King County Bar Association
Nancy P. Gibbs	1985-1986	Seattle-King County Bar Association
Thomas S. Zilly	1986-1987	Seattle-King County Bar Association
M. Wayne Blair	1987-1988	Seattle-King County Bar Association
Fred R. Butterworth	1988-1989	Seattle-King County Bar Association
Stew Cogan	1989-1990	Seattle-King County Bar Association
Matt Sayre	1990-1991	Seattle-King County Bar Association
Peter Greenfield	1991-1992	Seattle-King County Bar Association
Geoff Revelle	1992-1993	King County Bar Association

PHOTO CREDITS

The photographs reproduced in *From Profanity Hill, King County Bar Association's Story* are gratefully acknowledged and listed below.

Dust jacket, Jerry Gay.

Page 1. MOHAI, Seattle Historical Society collection.
Page 2. King County Superior Court collection.
Page 6. MOHAI, Seattle Historical Society collection.
Page 10. MOHAI, Seattle Historical Society collection.
Page 13. Washington State Library.
Page 15. Suquamish Tribal Museum, Photographic Archives.
Page 16. Grants, *History of Seattle*.
Page 17. Washington State Library.
Page 18. Grants, *History of Seattle*.
Page 20. MOHAI, Seattle Historical Society collection.
Page 23. MOHAI, Webster & Stevens collection.
Page 24. Washington State Library.
Page 27. Washington State Library.
Page 29. Grants, *History of Seattle*.
Page 31. University of Washington Libraries, Special Collections and Preservation Division.
Page 32. MOHAI, Seattle Historical Society collection.
Page 33. Karr Tuttle Campbell.
Page 35. University of Washington Libraries, Special Collections and Preservation Division.
Page 36. University of Washington School of Law.
Page 37. University of Washington School of Law.
Page 39. MOHAI, Seattle Historical Society collection.
Page 40. University of Washington School of Law.
Page 41. University of Washington School of Law.
Page 42. MOHAI, Webster & Stevens collection.
Page 44. King County Superior Court collection.
Page 46. MOHAI, Seattle Historical Society collection.
Page 47. Documentary Book Publishers Corporation archive.
Page 49. MOHAI, Webster & Stevens collection.
Page 51. MOHAI, Webster & Stevens collection.
Page 53. MOHAI, Webster & Stevens collection.
Page 54. MOHAI, Webster & Stevens collection.
Page 59. Documentary Book Publishers Corporation archive.
Page 60. The Boeing Company Archive.
Page 63. Tacoma Public Library.

Page 65. University of Washington Libraries, Special Collections and Preservation Division.
Page 66. *The Seattle Times*.
Page 67. MOHAI, *Seattle Post-Intelligencer* collection.
Page 68. The Boeing Company Archive.
Page 70. MOHAI, *Seattle Post-Intelligencer* collection.
Page 72. MOHAI, *Seattle Post-Intelligencer* collection.
Page 73. MOHAI, *Seattle Post-Intelligencer* collection.
Page 75. Documentary Book Publishers Corporation archive.
Page 76. MOHAI, *Seattle Post-Intelligencer* collection.
Page 78. Documentary Book Publishers Corporation archive.
Page 79. Washington State Bar Association.
Page 81. Schroeter, Goldmark & Bender.
Page 82. MOHAI, *Seattle Post-Intelligencer* collection.
Page 85. U.S. Ninth Circuit Court.
Page 86. MOHAI, *Seattle Post-Intelligencer* collection.
Page 88. MOHAI, *Seattle Post-Intelligencer* collection.
Page 90. Bettman Archives.
Page 93. MOHAI, *Seattle Post-Intelligencer* collection.
Page 96. *The Seattle Times*.
Page 97. Jerry Gay.

KING COUNTY BAR ASSOCIATION HISTORY SPONSORS

M any King County law firms and related service organizations have sponsored the King County Bar Association history book project. These firms and their chronicles are featured in the following pages.

Adolph & Smyth

Robert J. Adolph and Jeffrey A. Smyth formed their firm in 1987 to specialize in business litigation.

They serve construction, banking, and general business clientele, and they actively participate in high-profile cases, such as the aftermath of the *Exxon Valdez* oil spill in Alaska's Prince William Sound.

They have custom-designed their seven-lawyer firm to emphasize personal involvement with the cases. "Clients in Seattle hire lawyers for litigation, not law firms," says Adolph. "We're purely a service business. All we can sell is our time and talent and attention. Clients can leave their problems in our office and go run their businesses."

Adolph earned an undergraduate journalism degree from the University of Wisconsin because he liked to write, then he went to law school at Wisconsin. He relocated to Seattle in 1972.

Smyth's family has been in Seattle since the 1880s, when his great-grandparents came to town. Smyth, an undergraduate English major, began practicing in a Tacoma firm in 1975. He moved to Seattle because he "...wanted a steady diet of larger business." Smyth is the first member of his family to get a degree and follow a professional career. He formed his own firm in 1984, then joined with Adolph in 1987.

Business aside, the partners say they find their practice personally fulfilling.

"The law is an academic pursuit, and it draws into its fold a lot of bright and insightful people," says Smyth. "I enjoy it because it's a constant form of competition. I get to compete with some of the smartest people I've ever known in terms of written product, face to face in a courtroom. You get the best part of theater in performing to a jury, performing to judges. You get the pleasure of being paid to write interesting papers on interesting subjects. And in sixteen years, there has not been one day, including today, when there hasn't been something new, unanticipated."

They also don't restrain themselves from becoming emotionally interested in their clients' problems. "In order to be an effective advocate you have to have objectivity," says Smyth, "but you have to develop an intimate interest in a case before it will take on life for you."

Says Adolph, "Law is a very, very hard profession; extremely stressful. When you take up someone's problems, you have to be impervious to being bludgeoned. You have to not be intimidated, and always expect the unexpected. It's exhausting, frustrating, but very satisfying when you do solve a problem. The client is often absolutely furious when he comes here, because he feels he's been treated so unfairly," he continues. "He walks out of this office feeling, 'Finally somebody's thinking the way I am, somebody's going to do something about this.'" That's the way Adolph and Smyth want it.

The Alexander & Thomas Group, Inc.

The Alexander & Thomas Group, Inc., which was founded in 1987, is a contract attorney-placement service that provides experienced, prescreened attorneys that law firms and corporate law departments can hire on a temporary basis. The company represents more than seventy lawyers. As the company's literature puts it, "They help you complete your work, increase your revenues, and leave when the work is finished." The company's principals are Ellen Schreier Alexander, Tom Alexander, Robert J. Thomas, and Susan D. Reichert.

The contract attorneys have chosen to leave their traditional practices for a variety of reasons: some are raising children; some have second careers other than law; others have their own law practices, which they supplement with contract work.

Contract attorneys are available for short-term, part-time assignments, as well as longer-term, full-time projects. They can assist firms with legal research and writing; litigation: discovery, motions, and trials; contracts, wills, and documentation for real estate and business transactions; and projects involving special expertise such as tax, labor, and probate.

"We offer value by doing all of the legwork in advance, and by providing an attorney whose background specifically matches the project," says Tom Alexander.

Alexander & Thomas provides a firm with a general description of an available attorney who meets their requirements, and delivers the lawyer's resume. The law firm then interviews the lawyer and makes its own decision.

"This is a growing segment of our legal community," says Rob Thomas. "Contract attorneys are being hired by more firms because of the quality of their work, and because the firms can generate additional profits from existing overhead."

Barnard, Pauly, Kaser & Bellamy

Barnard, Pauly, Kaser & Bellamy is an intellectual property law firm. All attorneys in the firm have engineering and technology backgrounds, and are registered to practice before the U.S. Patent and Trademark Office. They restrict their law practice to matters relating to patents, trademarks, copyrights, and unfair competition, and related litigation and licensing.

The firm was founded in 1979 by Delbert J. Barnard, who had been in private practice in Seattle since 1962. Prior to coming to Seattle, Barnard worked for the U.S. Patent and Trademark Office; he has extensive experience in obtaining patents in most fields of technology.

Intellectual property law is a constantly changing field that is tied to new technology. When Barnard began his career, the cutting edge of technology related mostly to mechanical and hydraulic devices. Since then, inventions relating to electronics and computers have evolved in ever increasing numbers. Biotechnology is now emerging as an important field. Most patents do not involve pioneering breakthroughs, but rather refinements of existing processes or machines, or "solving the problems that everybody's cussing," as Barnard puts it.

The firm's philosophy is to seek a proper equilibrium between larger and smaller clients, and to develop a one-to-one relationship between client and attorney. "Personally, I'm a builder type," says Barnard. "I'm happy working on something that I start from scratch. I like to find clients with compatible personalities."

Joan H. Pauly, second to Barnard in seniority, joined the firm in 1981. Although, like Barnard, she has obtained patents in various fields, her focus is largely on patents that relate to new developments in aircraft manufacturing, including structures, systems, and controls. "I like the challenge of sophisticated technology," she says.

Bruce A. Kaser joined in 1983. He has prosecuted patents relating to microprocessor-controlled machines, electronic sensors, and test devices, and also handles a large number of both domestic and international trademark matters for the firm's clients. "This practice is rarely ever boring," he says. "It can be frustrating at times, but any frustration is generally offset by the satisfaction of being constantly involved with new and better ideas for solving existing technological problems."

Glenn D. Bellamy joined the firm in 1987. His academic background emphasized studies in biomedical technology. Bellamy's practice has emphasized preparation of patent applications and litigation of intellectual property issues. "Some people think this is a narrow practice, but I don't think so," he says. "If it's narrow, it's a window into another field. By definition, every patentable invention is new technology."

Teresa J. Wiant is the firm's newest attorney. She joined the firm in 1991, after graduation from Franklin Pierce Law Center in New Hampshire. She holds a bachelor of science degree in chemical engineering from West Virginia University.

Betts, Patterson & Mines, P.S.

"We are a firm of trial lawyers," says Mike Mines.

Betts, Patterson & Mines traces its roots to a firm started in 1899 by John W. Roberts. Fred Betts joined the firm in 1933, when it was Roberts & Skeel. Mike Mines joined in 1956, left a dozen years later, then remerged with the firm in 1976, when it was Skeel, McKelvy, Henke, Evenson & Betts. In 1979, that firm dissolved and Betts, Patterson & Mines was established.

The firm had about fourteen attorneys at first, and has seen a fairly steady growth pattern, paralleling the growth of the Seattle legal community in general. From 1983 to 1991, the number doubled. "The growth is as needed," says Mines, "we're not just growing for its own sake."

The firm's public profile was raised when it served as lead local counsel for bondholders in their action against the defaulting Washington Public Power Supply System. Although WPPSS was a highly publicized case, the firm has enjoyed more internal growth with other clients, including a solid client base of about forty insurance companies, such as State Farm. "In the 1950s, well over half of our business was insurance defense," says Mines. Insurance defense is still about a third of the business. But Betts, Patterson & Mines has expanded to represent diverse clients such as Associated Grocers, Fleetwood Enterprises (mobile homes), and Cooper Industries (a tool and equipment manufacturing conglomerate), as well as securities work.

Today, though litigation is the firm's specialty, its thirty-five lawyers also handle commercial transactions, real estate matters, tax law and estate planning, environmental and product liability cases, and complex bankruptcy matters. The corporate side of the firm is its fastest-growing department.

WPPSS aside, perhaps the most famous case involving a Betts Patterson attorney came in 1990. It was front-page news when Paul Carey obtained a restraining order against Little League officials, allowing 9-year-old Michael Hanner to refuse reassignment to another team and finish the season with his buddies on the Phillies.

James Stanley R. Byrd, Inc., P.S.

Stanley R. Byrd's law practice is limited to estate planning and asset protection. Estate planning includes protection from estate taxes and probate costs; asset protection comprises guarding against income taxes, creditors, and lawsuits.

Byrd was born in Rapid City, South Dakota, and earned his B.A. degree from Idaho State University. He lived in France and Belgium from 1959 to 1962, where he was a church representative fluent in the French language. He is married and has seven children.

A graduate of the University of Washington law school, Byrd was admitted to practice in Washington in 1967. After spending two years in the U.S. Army, he worked in a law firm for ten years before forming a two-person partnership. He handled a wide range of legal matters: corporate law, collections, contracts and business matters, criminal law, bankruptcies, probate, adoptions, and personal injury cases.

On July 1, 1982, he went into sole practice. It wasn't until 1988 that he emphasized his current specialty. "I came to the conclusion that I couldn't be everything to everybody, and I didn't want to try," he says. "Being competitive, I liked the challenge of court, but I think there's a better way. That better way is planning rather than litigating." Byrd feels that a specialist "is of greater value to the client. He's more knowledgeable, more efficient and more cost effective."

Byrd's typical client is the owner of a small or medium-sized business, who is retired or nearing retirement, or a professional concerned with lawsuits or the threat of lawsuits.

"It's fulfilling to see, usually in tangible terms, the benefit to the client of asset-protection law," Byrd says.

Byrd is admitted to practice in both the Eastern and Western Division of the United States District Courts for Washington, and the United States Court of Appeals for the Ninth Circuit. He has been active in the Washington and American bar associations in the sections of estate planning, probate,

trust, and real estate law. He is past president of the Seattle-King County Family Law Section, has served as a Superior Court Commissioner Pro Tem, was a Guardian Ad Litem, served as a Federal Bankruptcy Trustee and has been a community college real estate law instructor.

Related to his practice specialty, Byrd is also the founder of the Asset Protection Education Foundation, a nonprofit corporation whose purpose is to educate the public on how to protect assets from the five dangers to wealth: creditors, lawsuits, income taxes, probate, and estate taxes. "In this litigious society, it is only prudent to take advantage of all valid methods to protect one's assets," he says.

Cable, Langenbach, Henry & Kinerk

Cable, Langenbach, Henry & Kinerk is a nine-attorney firm (six partners and three associates) that specializes in complex commercial litigation and business transactions. The firm serves as Washington counsel for individuals, local businesses, and several large, nationally recognized companies.

The firm is one of several that trace their origins to Rummens & Griffin, which was founded in Seattle in the 1920s. By the 1970s, Rummens & Griffin had become known as Short, Cressman & Cable, and had grown to a thirty-lawyer firm located at 1001 Fourth Avenue. At that time, the firm concentrated on general civil matters, corporate law and real estate, and construction litigation.

In 1980, ten lawyers left Short, Cressman & Cable and formed Cable, Barrett, Langenbach & McInerney, with offices in the atrium of the Fourth and Blanchard Building in the Denny Regrade. The firm continued its emphasis on civil litigation, construction, and commercial matters. With the growth of the region and diversification of the business community, the firm expanded to twenty attorneys and increased its focus on real estate, taxation, securities law, and corporate transactional work. The firm also was in the forefront in handling plaintiffs' cases in the burgeoning fields of toxic waste and employment discrimination litigation.

The current firm was formed in 1987. The core of the practice remains general civil and commercial litigation and sophisticated business transactions in real estate and corporate areas. Individual partners also specialize in taxation, estate planning, employment matters, and professional associations.

The firm's two most senior partners, Don Cable and Read Langenbach, are active members of the legal community. Don Cable is a longtime resident of Mercer Island and a leading authority on mergers and acquisitions. Read Langenbach, who emphasizes real estate and general corporate law, is a former member of the Medina City Council and a veteran of numerous city planning and land use committees.

Cable Langenbach is located on the thirty-fifth floor of the Key Tower Building at 1000 Second Avenue. In recognition of its progressive office-space design, the firm received awards from the Institute of Business Designers and the American Institute of Architects.

Thomas J. Chambers

Thomas J. Chambers is one of Seattle's most active and well-known personal injury plaintiffs' litigation practitioners.

In 1989, he was awarded the Trial Lawyer of the Year Award by the Washington State Trial Lawyers Association. He is past president of the WSTLA and serves on the Board of Governors of the Washington State Bar Association and the Board of Governors of the WSTLA. A past member of the Board of Governors for the American Trial Lawyers Association, Chambers has been included in the book *Best Lawyers in America.*

Chambers attended Washington State University and the University of Washington School of Law, graduating in 1969.

He believes strongly in juries because, "that's the one protection that we have." Quoting deTocqueville, the jury system is "the way Americans represent themselves directly." As for trial work, "There's a sense of exhilaration and excitement in trying cases. Victories are nice; defeats are awful," says Chambers.

Chambers likes the atmosphere of the courthouse so much that he bought and refurbished an office building to look like a miniature courthouse in the style of Thomas Jefferson's Monticello.

Today, he spends about 25 percent of his time in lawyer-related activities, as opposed to actual legal practice. In order to give something back to the profession, Chambers envisions gradually moving to more of a mentoring role. As he puts it, "You can be concerned with how many seeds are in an apple, or with how many apples are in a seed."

Chambers enjoys feedback from other lawyers. Nevertheless, "I see the profession deteriorating into the bottom-line. We are losing the 'learned profession' status and are becoming just another business."

Chambers feels that attorneys come out of law school ill-prepared for the actual day-to-day practice. He'd like to see some kind of apprenticeship program, similar to what exists in British Columbia. Beyond that, he advocates more pro bono work since it is "one of the things that distinguishes law as a profession."

He already publishes a newsletter and also writes articles for journals and magazines; he has four volumes of publications collected in three-ring-binder notebooks; and he has written a two-volume book on personal injury trial practice. In addition, "I'm already making a series of how-to videotapes," such as "how to prepare a deposition." He is working on a tape on closing arguments.

"There's something special about doing plaintiffs' personal injury work," he says. "You're representing people against corporations, so there's a David and Goliath feeling to it. You have an opportunity to make a difference."

Chicago Title Insurance Company

Chicago Title Insurance Company, founded more than 145 years ago in Chicago, Illinois, is the nation's largest title insurer. Chicago Title, which opened its Seattle office in 1977, now employs 166 people at its main office in downtown Seattle (in the Columbia Center), with branches in Everett and Tacoma, as well as satellite offices in Bellevue, Federal Way, and Lynnwood.

Chicago Title Insurance Company provides property owners and mortgage companies with title insurance policies on property anywhere in the United States, Puerto Rico, the Virgin Islands, and Canada, through a network of more than four thousand locations. In Illinois, the parent company, Chicago Title and Trust Co., provides trust services that include estate planning with lawyers, executors and trustees under will, guardians and administrators, living trusts, investment counsels, land trusts, trustees for bond and note issues, and retirement trusts. In addition, it conducts an exchange trust business and administers 401(k) plans for many companies.

Both Chicago Title Insurance Co. and Chicago Title and Trust Co. trace their origins back to 1847 through direct succession to the business of several firms and corporations engaged in abstract and title business in Chicago, including Handy and Co., under which the business was continued until 1887.

In 1887, the state of Illinois passed the General Trust Company Act, granting to qualified corporations the right to act as executor, administrator, guardian, and trustee, and as fiduciary in other capacities. That same year Handy and Co. was succeeded by Title Guarantee and Trust Co., which qualified under the new act as a trust company.

In the next year came another action, which provided the protection commonly known today as real estate title insurance. The Title Guarantee and Trust Co. issued the first Title Guarantee Policy in Illinois, protecting the owner against loss of his title as guaranteed. Three years later, in 1891, the name of the company was changed to Chicago Title and Trust Co.

Chicago Title and Trust Co. grew with the city of Chicago. In the 1950s, the company expanded its business beyond the Illinois borders. To do title insurance on a national scale, in 1961 the company created a wholly owned subsidiary, Chicago Title Insurance Co.

In 1969, Chicago Title and Trust Co. became a wholly owned subsidiary of Lincoln National Corp. In 1985, Allegheny Corp., a New York-based company, purchased all of the outstanding stock of Chicago Title and Trust Co.

On January 21, 1987, Chicago Title and Trust Co. acquired SAFECO Title Insurance Co., a national title insurer. During the ensuing four years, Chicago Title's market share in King County was more than 25 percent of all insured transactions. In 1988, SAFECO changed its name to Security Union, a name derived from two predecessor companies of SAFECO Title.

In 1991, Chicago Title and Trust Co. acquired Ticor Title Insurance Company, which provided growth opportunities, especially in New York and California. With the acquisition, the Chicago Title and Trust Co. family of title insurers now includes Chicago Title Insurance Co. (CTIC), Security Union Title Insurance Co., CTIC of Oregon, Ticor Title Insurance Co., Ticor Title Guarantee, and Commonwealth Title Insurance Co. in Pierce County, Washington. The company expects continued growth from diversification and the existing agency network.

The hallmarks of the CT&T companies are expert personnel, a geographically vast title network, and top service. The company's record of profitability in each of the past ten years is unequaled in the industry.

Chicago Title Insurance Company, which sees itself as a service business, emphasizes customer service and a people-oriented corporate atmosphere.

"In the Puget Sound area, Chicago Title has been successful because of our people," says Jeff Knudson, vice president and Puget Sound Area manager. "We're a service business and our people have become established in the marketplace by focusing on our customer needs. The reason for Chicago Title's success is due to the job done by everybody at this company. If anyone is walking past a ringing phone, they pick it up. Everyone's involved in the effort here."

Chicago Title has been called "the attorney's title company." Many of the company's employees and agents are members of the legal profession. In addition, Chicago Title has its own legal department to assist in handling complex transactions and to provide underwriting and claims expertise when needed.

Title insurance is important to buyers, lenders, and others purchasing interests in real property to protect against loss or damage due to certain title defects that could later affect the purchased property rights. Examples of such covered defects are: forgeries in the chain of title, defective prior deeds, and recorded liens or encumbrances not shown in the policy. In the complex world of real property transactions today, Chicago Title provides valuable protection and outstanding customer service.

Chicago Title handles everything from the single-family, residential conveyance to the most complex types of projects—such as condominiums and condominium conversions; subdivisions; shopping centers; apartment, office and public buildings; and projects funded by industrial revenue bonds.

Chicoine & Hallett, P.S.

Chicoine & Hallett, P.S., is a Seattle firm that specializes in tax controversy matters. Its founders, Robert Chicoine and Darrell Hallett, each had extensive experience in government practice before founding the firm in 1983. Chicoine practiced as a Senior Tax Attorney for the Office of Regional Counsel, where he met and practiced with Mr. Hallett, before entering into private practice in 1977. Hallett had previously worked as a trial attorney for the Justice Department, served as Assistant District Counsel in Seattle, and was a Special Trial Judge for the United States Tax Court before he joined Chicoine for the purpose of developing a premiere specialty firm. Larry Johnson, who subsequently became a member of the firm, had accumulated ten years experience with the Office of Chief Counsel in Washington, D.C., and District Counsel's Office as a senior trial attorney.

The firm is one of the original boutique firms in the Seattle area, focusing on clients who have, or anticipate, tax-related disputes with federal and state authorities. Although the firm is small by design, it represents a large cross-section of society, often with significant tax deficiencies at stake. At any one time, it is not unusual for members of the firm to be working on matters for major corporations, local businesses, alleged racketeers, estates, entertainers, artists, or other law firms. Governmental agencies have also employed the firm to assist them in tax disputes and procedures. A large part of the firm's work involves criminal tax investigations and representing clients before the United States Tax Court.

The firm's attorneys are all considered experts in the field of tax, with over sixty years of accumulated tax experience. In addition, the firm works closely with former Internal Revenue Service investigators, collection officers, and appellate conferees to assist in audits, collection problems, and defending criminal prosecutions.

Providing quality service as efficiently as possible is an important philosophy of the firm. This philosophy is a major reason why the firm limits its practice to tax controversy. The attorneys of Chicoine & Hallett realize that often their clients are under a tremendous amount of pressure. "In most cases we have dealt with the situation before," says Chicoine. "We try to get to the heart of the problem, look for practical solutions, and give our clients a realistic assessment of their chances of success." Members of the firm have worked successfully over the years with many of the same International Revenue Service or governmental agents, so they have earned a level of adversarial respect that can help in achieving a satisfactory and timely resolution.

The nature of the firm's practice normally precludes continued client relationships once the tax dispute has been resolved, so the firm relies heavily upon referrals from other lawyers, accountants, and former clients. Speaking for the firm, Chicoine says: "Our reputation is extremely important to us. We believe that if we do our job well, have empathy for our clients, and offer them realistic solutions, we will continue to be successful."

Garvey, Schubert & Barer

Garvey, Schubert & Barer was founded by three classmates in 1966, two years after their graduation from the University of Washington law school. Six years later the firm opened a Washington, D.C., office. And in 1973 the partners stationed a lawyer in Japan. Both steps were "firsts" for the Seattle legal community. Its Portland, Oregon, office opened in 1982.

Garvey, Schubert & Barer now employs more than eighty lawyers in three offices. The firm represents clients before the federal government and in international legal matters, in addition to providing representation in commercial transactions and litigation.

John Hoerster, chairperson of the board of directors, characterizes the firm as "informal, with a sense of humor." Even the firm's formal statement of philosophy stresses this trait: "We decry hierarchy for the sake of hierarchy...we appreciate and encourage a certain amount of irreverence toward all matters concerning our firm, including this philosophy."

The firm's culture also emphasizes a willingness to weave policy from many voices. "Attorneys of all experience levels are expected to voice differences of opinion," says Hoerster. "One of Mike Garvey's favorite analogies compares the firm to the Stanford University marching band, whose members run in all directions but still play the same tune."

Garvey, Schubert & Barer's core practice areas are corporate and commercial law and litigation. The firm serves as primary outside legal counsel to: K2, a leading ski manufacturer; Stimson Lane, Ltd., the maker of Chateau Ste. Michelle and Columbia Crest wines; Totem Ocean Trailer Express, one of the region's two principal carriers to Alaska; Foss Maritime Co., the largest tug and barge company in Puget Sound; In Focus Systems, Inc., a leading manufacturer of liquid crystal display technology; and the Sisters of St. Joseph of Peace, Health and Hospital Services, a six thousand-employee healthcare system.

The firm has represented these clients in a broad range of commercial transactions, including acquisitions, an initial public offering, tax-exempt bond offerings, licensing and distribution agreements, and international distribution of products. In addition, Garvey, Schubert & Barer has served as advocate for these clients in a variety of disputes—from arbitration and mediation of small tort and contract claims, to administrative proceedings before government agencies, to patent and antitrust litigation in federal court.

The firm also practices in three significant areas not common among other firms: an international practice focused on the Pacific Rim, federal legislative and administrative representation, and public service.

The firm's Pacific Rim emphasis evolved from an early recognition of the significance to the Pacific Northwest of trade with Japan, the People's Republic of China, South Korea, and the former Soviet Union. In 1979, Stan Barer negotiated the resumption of shipping service between the People's Republic of China and the United States, after a hiatus of nearly thirty years.

Among other matters, the firm advises U.S. companies distributing products—ranging from skis to wine to wood products—in countries throughout the Pacific Rim, and it counsels major shipping interests on customs matters. Effective representation in international transactions requires a combination of legal skills, language abilities, and cultural understanding. As a result, members of the firm speak Japanese, Chinese, Russian, and Korean, and a number of the firm's attorneys have lived and worked in Pacific Rim countries.

The firm's practice before the U.S. Congress and federal agencies spans many areas of federal regulation, including international trade, natural resources, housing, and maritime and other transportation. In representing clients dealing with the federal government, Garvey, Schubert & Barer attorneys rely on prior experience in the public sector. Attorneys in the firm have held posts such as Deputy Secretary of Transportation and General Counsel of the National Oceanic and Atmospheric Administration; others have served as senior aides to members of Congress and staff directors of congressional committees.

Commitment to public service is a notable component of Garvey, Schubert & Barer's practice. It is a policy of the firm to encourage each lawyer to devote 10 percent of his or her time to public service work. "Lawyers have a responsibility to clients who can't afford legal services," says Hoerster. The unusual aspect of the policy is that the firm's billing system, in generating internal management reports, automatically treats these hours as chargeable hours and translates them into billings. The firm modified its billing system in this manner because "public service work is important to the firm, not simply an 'extracurricular' activity undertaken by individual lawyers on their own time."

The firm has assisted Indian tribes in litigating their status under treaties, undertaking economic development of tribal resources, and drafting tribal codes. The firm has also cooperated with Evergreen Legal Services on a number of cases, including one challenging school board election practices that disadvantaged minority candidates, and another on behalf of homeless children seeking assistance from the Department of Social and Health Services. The firm

devoted many hours to public service legal work in 1991.

Garvey, Schubert & Barer plans to continue its long-term objective of building a Pacific Rim practice. "We also intend to reinforce our core, 'bread and butter' commercial and litigation practices, which involves representing small and medium-sized businesses in the Pacific Northwest," says Hoerster. "We're comfortable with the size of the firm and we'll continue to grow at a moderate pace. Beyond these predictions, it is difficult to say what the future holds. We're opportunistic, we're risk takers, we do new things."

Heller Ehrman White & McAuliffe

With seventy-five lawyers, the Seattle office of Heller Ehrman White & McAuliffe is larger by itself than all but a few other Washington State firms. And with additional offices in Tacoma, Portland, and Anchorage, Heller Ehrman is now a major presence throughout the Northwest. Yet it was only ten years ago, in January 1983, that Heller Ehrman gained its first lawyer north of the Golden Gate Bridge. The firm's growth is a story of planning—and luck.

In 1982, Heller Ehrman was already ninety-three years old and well established as a premier San Francisco firm. Successive senior partners had long represented such Bay Area institutions as Wells Fargo Bank and Levi Strauss (both of these companies even set up temporary headquarters in Mr. Heller's house after the 1906 earthquake), and prominent public agencies such as those that built the Bay Bridge and the Golden Gate Bridge itself. But the firm's co-presidents, Vic Hebert and Larry Popofsky, had wider vision: they wanted Heller Ehrman to become known as a "West Coast" law firm, not just a San Francisco one.

At that time, Eric Redman was a Seattle lawyer (and former aide to Senator Warren G. Magnuson) who had just left a partnership at a major Seattle firm. The Washington Public Power Supply System (WPPSS) litigation had erupted unexpectedly and produced a conflict involving Northwest aluminum producers (ALCOA, Kaiser, Reynolds, Intalco, and others), the electric power clients for whom Redman was then a leading lawyer.

The aluminum producers stuck with Redman, who had represented them in court and before Congress for many years. They actively aided him in finding a new firm. But the clients imposed one condition: Redman could not join any of the large firms then active in Washington State, all of which

represented parties adverse to the aluminum producers in the WPPSS litigation.

The stage was set for a large new law firm to enter the Northwest market. Working with his clients, Redman narrowed the choice to two firms, one of which was Heller Ehrman. "I chose Heller Ehrman for two reasons," Redman recalls. "Talent and vision. The firm already had the most talented lawyers and successful litigators I'd ever met. And the idea of a West Coast law firm, not just a Seattle firm, appealed to me at once."

So Heller Ehrman opened its doors in Seattle and Portland (the region's electric power capital, thanks to the Bonneville Power Administration) on January 1, 1983. At the time, no other firm with its largest office outside Washington had a permanent office in the state. Heller Ehrman's unprecedented move caused controversy.

"One prominent state bar official called me a 'fifth columnist,'" Redman says. "He accused me of throwing open the gates of the city to the Californians. In fact, of course, we staffed the office with local lawyers." It's a pattern Heller Ehrman has followed in each of its offices, now seven in number. "We've never been carpetbaggers," notes Jessica Pers, an intellectual property litigator in the firm's San Francisco office who recently became Managing Partner of the entire firm.

At first Redman was alone in the Seattle office. In the Portland office, Michael C. Dotten, an electric power lawyer who left Bonneville to join the firm, was also alone at first. But that changed quickly.

The growth of Heller Ehrman's Northwest offices was not propelled by the WPPSS litigation. Ironically—or "fortunately," as Redman says—the Northwest aluminum producers managed to avoid becoming parties to the WPPSS cases in the end. But the Northwest aluminum producers had a host of other needs, and there was plenty of work for Heller Ehrman lawyers. The Northwest offices began to grow.

Two years later, the firm's Seattle office made another leap. In January 1985, Ralph Palumbo, one of the earliest and most prominent environmental specialists in the Northwest, joined the firm as a lateral partner. "The aluminum producers wanted to support the office," Redman remembers, "so they sent us environmental work. But they always insisted that our firm associate Ralph, whom they considered the best environmental lawyer in the region. Finally Ralph was persuaded to join us."

Palumbo's environmental clients included Northwest giants such as PACCAR, Weyerhaeuser, various pulp and paper companies, and, of course, the aluminum producers. Peter Weiner, a former top official in the administration of California governor Jerry Brown, opened the firm's environmental practice in California in the same year. Tacoma-based Mike Thorp, an environmental lawyer of national stature and the chief environmental counsel for worldwide mining giant ASARCO, joined Heller Ehrman a few years later. Today, according to industry data, Heller Ehrman's one hundred environmental lawyers give the firm one of the largest environmental law departments in the United States.

The firm's West Coast strategy and its potential benefits were put to the test almost immediately. Larry Popofsky and Peter Wald, two San Francisco litigation partners, led the team that persuaded the U.S. Supreme Court to review a lower court decision and grant the Northwest aluminum producers a key victory in 1984 in the landmark electric power and administrative law case *Aluminum Company of America et al. v. Central Lincoln People's Utility District et al.* "Having lost the case myself in the Ninth Circuit," Redman says, "I was not only relieved, but very, very glad to be practicing law with Larry and Peter."

At the same time, the Penn Square loan disaster and the losses consequently sustained by Seafirst Bank resulted in Heller Ehrman being asked to field a large team of high-powered litigators in the U.S. District Court in Seattle on behalf of Seafirst. Richard Cooley, newly installed as head of Seafirst, had come from Wells Fargo and, in addition, had been a client of Heller Ehrman personally. Cooley knew the firm's San Francisco litigators well, and wanted the firm representing Seafirst in court in Seattle.

A trial team led by Steve Bomse of San Francisco and including others such as George Greer, a litigation partner in the Seattle office, scored singular courtroom successes for Seafirst, producing recoveries from insurance companies and other defendants of many tens of millions of dollars. "It was a victory on all counts," Greer notes.

The Seafirst case, as well as the firm's success on behalf of Johns Manville against JM's insurers in the asbestos litigation, gave birth to Heller Ehrman's insurance coverage litigation practice (on behalf of insureds, not insurers). Thanks in part to environmental insurance coverage litigation, the firm now enjoys the largest insurance coverage practice of any firm in the U.S. The Seafirst case also provided Heller Ehrman's first experience at something else: "cross-staffing" major litigation. Cross-staffing means using the best available talent from

any of the firm's West Coast offices (now located in Seattle, Tacoma, Portland, Anchorage, San Francisco, Palo Alto, and Los Angeles) for each particular case. "Our clients are generally large and sophisticated," says Tom Brewer, a Seattle litigation partner. "They participate actively in selecting the team of Heller Ehrman lawyers they feel will produce the best result at the lowest cost."

Heller Ehrman's major cross-staffed litigation in recent years includes the firm's representation of Ernst & Young in the massive Lincoln Savings litigation; Bank of America (Seafirst's corporate parent) in the student loan and other cases; and Alyeska Pipeline Service Company, the operator of the Trans Alaska Pipeline, in the criminal defense phase of the *Exxon Valdez* litigation.

In 1988 the Seattle office of Heller Ehrman again made waves with the city's first three-way law firm merger. Joining the firm's Seattle office in the downtown financial district were Wickwire, Goldmark & Schorr from Pioneer Square and Syrdal, Danelo, Klein, Myre & Woods from the Denny Regrade. For several months, before the three former firms could get together under one roof in their present home, the Columbia Center, the firm's offices were known locally as Heller North, Heller South, and Heller Central.

The 1988 merger brought Heller Ehrman a host of major environmental and timber industry clients, as well as many new partners and associates. Unlike some mergers, this one worked: four years later, the Seattle office has again doubled in size. The merger also brought the office new specialties and practice group leaders, such as Otto Klein and the Employment Law group, Kevin Kelly and the Biotech group, and John Phillips and the Environmental Litigation group. The Seattle office's environmental group also gained additional leaders with strong practices such as partners Dan Syrdal and Duane Woods.

After the merger, Heller Ehrman added three lateral partners in Seattle. Bruce Pym, long a key Northwest lawyer for Security Pacific and ARCO, among other clients, brought major corporate, banking, and securities law expertise. Jack McCullough brought his land use practice and major development interests. Patrick Dunn brought both his legislative and community affairs experience and the largest lobbying practice in the state. The opening in 1989 of the firm's Anchorage and Tacoma offices (again with local lawyers) also markedly increased business in the Seattle office.

Like the firm as a whole, the Seattle office of Heller Ehrman values—and rewards—community service, civic involvement, and pro bono activity. Lawyers

in the Seattle office have twice won the firm's coveted Guggenhime Award, presented annually to the Heller Ehrman lawyer whose pro bono efforts best exemplify the spirit of the firm's late senior partner Richard Guggenhime, widely credited with having launched pro bono activity in the U.S. legal profession. On the occasion of the firm's 100th anniversary in 1990, the firm endowed a pro bono chair at Stanford and donated $100,000 to organizations helping the homeless on the West Coast, including the Fremont Public Association in Seattle.

"We've been very fortunate," says Klein, who now manages the Seattle office. "We're Northwest lawyers, we've done well here, our clients are very loyal, and we're part of a much larger firm whose long traditions of excellence and public service we've been proud to share."

Karr Tuttle Campbell

In 1904, when Day Karr and George W. Gregory formed their law practice, they walked the wooden stairs up Profanity Hill to argue cases before King County Superior Court judges. Today, the county courts are located on Third Avenue, and the firm, now known as Karr Tuttle Campbell, is located in the Washington Mutual Tower.

Karr and Gregory were studies in contrasting, though complementary, personalities. Karr was an reserved perfectionist with an eye toward detail and a law degree from Kansas Law School. The extrovert George Gregory was an All-American football player from the University of Michigan who was extremely competitive.

Karr & Gregory was like others of its day—it offered general legal services. There were no specialty firms then. When the Panic of 1907 dimmed Seattle's bright economy, the partners turned to moonlighting to supplement their incomes. Gregory coached a local football team and Karr worked as a part-time clerk in a cigar store. Years later Karr became the first regional director of the Securities and Exchange Commission, which helped him garner considerable securities law expertise, but to avoid any conflict of interest, or appearance of impropriety, the firm turned down securities work until the late 1950s.

In 1930, Clarence H. Campbell joined the firm. A year later he took over as supervisor of claims for Karr & Gregory's largest client, The Fidelity and Casualty Company of New York, but he still maintained a relationship with the firm.

The firm's second generation began following the death of George Gregory, during the dark days of the Depression. Day's son, Payne, was fresh from the George Washington University School of Law when he joined the firm in 1932. Four years later Howard Tuttle, a former University of Washington student body president and law school graduate, joined the firm. Tuttle served as president and member of the board of trustees of the UW Alumni Association and he was well known in the community. At about the same time, another University of Washington law school graduate, Carl Koch, joined the firm. Several years later firm members Koch, Clarence Campbell, Tuttle, and F. Lee Campbell (no relation to Clarence) were called to active duty in World War II and did not return until its conclusion.

After the war Karr, Tuttle & Campbell focused its skills on peacetime clients, such as Gai's Bakery, Rosella's Fruit and Produce, Evergreen Washelli, Bekins Moving and Storage, the University Bookstore, and numerous insurance companies.

In the early 1950s the firm's clients began requesting probate, estate planning, and trust services and in 1953, a law school classmate of Tuttle's, Muriel Mawer, was hired. Mawer and her classmate Maryhelen Wigle, who had finished second and third in their law school class of 1935, formed the first women's law partnership in Seattle. It was one of the first such firms in the nation. During the war Mawer had worked in the Office of Price Administration and by the time she joined the firm she was an experienced probate, estate planning, and trust attorney. Mawer became a partner in 1962 and practiced until 1983, when she became of counsel.

By 1970 Karr Tuttle had become a full-service regional law firm and in 1977 it was incorporated. In 1986 it merged with Sax & MacIver and consolidated the two firms' strong banking practice. Its name was changed to Karr, Tuttle, Koch, Campbell, Mawer, Morrow & Sax, P.S.

The firm had always encouraged its lawyers to pursue interests outside the office. Payne Karr served as chairman of the Seattle Transit Commission, president of the Seattle Chamber of Commerce, and president of the International Association of Insurance Counsel (IADC). Both Karr and F. Lee Campbell served as presidents of the Washington State Bar Association. Karr, F. L. Campbell, Bob Piper, and Craig Campbell (no relation to Clarence or F. Lee) are members of the American College of Trial Lawyers. Payne and Robert Payne Karr, who joined the firm in 1961, have served at the national level as officers of the IADC.

This tradition of outside service continues today: Terry Lukens, who practices in the firm's Bellevue office (opened in 1984), served on Bellevue's city council and became the city's mayor. Numerous other lawyers in the firm devote their time and talent to various professional and community organizations. In 1992 the firm's commitment to community service was recognized when it received the Seattle-King County Bar Association Pro Bono Service Award for providing legal services to homeless people living temporarily in Seattle Emergency Housing shelters.

In the last sixty years, Karr Tuttle Campbell has expanded its litigation practice, which now makes up almost 60 percent of its business. The firm is recognized for its expertise in numerous areas, such as general insurance claims, product liability, aviation and environmental law, hazardous waste disposal, employment relations matters, intellectual property, bankruptcy, and others. The firm's fifty-five lawyers represent nationally known clients, such as General Motors, Siemens Power Corporation, Bethlehem Steel, and General Electric, as well as prominent local businesses such as Gai's Seattle French Baking Company, Group Health Cooperative, Shah Safari, and Unisea.

As the firm prepares to celebrate its ninetieth anniversary, Bob Karr, grandson of founder Day Karr, notes, "We're one of a handful of third-generation firms in the area. Our profession has become complex and we look forward to the challenges of practicing law and meeting the changing needs of our clients in the 1990s."

Keller Rohrback

The firm now known as Keller Rohrback was established when its founder, George Kahin, entered private practice in Seattle's Central Building in 1918.

Kahin, a Harvard Law School graduate, worked as a solo practitioner until 1924, when he formed a partnership with Keith L. Bullitt. In 1929 Lumbermen's Mutual Casualty Company retained Bullitt & Kahin, launching the firm's insurance practice, which has continued and expanded up to the present time. Today, Keller Rohrback still represents Lumbermen's, along with more than twenty other major insurance carriers.

In 1930, the Bullitt & Kahin partnership was dissolved and John D. Carmody, an experienced trial lawyer in the Seattle City Attorney's Office, joined Kahin to form Kahin & Carmody. Kahin & Carmody practiced together throughout the 1930s and 1940s, and were joined by Joe S. Pearson in

1948, when the firm changed its name to Kahin, Carmody & Pearson.

Mr. Pearson was killed in a 1950 automobile accident, and Erle Horswill and Burton Waldo joined the firm to fill the gap left by Pearson's death. The firm changed its name to Kahin, Carmody & Horswill that year, and hired a promising young associate named Pinckney M. Rohrback. In 1953, Mr. Carmody retired from the firm to become general counsel for the New World Life Insurance Co., which was later acquired by Farmers Insurance.

In 1954, well-known real estate lawyer Robert K. Keller joined the firm. Keller was a true leader in the real estate community; he represented the North End Brokers Association, Inc. (now known as the Puget Sound Multiple Listing Association), from the organization's inception in 1958, until his death in 1992.

By the late 1960s, the firm was among Seattle's most prominent. Pinckney M. Rohrback served as president of the Seattle-King County Bar Association from 1968-1969; four of the firm's twelve attorneys were featured in the 1968 *Who's Who in America*; and in 1972, Governor Daniel J. Evans appointed Mr. Horswill to a judgeship on the King County Superior Court. The firm continued on its path of steady growth throughout the 1970s and 1980s. The firm now has more than thirty-five lawyers, and maintains offices both in Seattle and Bremerton, Washington. In 1986, the firm shortened its name to Keller Rohrback.

Today, the firm continues its prominent presence in the insurance bar, but has expanded its practice to a multitude of other areas as well. Keller Rohrback lawyers serve as members of the International Association of Defense Counsel, the Federation of Insurance and Defense Counsel, the American College of Trial Lawyers, the Washington State Trial Lawyers Association, the American Trial Lawyers Association, and the Washington Defense Trial Lawyers Association. The firm continues to represent numerous substantial insurance companies, many of which have been loyal clients for dozens of years. The firm has also achieved recognized expertise in regional banking, environmental, real estate, commercial litigation, product liability, construction law, securities, antitrust, class actions, estate planning, professional services, and ERISA.

While Keller Rohrback continues to earn its reputation as one of the region's leading law firms, its practice now extends nationwide through its efforts in prominent class-action litigation, as national counsel for the plaintiff class in the *Exxon Valdez* oil spill litigation, and in numerous class-action price fixing suits (including the Airline Ticket Antitrust litigation, which was the largest class action in the history of United States jurisprudence). The firm's product liability defense practice has also expanded throughout the region through its representation of clients such as Honda Motor Company, Bell Helmets, Subaru, and Suzuki. The firm now serves as local counsel for many Fortune 500 companies with litigation matters in the Pacific Northwest.

The firm's reputation is also growing within the Pacific Rim business community, where Keller Rohrback's long-standing ties to the Chinese-American and Korean-American communities serve as a natural bridge to the Far East.

In addition, the firm has continued its distinguished history of community service. Keller Rohrback attorneys are frequently called upon as authors and speakers in continuing legal education activities. From the 1960s to the present, in an almost unbroken line, Keller Rohrback attorneys have served at the highest levels of the Seattle-King County Bar Association. As recently as 1988-1989, Fred R. Butterworth served as president of the organization; partner Benson D. Wong presently serves as the SKCBA treasurer.

The Keller Rohrback of today might be hard for George Kahin to recognize. The firm now occupies offices on the thirty-second and thirty-first floors of the Washington Mutual Tower. Although the firm has undergone many changes in the course of its seventy-four-year history and its thirteen name changes, today's Keller Rohrback strives to carry forward the standards of integrity, hard work, and zealousness that were set by the firm's founders, and are so well embodied by the lawyers who have led the firm to its current position of distinction.

Lane Powell Spears Lubersky

Lane Powell Spears Lubersky traces its history back to 1889, when William A. Peters of Pennsylvania joined the firm of Strudwick, Peters & Collins. The firm has subsequently undergone many changes to its name.

Two years later, in 1891, the name of the firm was changed to Strudwick, Peters & Van Wyck. In 1893 Van Wyck returned to San Francisco and the firm continued as Strudwick & Peters until 1900.

John H. Powell arrived in Seattle shortly after the 1889 fire to practice law with his sister's husband, Julius Stratton, in the firm

of Stratton, Lewis & Gilman. Another young man in the office was Jay C. Allen, and he and John Powell started their own firm of Allen & Powell after a few years, which continued until 1900.

In 1900 William A. Peters and John H. Powell entered into partnership under the firm name of Peters & Powell, with offices in the Dexter Horton Building.

Robert H. Evans joined the firm as a partner on November 10, 1925, and John J. Jamison was employed in 1926 and became a partner on April 15, 1927. W. Byron Lane was employed as an associate in 1928. William G. McLaren joined the firm as a partner on April 1, 1929, at which time the name of the firm was changed to Peters, Powell, Evans & McLaren.

The firm was for many years counsel for both the Dexter Horton National Bank and the Washington Mutual Savings Bank, but in either 1928 or 1929 there arose a controversy between those two institutions, and the firm gave up representation of the Washington Mutual Savings Bank. Also, the firm was very active in the municipal bond business, along with the Thorgrimson firm and Shorts & Denney.

William A. Peters died on November 1, 1929, at about 68 years of age, and John H. Powell died on March 10, 1930, at the age of 63. Immediately prior to the death of William A. Peters, the partners in the firm were Messrs. Peters, Powell, Evans, McLaren, and Jamison, and the associates were R.W. Reid and W. B. Lane.

Laurance A. Peters, the youngest child of William A. Peters, joined the firm as an associate on September 1, 1930, at which time the name of the firm was changed to Peters, Evans & McLaren. Laurance became a partner on August 1, 1932, and left the firm on August 10, 1933, to pursue a career in traveling and writing. At that time the name of the firm was changed to Evans & McLaren.

George V. Powell, the youngest child of John H. Powell, went to work for the firm in 1933 while still at law school, after having worked for about a year in the office of Tanner & Garvin. Upon passing the bar exam in 1935, he became an associate.

On May 1, 1936, Norman Littell joined the firm as a partner and the name was changed to Evans, McLaren & Littell. Norman Littell had formerly been associated with the Bogle firm in Seattle and more recently the United States Attorney General. At the time Mr. Littell joined the firm, Mr. Reid and Mr. Jamison had left, Reid to go to Olympia and Jamison retiring to live in Pennsylvania.

On March 1, 1939, Norman Littell left Seattle and W. Byron Lane became a partner, and the name of the firm was changed to Evans, McLaren & Lane.

On March 1, 1946, upon George V. Powell's return from navy duty, he was made a partner in the firm, and the name of the firm was changed to Evans, McLaren, Lane & Powell.

In September 1948 William T. Beeks, an admiralty specialist, joined the firm as a partner, and the name of the firm was changed to Evans, McLaren, Lane, Powell & Beeks.

In 1961 Mr. Beeks left the firm to accept an appointment as United States District Judge, and the firm name was changed to Evans, McLaren, Lane, Powell & Moss. Gordon W. Moss had joined the firm as an associate in 1948 and became a partner in 1959.

On February 1, 1966, Pendleton Miller and Wilbur J. Lawrence, who had formerly been members of the firm of Grosscup, Ambler, Stephan & Miller, became partners in the firm and the name of the firm was changed to Lane, Powell, Moss & Miller.

In 1979, the firm expanded to Anchorage, Alaska, by merging with the Anchorage firm of Ruskin, Barker & Hicks. Mr. Ruskin left the firm in 1982, and the Anchorage office then became known as Lane Powell Barker & Hicks. In 1986 the firm opened an office in Mount Vernon, Washington.

On November 1, 1987, the firm merged with the Seattle firm of Cohen and Kaplan, a firm of four attorneys specializing in business, probate and estate planning, and commercial litigation.

In 1988 the firm opened an Olympia office with one attorney, and has since expanded to four attorneys.

The firm also opened a London office in 1988. This office was opened to serve the firm's needs in relation to the London insurance market, which had become a significant client base and was initially intended to be a servicing office with a permanent staff but no lawyers being assigned on a permanent basis.

The name Lane Powell Spears Lubersky results from the June 1, 1990, merger with the Portland-based firm of Spears Lubersky Bledsoe Anderson Young & Hilliard, a full-service law firm with eighty-six attorneys founded in 1889.

Since 1990 the firm has added a Los Angeles office, which now has fifteen attorneys, and placed attorneys in law firms in Tokyo and Osaka.

The legal profession has come a long way since 1889. George V. Powell, of counsel, now eighty-two years old, cites copiers and messenger services as the greatest changes in the legal profession. "We didn't have copy machines. Secretarial work was awful, hard work," he says in sympathy with the secretaries who slogged through the dark ages of carbon copies and manual typewriters. "They didn't have these messenger services then, and serving papers was the job of the law clerks and law students."

George was a Washington State representative from 1947 to 1953. From 1952-1964, he was a Commissioner on Uniform State Laws. He was a member of the Board of Governors of the Washington State Bar Association from 1963-1965. In addition, in 1965 he was appointed by Governor Dan Evans to the Board of Regents of the University of Washington.

George V. Powell is just one of the many attorneys at the firm who have played significant roles in the community over the years and in the present. Others include William T. Beeks, William J. Walsh, Jr., Hon. Thomas S. Zilly, Raymond W. Haman, D. Wayne Gittinger, David C. Lycette, and James L. Robart.

LPSL Today

LPSL is a major regional law firm of over 240 attorneys, offering a broad range of legal service to local, national, and international clients in the areas of business law, employment law, general litigation, maritime and aviation, and tort and professional liability.

Clients of LPSL include Afognak Native Corp.; Alaska Pulp Corp.; American President Lines, Ltd.; Amtrak; Associated Aviation Underwriters; The Atlantic Cos.; Burlington Northern Railroad Company; The Callison Partnership; Canron Construction Corp.; Castle & Cook, Inc.; Cavenham Forest Industries; Ciba-Geigy Corp.; CIGNA; Connaught Laboratories, Inc.; Continental National American Group; Cook Inlet Region Inc.; Digital Equipment Corp.; Emerson Electric Co.; First Interstate Bank; Fred Hutchinson Cancer Research Center; Georgia-Pacific Corp.; The Hartford Insurance Group; The Home Insurance Group; Honeywell, Inc.; James River Corp.; Key Bank of Puget Sound; Kohlberg, Kravis & Roberts; Maryland Casualty Co.; Mitsui & Co., Ltd.; The Mutual Life Insurance Co. of New York; New England Mutual Life Ins. Co.; The New York Life Ins. Co.; Nordstrom, Inc.; Prudential Securities; Simpson Investment Company and Affiliates; Southeastern Aviation Underwriters, Inc.; Texaco, Inc.; Trident Seafoods Corp.; Underwriters at Lloyds, London; Union Pacific Railroad Co.; W. R. Grace & Co.; Washington State Physicians Insurance.

In the international arena, LPSL is expanding its visibility and promoting its expertise in international tax and transactions, and representation of foreign investors. LPSL has established contacts throughout the Far East, including formal affiliations with the law firm of Nakagawa & Takashina in Tokyo, Japan. The affiliated office in Tokyo brings expertise and growing opportunities for representation of Japanese and other Asian clients. LPSL regularly represents business engaged in international trade and investment, including representation of a number of Asian clients in the forest products, fishing and seafood industries, and in the purchase of U.S. real estate and business interests. Membership in the World Law Group also provides our clients with top quality and efficient legal knowledge and expertise throughout the world.

Pro Bono and Community Service

LPSL is dedicated to extending the reach of legal services to the broader community. The firm's lawyers participate in many professional, pro bono, and community service activities. LPSL has consistently ranked high among firms in the Northwest, and has been recognized by the King County Bar Association and the Multnomah County Bar Association for its outstanding contribution to pro bono service.

At the 1992 Washington State Bar Association Convention, LPSL was presented the Affirmative Action Award. It is only the second time the award has been given. It is presented to an individual or law firm that has made a significant contribution to affirmative action in employment of ethnic minorities, women, or the disabled in the legal profession. LPSL was named because of the extensive service it has provided to the Northwest Minority Job Fair.

LPSL lawyers serve on the boards of and act as counsel to many nonprofit charitable and cultural organizations. Among those organizations are Volunteer Lawyers for the Arts, Seattle's Pike Place Market Historic Commission, Multifaith AIDS Project of Seattle, Fred Hutchinson Cancer Research Center, Oregon Symphony, Portland Opera, Waterfront Classics, Portland Theater Alliance, Portland State University Foundation, Seattle Central Community College, Oregon Museum of Science and Industry, Linfield College, Meridian Park Hospital Foundation, M.S. Society of Oregon, and many others.

Ed Harnden, managing partner, says, "We eagerly look forward to the next 100 years being as exciting and challenging as the last 100 years."

Lasher Holzapfel Sperry & Ebberson

Lasher Holzapfel Sperry & Ebberson acts as general corporate counsel, providing general business and litigation services to a primary clientele of locally owned private businesses and entrepreneurs.

The firm's roots go back to 1973, and after a merger it became known as Lasher & Johnson, in 1976. The firm's partners, realizing the firm's name was too easy, changed it to Lasher Holzapfel Sperry & Ebberson in 1989.

The firm offers legal services in the areas of law that a business client typically needs: corporate, business and tax law, commercial litigation and alternative dispute resolution, real estate, pension and employee benefit plans and administration, and management and employee relations. The firm also recognizes that business clients have many needs and provides representation for bankruptcy and creditors' rights, estate planning and probate, family law, and personal injury.

"Our market niche has been very successful," says Shannon Sperry, who focuses her practice on real estate and labor law. "We're recognized as the firm that represents private companies, and our clients are loyal. We get a great sense of fulfillment out of helping make their businesses successful." Many of the attorneys in the firm have experience as business owners themselves, so they are better able to understand and achieve their clients' objectives.

Lasher Holzapfel Sperry & Ebberson's support facilities include computerized research, data processing and word processing, plus a large paralegal staff. "We've set up systems to efficiently handle the routine legal work," says tax and business attorney George Holzapfel. This technical base makes it possible for LHS&E to efficiently serve its many clients, which include entrepreneurs, venture capitalists, real estate developers and investors, financial institutions, contractors, a major commercial airline, manufacturers, computer software developers, and numerous retail and service businesses.

LHS&E offers the professional nuts and bolts of ongoing legal support for businesses—with a plus: the human values that sometimes get lost as professional businesses grow. As senior litigator Linda Ebberson says, "We've turned down a number of merger offers. We're flattered, but we like the congenial atmosphere we have here. Our lawyers are top quality, Law Review, CPAs, etc., and chose to join a smaller firm." There is a noticeable camaraderie among support staff, as well, where the quality of work product is important and in fact is enhanced by mutual pride in working together to achieve their clients' goals.

As the firm has grown from the original five attorneys to its present size of twenty, it has done so in an egalitarian and progressive way. Nearly half the partners are women, and balance between work and personal life is encouraged. The vitality of the group is evidenced by the combination of depth of legal experience and youthfulness of its partners and associates, as well as their active participation in local, state, and national bar associations, service on boards, councils, and committees, and time spent in teaching and lecturing in their areas of expertise. And where else? With their families and on the ski slopes, in aerobic workouts, and bicycling marathons!

"We try to strike a balance in our lives. We strive to be the best lawyers for our clients, and at the same time keep our perspective on life. In the long run, we do a better job for our clients, " says founding partner Earl Lasher.

Legal+Plus Software Group Inc.

Legal+Plus Software Group Inc. was started in 1988 by Stephen and Timothy Sooter. Stephen Sooter is a 1987 graduate of University of Puget Sound School of Law; Tim is the computer programmer. Their first product, SupportCalc,™ was written to calculate and produce paperwork for the new Child Support Schedule. SupportCalc™ now has one thousand current users in six hundred law firms throughout Washington State, as well as many county courts and state offices, including the Office of Support Enforcement and the Washington State Attorney General.

"Obviously we have met a need in law for automation. There are one thousand members of the Family Law Section of the Washington State Bar, and one thousand users of SupportCalc.™ But automating only the Child Support Schedule limited the usefulness of what we had developed," says Stephen Sooter, the older brother. "We began looking for other applications for our developing technology."

They did not have to look far. In 1989, the Washington legislature passed a law requiring usage of state-developed mandatory pleading forms in all family law cases. When these forms went into effect on January 1, 1992, the Sooter brothers were ready.

"Developing good software to produce the ninety-seven mandatory family law pleading forms developed by the Pattern

Forms Committee was a tremendous personal challenge," says Tim Sooter. "After looking at computer software technology that was nationally available, it was clear to us that nothing existed to meet the needs of Washington attorneys faced with their new mandatory forms." So the Sooter brothers wrote their own computer software to meet the need: Forms+Plus.™

Forms+Plus™ is now used in Washington State by several hundred law firms to produce the mandatory family law pleading forms. Forms+Plus™ integrates all information among the forms, so that information is never typed twice. "Besides filling out forms in record speed, information accuracy is assured," says Stephen.

Legal+Plus Software Group Inc. was recently honored by being one of only five vendors invited by the American Bar Association to display at its annual Family Law Convention in Washington, D.C. The convention delegates were very receptive to Forms+Plus.™ "They wished they had Forms+Plus™ working in their states to fill out forms," said Tim. The Sooter brothers now have plans to expand Forms+Plus™ throughout the United States.

LeSourd & Patten, P.S.

LeSourd & Patten was one of the first law firms in Washington State to make tax law a substantial portion of its practice. No other firm of attorneys concentrated on tax matters to the same extent, especially in resolving disputes with the Internal Revenue Service.

The firm's roots go back to 1922, when it was founded as Stratton & Kane. Fran LeSourd, currently of counsel, joined the firm in 1939, when it had ten attorneys, a sizable firm for that time. In 1960 LeSourd, Woolvin Patten and Brock Adams, the future U.S. senator, split from the original firm to form LeSourd, Patten & Adams. "We wanted to be small," says LeSourd.

LeSourd himself was a University of Washington student when he made the decision to become an attorney. "I was working over the summer setting chokers for a logging operation in the Cascades. There was an old guy there that had been a 'High Climber' in the woods at big money; but when he got old, he was reduced to making beds. Before going to the woods, he said, he had been a telegraph operator working next to Henry Ford. At this point I began to realize that I wanted a career where my value would increase over time, not decrease."

After graduation in 1932, LeSourd worked briefly for the Chadwick firm in Seattle, and then went to Washington, D.C. and the Tax Division of the Department of

Justice, trying tax cases all over the country. In 1939 he returned to Seattle, preferring to raise a family here.

LeSourd met his partner Woolvin Patten when they were on opposite sides of a 1955 criminal tax case. Patten, acting on behalf of the IRS, was prosecuting an Issaquah dairyman for tax evasion. The dairyman blamed his public accountant, who had already served time for tax evasion on his own return. LeSourd represented the accountant, and secured his acquittal. After the trial, the opposing attorneys decided to join forces. "Woolvin and I had such regard for each other's trial abilities that we got together," says LeSourd.

Today, the firm's attorneys continue to focus on tax, business, and estate planning; civil and criminal tax litigation; pension and profit sharing; real estate; and environmental and business litigation. Among their assets are two attorneys who are also CPAs, and four with LL.M.'s in Taxation. In an age of law firm mergers, LeSourd & Patten plans to stay small and specialized.

Mikkelborg, Broz, Wells & Fryer

Mikkelborg, Broz, Wells & Fryer is a midsized downtown civil litigation firm, specializing in business, maritime, immigration, employment, and the fishing industry. The firm's emphasis on these fields is partially a result of the original partners' extensive service in the law departments of various federal and state agencies.

The firm was founded in 1961 in Seattle by three former assistant United States attorneys: Richard F. Broz, Jeremiah M. Long, and Jacob A. Mikkelborg. They were soon joined by two former assistant attorneys general for the state of Washington—Robert O. Wells, Jr., and Douglas M. Fryer. All had extensive backgrounds with state and federal agencies in addition to their immediate past government employment.

The firm's early practice, which included several high-profile cases of the mid-1960s, reflected the partners' varied experience as government lawyers. These cases included the nationwide antitrust cases against the manufacturers of electrical equipment and the city of Anchorage case against Lloyds Underwriters for damage—sustained during the 1964 Good Friday earthquake—to the port of Anchorage. The firm served as special counsel to the Washington State Bar Association for many years.

In 1968, Broz left private practice when he was appointed to the King County Superior Court bench by Governor Daniel J. Evans. Upon rejoining the firm in 1971, he chaired the Washington State Bar Association's Committee on Automobile Reparations.

Broz and Wells later drafted the Association's tort reform proposals, including the abolition of the contributory negligence and host-guest doctrines, which were enacted into law in the early 1970s. Broz, alluding to the firm's substantial background in admiralty law, comments that contributory negligence was appropriately replaced by the more equitable comparative negligence rule applicable to maritime cases.

During the seventies and eighties, the firm continued to expand its trial practice, adding experienced lawyers as necessary. Douglas M. Duncan joined the firm from the law clerk staff of U.S. Court of Appeals Judge Eugene Wright. Richard L. Phillips and Margaret Doyle Fitzpatrick came on board following service as deputy prosecuting attorneys, and Jeffrey L. Jernegan became a litigator specializing in maritime and business law.

In the 1980s, the firm acted as lead counsel in the multi-district Bristol Bay Anti-Trust litigation, which culminated in a successful trial and defense verdict. As a result of the rapid expansion of the fishing industry, the firm attained a position of leadership as counsel to many new fishing businesses.

In the 1990s, the firm acted as special counsel to the federal government of Canada, in the oil spill litigation arising out of the *Nestucca* collision in December 1988 off Grays Harbor.

While founding partner Jacob A. Mikkelborg has retired, and Jeremiah M. Long has established a separate practice specializing in real estate transactions, original partners Broz, Wells and Fryer continue to practice in the firm, building on the original concept of a mid-sized law firm specializing in civil litigation, with concentrations in maritime, insurance, business, antitrust, and immigration law.

Managing partner Douglas M. Fryer notes that as the firm completed its first thirty years, its practice had expanded into such diverse areas as employment, environmental, and bankruptcy matters, reflecting the changing requirements of the firm's clients. As examples, Fryer cites the firm's recent representation of the prevailing side before the U.S. Supreme Court in the Wards Cove Packing Company case (a landmark decision in employment law) and its participation in developing areas of the law such as employment discrimination and alternative disputes resolutions.

Wards Cove was also a landmark decision in civil rights litigation. The racial discrimination class action suit began in 1971 and was finally affirmed by the U.S. Supreme Court in 1989. In 1986 the firm won the largest individual award for discrimination in state history in a case against Fuji Photo Lab.

The firm was also involved when the West Seattle Bridge was struck and jammed open. As Broz says, "There's no such thing as a small ship collision."

In another case, which has become part of Seattle's legal lore, Broz and Mikkelborg prosecuted the defendant in *U.S. v. Odd John Solnordal.* Solnordal had sunk the *Cape Douglas* in 660 feet of water off Three Tree Point, south of Elliott Bay, claiming the vessel had been damaged and sunk. Following investigations by Mikkelborg and Broz, subsequent investigations by the Coast Guard and FBI, and the raising of the vessel by a salvage master, Solnordal was indicted on the rare charge of "barratry"—the sinking of a vessel by her master.

Mills & Uchida Court Reporting, Inc.

Mills & Uchida was founded in 1978, when Mike Mills and Pat Uchida, colleagues in a Seattle freelance court-reporting firm, formed their own enterprise.

Mills started as an official court reporter in 1964, in Corpus Christi, Texas, before moving to the Northwest in 1973. Two years later, he switched from official to freelance court reporting and became an associate with a Seattle freelance firm. Pat Uchida, a native of Seattle, has been practicing her craft since 1974. She was an associate at the Seattle court-reporting firm when she met Mills.

The catalyst for forming Mills & Uchida Court Reporting, Inc., was their appreciation of computer-aided transcribing systems of stenographic notes. At first, the firm consisted of just Mills and Uchida, but it has grown over the years to fifteen reporters. There are also two staff employees who handle the calendar schedules, copying, indexing, billing, delivery, and filing of transcripts and exhibits.

In 1985, Mills and Uchida began changing over from the original mini-computers to PC technology. They have continued to upgrade their computers, and they now utilize a portable hard-drive system, which allows the firm's reporters to carry their work around on a "Passport" hard drive and plug into their home computers. The firm also uses portable computers for traveling jobs, so that the reporters can be working on transcripts while they are out on the road, rather than having to do all the work upon their return.

The computer system gives greater quality control than the old dictation/ transcription system. The reporter "writes" the deposition, then "translates" it, does all the first-pass "scoping," and proofreads a rough-draft hard copy, before additional inputs and corrections for the final draft. This provides three extra levels of QA/QC for the reporter's product.

New services and products are continually being offered to the legal community. Transcripts can be provided in ASCII format on diskettes or sent via modem anywhere in the world. Transcripts can be compressed from typewritten format to three-column magazine format; eight pages of transcript can be printed on a double-sided sheet of paper.

The firm is committed to providing the highest-quality transcripts available anywhere.

Miracle, Pruzan & Pruzan

Miracle, Pruzan & Pruzan, which specializes in personal injury law, was co-founded before World War II by Hugh Miracle and Kenneth Tredwell. Howard Pruzan, who clerked for the firm while in law school, joined it in 1948, just as the practice of personal injury law was beginning to develop.

Miracle and Pruzan were actively involved in the evolution of the field. Steve Pruzan, Howard's son, joined the firm in 1975, after graduating from Gonzaga Law School. Hugh Miracle retired in 1977. Another Gonzaga Law School graduate, James E. Baker, joined the firm in 1986, and he is now a partner.

In the early days, the two partners complemented each other: Miracle was a colorful character who enjoyed the theatrics of a court trial, while Howard Pruzan was the academic, "more interested in the book end, the appellate end. We made some good law," explained Pruzan, then he cited several tort precedents.

Steve Pruzan specializes in medical malpractice. He enjoys the competition of law, but also is fascinated by medicine. "That's the fun part, to learn something outside of law," reveals Pruzan.

Because personal injury involves representing individuals—rather than corporations or business entities—the attorneys have the opportunity to closely observe human behavior. They also see the resiliency of human nature. For example, a dramatically injured client who refuses to succumb to life's setbacks can reaffirm the attorneys' own optimism about humanity—not to mention the effect it has on a jury. According to Pruzan, "Juries love resiliency. They love to see somebody who's trying. The less you complain, the better you do."

Because the nature of their practice frequently brings clients who are down and out, the attorneys praise the contingent fee system, which offers a day in court to everybody, not just corporations that can afford hourly rates. "I think it's fair to say that we've regarded this as more of a calling than just a money-making endeavor," says the senior Pruzan.

The firm possesses a belief in the courts and the legal system in the face of society's increasingly litigious tendencies. First, suggests Steve Pruzan, "People have a heightened awareness of their rights. I think that's good."

"Negotiations aren't always fruitful, but I'm all in favor of the idea of peaceful solutions," notes Howard Pruzan. "But there are times when a dispute has to be adjudicated in a formal manner."

Besides the increasingly complex legal landscape and ongoing legislative review of malpractice law, Howard Pruzan laments that, over the years, the friendly competition and inter-lawyer relationships have diminished. "I used to know most of the lawyers. Now, I know maybe a few out of a hundred. But it's still a source of pride to be held in high regard by the opposite side."

The firm plans to maintain its current size and direction. "We enjoy being a small firm," says Steve Pruzan.

Dean Moburg & Associates, Inc.

Dean Moburg & Associates, Inc., has been in business longer than any other Seattle court-reporting firm. The company was founded in 1928 by Bruce Moburg, then was taken over by his son, Dean Moburg. The firm was acquired in 1981 by Robert Keblbek, B. J. Meek and Eric Nutt; since 1988, the offices have been located in the Washington Mutual Tower, 1201 Third Avenue.

Among the approximately eighty-five court-reporting companies in Seattle, Dean Moburg & Associates is the oldest and among the largest, with twenty-one professional registered court reporters.

Today court-reporting companies offer many more services than what Bruce Moburg envisioned when he founded the firm over sixty years ago. Court reporters often specialize in technical areas such as medical and maritime, as well as arbitrations, antitrust, labor, airline, and admiralty. Court reporters provide transcripts on computer discs and hard-copy, as well as video and cassette transcriptions.

The main attributes of a court-reporting business are the same as they've always been: accuracy, reliability, and on-time delivery. Dean Moburg & Associates promises to provide all those qualities, plus a full range of court-reporting services and daily computerized copy. It also promises to be always available.

Objective Medical Assessment Corporation

Objective Medical Assessment Corporation (OMAC) is a medical-legal resource that provides medical panels and single-physician examinations for plaintiffs and defendants. The company has over four hundred physicians who are consultants to claims administrators and attorneys and who perform clinical trials.

OMAC was started in Tacoma in 1981 by Dick Nelson and medical director Dr. Louis A. Roser. Nelson, who had been Medicaid Director for the state of Washington and responsible for the Social Security Disability Program, observed a revolving door of medical, legal, and administrative cycles that was victimizing to the people caught in it. "I thought if we could provide medical-legal opinions in the private sector, if we could interdict, we could make a difference," he says.

OMAC now has nine clinics throughout the state, with sixty-five employees. Corporate headquarters are in the Westlake Tower in Seattle.

Bob McCluskey, an attorney, joined the company in 1990 to provide direction to the medical-legal business and other client services.

"We provide advice, counsel, and medical opinion for non-medical clients," Nelson says. "The medical-legal field is expanding. There are questions on the health-care horizon, and we continue to look for new jurisdictions in which to operate." In providing services to attorneys, OMAC serves "as a resource to those with responsibilities in the judicial system."

Oles, Morrison & Rinker

Oles, Morrison & Rinker is the largest firm in the Pacific Northwest with a principal specialty in the construction field.

The firm, which also remains in general practice, was founded in 1893 by John T. Condon and George E. Wright. The original offices were in the Burke Building, in what is now the historic Pioneer Square area of Seattle. Condon Hall at the University of Washington law school is named for Condon, who became dean in the late 1890s. Among the partners in the early part of the century were Hugh Caldwell, who served as corporation counsel of Seattle in the World War I era, and William Askren, later of the Washington Supreme Court.

Edward Allen, another early partner, was an acknowledged authority on fisheries and international law. He was deeply involved in the commercial fishing industry as general counsel to the Alaska Salmon Industry. As a member for several decades of the International Fisheries Commission, he was part of the delegation that negotiated the fishery treaties with Japan, and was a U.S. delegate to the United Nations Food and Agriculture meetings in Rome.

Gerald DeGarmo joined in 1930. His work in the field of heavy construction set the character of the firm. DeGarmo was attorney for the consortium that built the Grand Coulee Dam, and his clients included Kaiser Industries, Morrison Knudsen, and Peter Kiewit.

Stuart Oles, who followed in DeGarmo's footsteps, was involved in major construction litigation throughout America and abroad. Oles is now counsel.

"The philosophy of the firm has been to emphasize a thorough understanding of the industry itself," says Oles. "Our people become part of the construction team, so we feel we know more than anybody about the technical problems."

Construction has become an increasingly complex thicket of regulations, especially when the government is involved. Nevertheless, Oles has great faith in the judicial process, even in the face of highly complex and technical cases. "I think juries are better than they're given credit for. You get a good old retired carpenter on a jury and he understands it when you start unrolling construction plans. Then courtroom theatrics come into it. You're putting on a morality play and everybody has their part."

On the down side, over the years Oles feels that "litigation has become less pleasant." He despairs over the loosening of restrictions on lawyers' advertising. And "I still think it's grossly unethical to go to another person's client and say, 'I can do it better.' "

For all the frustrations, though, he never considered another profession. "In my case, it's been a lot of fun," he says. "I've had opportunities to travel around the world. I've walked through sewers in Cairo, and I've helped build roads in Puerto Rico. It's an interesting activity, especially dealing with contractors, who are great people."

Perkins Coie

The Perkins Coie firm began as Donworth & Todd in 1912, when law was simple and its language was less complex. Its founders were two classic western lawyers who had sought and dispensed justice from opposite sides of the bench. George Donworth was a federal judge and Elmer Todd was a United States attorney. When Todd told Donworth of an offer from the Bogle firm to enter private practice, the judge countered with his own plan, and the two opened their own office.

Their reputation soon attracted a major client, Seattle and Lake Washington Waterway Company, which offered stock and bonds to raise money to build a canal between Elliott Bay and Lake Washington. The canal was never completed, but earth was moved, land was filled, and valuable waterfront real estate was created and sold.

The firm began representing William E. Boeing when his company was less than two years old. It learned the new language of air frames, engines, avionics and aviation, and it assisted Boeing in forming The Boeing Airplane and Transport Corporation, and later, Boeing Air Transport, Pacific Air Transport and in 1929, United Airplane and Transportation Company, which was the predecessor to United Airlines. The firm continues to serve as The Boeing Company's outside general counsel.

The firm became a magnet for attorneys with a passion for business. Its distinguished alumni include William M. Allen, who began with the firm in 1923 and resigned in 1945 to become president of The Boeing Company. Todd himself, at the invitation of his client Alden Blethen, retired in 1943 to become publisher of Blethen's newspaper, *The Seattle Times.* Since then the list has grown to include other business executives: Lowell Mickelwait, Boeing; John Ellis, Puget Power; Richard Albrecht, Boeing; Christopher Bayley, Burlington Northern; Tom Alberg, McCaw Cellular; and William D. Ruckelshaus, Browning-Ferris Industries, who headed the Environmental Protection Agency during the Nixon administration and later returned to practice environmental law at Perkins Coie.

Other Donworth & Todd lawyers have had distinguished careers. Among them are Frank Holman, who served as president of the American Bar Association, Alfred Harsh, who became dean of the University of Washington School of Law, and Donworth's son, Charles, who in 1956 became Chief Justice of the Washington State Supreme Court.

The firm went through fourteen name changes before becoming Perkins Coie in 1985. It has grown to more than 335 attorneys in nine offices, including two in the Far East—Taiwan and Hong Kong. A sixteen-member executive committee, headed by Managing Partner Robert Giles, acts as the firm's board of directors, establishing policies and goals and overseeing legal operations. All of the firm's non-legal activities are overseen by Executive Director Guy Bennett.

Perkins Coie represents a long, distinguished list of clients. Some are old—Boeing, Puget Sound Power & Light Co., and Weyerhaeuser—and many are new—Immunex, Heart Technology, and McCaw Cellular Communications. Now, the firm's attorneys are fluent in the specialized languages of business, banking, government regulations, computer hardware, software, biomedicine, engineering, and disciplines that Donworth and Todd never dreamed of in 1912.

Preston Thorgrimson Shidler Gates & Ellis

The Preston firm is the oldest in Seattle, dating from 1883, when Harold Preston opened a law office. It has gone through many changes in name and personnel (the partnership with O. B. Thorgrimson was formed in 1912). Preston is now a full-service firm with more than 230 attorneys in seven offices, both public and private clients, and annual billings in excess of $40 million.

In early 1990, Preston Thorgrimson Ellis & Holman merged with Shidler McBroom Gates & Lucas, a firm founded in 1927. The Preston firm had developed a national reputation for its municipal work, especially as bond counsel for public entities. Shidler, a smaller firm, had extensive experience in corporate law casework and was general counsel to a number of local publicly traded companies, including Microsoft. It was also known for its litigation department, which has handled such high-profile matters as the WPPSS securities case and the Microsoft/Apple litigation. Besides combining these practices, the merger turned two modest-sized firms into one of the largest in the Pacific Northwest, with offices in Seattle,

Bellevue, Tacoma, Washington, D.C., Spokane, Portland, and Anchorage.

The firm's municipal department maintains the oldest and largest municipal finance practice in the Pacific Northwest. The firm has participated in drafting legislation at the federal, state, and local levels and serves as utility and enterprise counsel to local governments, including Seattle, Tacoma, Everett, and Bellevue, Anchorage, Fairbanks, Portland, Eugene, and Corvallis.

Among the Litigation Department's more prominent cases was its representation of the state of Alaska in its suit against the Exxon Corporation arising from the 1989 oil spill in Prince William Sound. Preston is general counsel to Metro in land use and construction litigation, most recently in cases arising out of the downtown bus tunnel project and new secondary sewage treatment facilities. The firm served as one of three co-lead counsels for the plaintiffs in the WPPSS securities litigation. Preston also has an active media, communications, and first amendment practice and an intellectual property practice involving copyrights, trademarks, patents, and trade secrets.

Business department clients include a number of prominent Northwest corporations: Microsoft, Univar, PENWEST, Ltd., Starbucks Coffee, and KIRO, Inc. Like many Seattle firms, Preston Thorgrimson Shidler Gates & Ellis maintains an active Pacific Rim practice.

Throughout the firm's history, partners have been involved in civic activities. Harold Preston, the firm's founder, was a state senator and later, in 1911, was the draftsman and the major advocate of the state's Workmen's Compensation Law, a radical notion at the time. The firm's partners have included state supreme court judge Charles Horowitz, federal court of appeals judge Betty Fletcher, and James Ellis, the prominent civic activist and former chair of the American Bar Association Section on Urban, State, and Local Government Law. Harold Preston, O. B. Thorgrimson, John N. Rupp, and William H. Gates all served as President of the Washington State Bar Association and as president of the Seattle-King County Bar Association. John Gose served as the chair of the American Bar Association Real Property Probate and Trust Section.

A partner in the firm, Fred Tausend, was named 1991 Lawyer of the Year by the Seattle-King County Bar Association. He acted as lead counsel for the Pike Place Market Development Authority in its high-profile two-year dispute with its New York investors. The firm received the Seattle-King County Bar Association Pro Bono Award in 1987 and the Charles Goldmark Foundation Award in 1989. Six of the firm's attorneys shared in the 1989 Civil Libertarian Award for volunteer services to the ACLU.

Over the years, starting with Judge Horowitz in 1927-29, six of the firm's lawyers have been Rhodes Scholars at Oxford—probably a record for a Seattle law firm.

Within its own offices, Preston has recognized the changing society and encouraged a more diverse, multicultural atmosphere, encompassing ethnic minorities, handicapped persons, and alternative lifestyles. As managing partner Kirk Dublin said in an interview, "I have a basic belief that any firm our size should do its best to mirror the communities in which it works."

Two of the firm's senior attorneys, Bill Gates and Jim Ellis, reflect on their careers:

"One is inclined to regret the passing of the 'good old days' when we were all generalists and when we knew almost every other lawyer in town," says Gates. "However, there are some really good things about current law practice. The profession is attracting the best and brightest from college ranks—spectacular young people with superb ideals. We deliver extraordinarily sophisticated advice and documentation virtually on demand. Also, I believe today the relationship with clients is characterized by informality and mutual interest in achieving practical results, where in the past there was more formality and less effective communication."

His own practice became steadier and more staid, too. "I did trial work for the first fifteen years of my career," says Gates. "When you do more business work, the thrills and excitement are fewer and farther between."

Nevertheless, a big resourceful firm has many advantages, too. "The amount of specialized knowledge available to a client is very impressive," says Gates.

Jim Ellis has been a high-profile civic activist for four decades. Known as the Father of Metro, he has been a leader in such major local projects as cleaning up the pollution in Lake Washington; creating a regional public transit system; founding Forward Thrust, the force behind such major projects as the Kingdome, the Aquarium, Freeway Park and Waterfront Park; preserving thirteen thousand acres of farmland; and building the Washington State Convention Center.

"There were wonderful moments in these community efforts," says Ellis, "but being in the spotlight is a mixed blessing. It gives you

a stronger voice on issues but it also makes you a target for public attack."

Like Gates, Ellis has seen his practice narrow over the past few decades. "I enjoyed the wide range of matters which a lawyer could perform when the law was simpler. But the ability of this firm to undertake complex matters is far greater today and the competitive world requires that ability."

He says you can't separate the activist from the attorney. "You need the support structure of a civic-minded firm. It's second only to the family," he says. "This firm provides the activist lawyer an opportunity to secure close allies and to test ideas. It recognizes public service as a firm goal. And it's willing to subordinate dollars to that goal."

Revelle Hawkins

Revelle Hawkins, P.S., was founded in 1978, in Bellevue, Washington, and it has grown to become the largest law firm on the Eastside.

Revelle Hawkins provides a wide range of legal expertise, including alternative dispute resolution, bankruptcy, business, civil and criminal litigation, computer law and high technology, corporation, environmental law, escrow, family law, government contracts, health law, land use, probate and estate planning, real estate, and taxation.

The firm has developed an Arbitration and Mediation department, which specializes in finding amicable and speedy resolutions for disputes before contested matters enter the costly process of court solutions.

Among its unique services, Revelle Hawkins, through its subsidiary Revelle Escrow, Inc., is one of the largest non-institutional escrow businesses in Washington State.

Revelle Hawkins represents a broad base of private and corporate clients, including the Washington Association of Realtors, the Seattle-King County Board of Realtors, Attachmate Corporation, Chicago Title Insurance Company, and Coldwell Banker, as well as many of the Eastside's largest institutional lenders, mortgage companies, developers, and commercial and residential real estate companies.

Its estate planning, tax, and trust attorneys work with individuals interested in defining and preserving their estates. The firm's expertise includes the preparation of wills, estate and gift tax returns, trusts, and other related documents.

Revelle Hawkins also represents its clients in matters of dissolution, custody, adoption, and modification orders. In these specific areas, the firm is the leader in alternative dispute resolution, and a number

of the firm's attorneys are active in advancing the practice of arbitration and mediation.

The firm's attorneys are committed to their community as well as their profession and they participate in a variety of professional and community activities.

Revelle Hawkins members include the past chairman of the Washington State Bar Association's Family Law Section, a retired Superior Court judge, a director of the National Association of Realtors, a director of the Escrow Association of Washington, the past president of the East King County Bar Association, the president of the King County Bar Association, and the president of the State Board of Washington Women Lawyers. Several of the firm's members are also committed to active participation in the Eastside Legal Assistance Program, the Youth Eastside Service organizations, and United Way.

Schroeter, Goldmark & Bender

For three decades, the law firm of Schroeter, Goldmark & Bender (SGB) has fought for the rights of injury victims and defended the rights of the accused.

The seed of what was to become SGB was sown in 1962 by Leonard W. Schroeter. After graduating from Harvard Law in 1951, Schroeter worked for Thurgood Marshall and the NAACP on the segregation-shattering *Brown v. Board of Education*. Upon moving to Washington, he served as northwest director of the Anti-Defamation League and later as president of the Washington State American Civil Liberties Union. He chose to represent personal injury victims in private practice to carry on a lifelong career of siding with those who most needed quality representation. As a trial lawyer, he was respected by his colleagues and feared by his opponents, and he was elected president of Washington State Trial Lawyers Association (WSTLA).

Schroeter was later joined by Dean Bender (1933-1988), who shared a preference for the underdog. Bender, though less flamboyant than Schroeter, brought an understated competence to the firm. He too ascended to the presidency of WSTLA, as would later partner J. Murray Kleist.

Perhaps the best known of the three named partners was the late John Goldmark (1917-1979). After graduating with honors from Harvard Law, Goldmark returned to his native Washington to ranch in Okanogan. Always politically active, Goldmark was elected to the state house and senate, and he was widely reputed to be in line for the governor's mansion. His political career was ruined by libelous accusations of right-wing opponents. Judge William Dwyer has chronicled Goldmark's struggle and victory in the acclaimed book *The Goldmark Case*. His political career in tatters despite his victory, Goldmark found his interest in law renewed. He decided to link his brilliant legal mind with fiery Schroeter and the steady Bender, and SGB was formally created.

The firm attracted, and continues to attract, legal talent from the best law schools across the nation. Yale, Berkeley, New York University, Columbia, University of Chicago, University of Washington, and Harvard are just some of the law schools that make up SGB's prestigious resume. Although Goldmark and Bender are now gone, the firm's traditions live on through senior partners such as Croil Anderson and Paul Whelan. Attracted to the firm's unique blend of high-quality trial work and commitment to representation of victims, Anderson and Whelan are in their third decade in SGB's home, in Seattle's historic Central Building. Schroeter, though now of counsel, still shows more energy than any eager young associate. He keeps the conscience for the firm, as well as adding to its national prominence through his membership in the Inner Circle of Advocates, a group of the top one hundred personal injury trial lawyers in the nation, and through leadership in the national American Trial Lawyers Association and the Trial Lawyers for Public Justice. Two other partners have recently been honored with high awards: Mike Withey, as 1990's Trial Lawyer of the Year for Washington, and Jeff Robinson, as one of the Top Ten Lawyers in Washington by the 1991 Judges Choice.

The firm prides itself on its ability to handle small automobile accidents, workers' compensation, and social security disability in the same competent way it handles large and complex litigation. However, its national and regional reputation were made by leading the fight against the asbestos manufacturers, toxic polluters, malpracticing doctors, and a variety of manufacturers of defective products like the Dalkon Shield, L-Tryptophan, and most recently, breast implants. Whether working for justice for politically motivated slayings in the famous case of *Domingo & Viernes v. Ferdinand & Imelda Marcos*, in which the jury returned a $15.1 million verdict, or exposing experiments on workers through *Strom v. Boeing* on CBS's "60 Minutes" SGB seeks to meld its legal skills with the goal of enhancing social justice. Over three decades, SGB has grown to become the largest plaintiffs' personal injury law firm in the Pacific Northwest. Since most of its fights are against large insurance companies and corporations, that size comes in handy, as does the firm's commitment to remain on the cutting edge of technology.

SGB sees the fight for victim's rights as far from over. New challenges face the firm every year. Recent revelations of the horrors of breast implants have again thrust the firm into the local and national spotlight on the toxic consequences of a defective product. As Croil Anderson, SGB's president, says, "There's nothing like a good fight for a good cause".

Short, Cressman & Burgess

Formed in 1915 by two ambitious young lawyers, Short Cressman & Burgess is today a full-service, general practice law firm of over 50 attorneys.

The firm's founders were George Rummens and Tracy Griffin, two colorful and legendary trial attorneys. Both Mr. Rummens and Mr. Griffin served as president of the Washington State Bar Association. In 1946, after serving in the U.S. Army in World War II, Kenneth P. Short joined the firm. Three years later, another young trial lawyer, Paul R. Cressman, joined Rummens and Griffin. Mr. Short and Mr. Cressman went on to lead the firm's modern-day expansion, becoming leaders in local and state bar associations. Both served on the board of trustees of the Washington State Bar Association, with Mr. Short later serving as its president. In 1961, John O. Burgess joined the firm that now bears his name. Originally planning to be a tax attorney, Mr. Burgess soon became a trial lawyer, following in his predecessors' footsteps. He is now regarded as one of the finest trial lawyers in the Pacific Northwest.

The firm grew dramatically in the late sixties. Short, Cressman & Burgess served as the principal draftsmen of the King County Charter in 1969. The firm's growth continues today, both in the number of attorneys on staff and the breadth of the firm's practice.

"From its beginnings earlier this century, the firm's credo has been to provide its clients high-quality legal services promptly and efficiently," says James A. Oliver, the firm's managing partner. "This commitment remains unchanged as the firm expands its traditional practice areas, and continues its success in developing new areas of practice."

Although it began as a firm devoted to trial work, today Short, Cressman & Burgess' practice is evenly divided between general litigation and legal services in the areas of business, commercial, international, and real estate law.

The firm's broad civil practice includes general litigation, construction, corporations, partnerships, tax, deferred compensation, business planning and business regulations, insurance, banking, lending and secured transactions, mergers and acquisitions, employment law, municipal law, securities, real estate, environmental and land use, hazardous waste, fisheries, admiralty, maritime, immigration, U.S. Customs, international transactions, insurance defense, professional malpractice, products liability, creditor and debtor rights, bankruptcy, family law, landlord-tenant law, estate and trust matters, and probate.

Short, Cressman & Burgess' reputation and excellence as a litigation firm has never diminished. Nearly one-half of the firm's lawyers devote their practice to litigation and alternative dispute resolution. The firm represents local, regional, and national clients in both state and federal courts. Two of the firm's senior partners are Fellows of the American College of Trial Lawyers. Two former members of the firm are a Washington State Supreme Court justice and a King County Superior Court judge.

The firm's construction law practice dates back to its inception in 1915. The firm remains one of the region's premier construction law firms, involved in significant construction litigation and alternative dispute resolution throughout the Northwest. The firm's Construction Section is composed of fifteen lawyers, who represent owners, design professionals, sureties, subcontractors, and suppliers involved in both public and private projects. The firm has represented clients involved in a variety of construction projects, including road and utility construction, military facilities, state and federal courthouses, performing arts centers, hospitals and medical facilities, jails and correctional centers, schools, university facilities, domestic water and waste-water systems, office buildings, shopping centers, apartment complexes, and condominiums. Recently, the firm has added marine construction litigation to its practice.

The firm also maintains an active practice in the area of employment law, advising clients on matters involving employment contracts, personnel practices, compliance with discrimination laws and regulations, wage and other regulatory matters, and labor/management relations.

The firm clients include employers in the hospitality/hotel/restaurant industry, financial institutions, construction firms, manufacturing companies, medical/dental practices, hospitals and medical centers, timber and forest product companies, insurance brokerages, and seafood processors.

The other half of the firm's lawyers practice in the areas of business, commercial, international, and real estate law, with experience in all facets of corporate and commercial transactions. On the business side, the emphasis is on banking/trust, lender/borrower, corporate acquisition, and refinancing/restructuring practice. The firm has represented banks and lending institutions for over fifty years.

Lawyers in the firm's merger and acquisition practice have represented privately held and public companies buying or selling businesses valued from less than $50,000 to more than $20 million.

The firm's international section represents a diverse client basis, with a focus on business transactions in the Pacific Rim. Several members of the firm speak Chinese. The firm's lawyers represent U.S. companies doing business abroad. Other clients are companies, financial institutions, and individuals based in Hong Kong, Taiwan, and the People's Republic of China who are doing business in the United States. Members of the firm are active in the Japan-America Society, the China Relations Counsel and the Korean American Trade Club of Washington.

Through its Real Estate Section, the firm has a diverse real estate, development, lending, and secured transaction practice. The fastest-growing area of the firm's practice has been in environmental, hazardous waste, and land use matters. Before joining Short Cressman & Burgess, several firm members served tenures with the U.S. Environmental Protection Agency and the Washington Department of Ecology. Clients are assisted by members of the firm's environmental/land use practice group in regulatory matters, permit and EIS processes, and administrative hearings.

"One of the hallmarks of the firm is its youth," says Oliver. Most of the senior attorneys are in their early fifties and late forties. Reflecting Seattle's cosmopolitan population, the firm's lawyers come from fifteen states and Hong Kong, thirty universities, and twenty-four law schools.

Another hallmark of the firm is its commitment to the Seattle-area community. The firm's lawyers provide pro bono legal services through such agencies as the Seattle-King County Bar Association and Legal Action Center. The firm participates in the MENTOR Program, sponsored by the Washington State Bar Association, which promotes law-related education for high school students. Firm members are active in a number of charitable organizations and foundations, including United Way, The Arthritis Foundation, Children's Home Society, the Woodland Park Zoo, and the Museum of Flight. One lawyer is presently a member of the Bainbridge Island City Council.

"Short Cressman & Burgess marked its 75th anniversary in 1990," notes Oliver. "We look forward to celebrating our centennial in the next century. And I know that if they were with us, Mr. Rummens and Mr. Griffin would look back on their legacy with a great deal of pride."

Smith & Leary

Smith & Leary was formed in 1986 as a partnership between James A. Smith, Jr., and J. J. Leary, Jr. Smith & Leary focuses on civil litigation in state and federal courts, with emphasis on securities, timber, construction, employment, contract, and Native American matters. The firm also represents professional athletes in business dealings and contract negotiations, and is litigation counsel for a National Basketball Association franchise. The firm is determined to remain small, while handling diverse and complex litigation typically performed by much larger law firms.

Jim Smith's extensive litigation background has included appearing before the United States Supreme Court on securities issues of first impression as well as successfully pursuing timber claims on behalf of landowners against major corporations in the Northwest and in the South.

J. J. Leary's practice is a balanced and complementary mix of commercial litigation and business transactional work involving domestic and Native American corporations. He especially enjoys construction litigation and partnership and shareholder disputes.

Because of its unique practice, Smith & Leary's clients have originated from referrals from other firms and former clients. The firm has been fortunate in having the opportunity to be very selective in choosing its cases. While the firm emphasizes plaintiffs' litigation, its caseload is typically a blend of work for both plaintiffs and defendants. The guiding consideration in assuming representation is whether the case is interesting, challenging, and meritorious.

The firm is hardworking and it obtains results.

Smith & Leary's professionalism is tempered by informality, including an "office dog," Bosley, a labrador retriever who comes to work each day with J. J. Leary. The firm's offices are located in a building in the historic Pioneer Square area of Seattle, within walking distance of the courthouse and downtown office buildings. The building itself is not the typical law firm high-rise. Instead, it's a restored structure on a tree-lined brick pedestrian mall surrounded by art galleries, coffeehouses, and bookstores.

The firm's "work hard, play hard" practice peaks each year with the annual Smith & Leary party, complete with a rock n' roll band, outside on the deck that surrounds the offices. It is attended by lawyers, judges, clients, family, friends, and neighbors.

Stokes, Eitelbach & Lawrence, P.S.

Stokes, Eitelbach & Lawrence, P.S., is a mainstream business and commercial law firm that strives to provide the personal service associated with the small-firm environment.

The firm was founded in 1981 as Monroe & Perry by Dick Monroe and Wayne Perry. The initial practice was essentially two clients: McCaw Cellular Communications and Omni Enterprises, an Alaska retailer. "We wanted a more entrepreneurial experience," says Monroe. "It definitely was that."

In 1985, Wayne Perry left the firm to become an officer of McCaw Cellular Communications, Inc., which continues as one of the firm's clients. In 1986, the firm became a professional service corporation and changed its name to reflect the addition of three principals—Bob Stokes, Sarah Eitelbach, and Doug Lawrence. The firm name was changed in 1992 to reflect Dick Monroe's position "of counsel" to the firm. Since 1986, Rob Thomas, Steve Brown, Carolyn Cairns, Sandra Perkins, and Phil Ginsberg have become principals in the firm.

A majority of the firm's attorneys left larger firms for the more congenial atmosphere of a small firm. Because of their large-firm experience, they maintain a sophisticated commercial practice. The firm has emphasized hiring women; three of the eight shareholders are women.

Stokes, Eitelbach & Lawrence stresses the working relationship between attorney and client, responsiveness and efficiency. "We have structured our systems so that we are accessible to our clients and can respond quickly to their needs," says Rob Thomas.

JANUARY 1972
JOSEPH SINCLITICO
NAMED FIRST
LAW SCHOOL DEAN

❝

I have been asked what kind of legal education we will develop and what our overall educational philosophy will be. I will answer that very simply. Our law school will be neither liberal nor conservative, nor on dead center. We will take our educational position where common sense and good reason dictate we should be.

❞

DEAN JOSEPH SINCLITICO
IN AN INTERVIEW
WITH NEWS REPORTERS

SEPTEMBER 1972
UNIVERSITY OF
PUGET SOUND WELCOMES
FIRST LAW CLASS

❝

This school, in a very short time, will take a place among the finest law schools in this country. Every one of the people who, in a remarkably short time and under great pressure, provided the planning and execution of this great project of such great value to the University, the Puget Sound area, and to this entire state, is entitled to the commendation and gratitude of all the people this school will serve presently and in all the years to come. I consider it a great privilege to have had even a very small part in making this day come true.

❞

JUDGE GEORGE BOLDT
FOUNDING CHAIRMAN
OF THE LAW SCHOOL
BOARD OF VISITORS

FEBRUARY 1973
LAW SCHOOL GETS
EARLY ACCREDITATION
FROM THE AMERICAN
BAR ASSOCIATION

❝

The University of Puget Sound may have set some sort of record in taking its law school from the 'drawing boards' to the operational phase. Some might have suggested that the school should not be started so fast and so large. But skeptics may again have been confounded.

❞

PROFESSOR MILLARD RUUD
CONSULTANT TO THE COUNCIL
OF THE SECTION
ON LEGAL EDUCATION
AMERICAN BAR ASSOCIATION

APRIL 1975
FIRST UPS LAW
GRADUATES MAKE STATE
BAR EXAM HISTORY

❝

The first graduates of the University of Puget Sound's new law school to take the state bar exam had a passing rate of 91 percent, university officials have announced. A total of 239 law graduates from all schools took the February 1975 exam and 164 passed, for an overall passing rate of 69 percent.

❞

EXCERPTS FROM A SEATTLE
POST INTELLIGENCER ARTICLE
BY REPORTER SOLVEIG TORVIK

THE
UNIVERSITY
OF PUGET
SOUND

At 20

SCHOOL
OF
LAW

SEPTEMBER 1980
MORE THAN 2,000 PERSONS
PARTICIPATE IN DEDICATION
OF THE NORTON CLAPP
LAW CENTER

❝

And so, as you dedicate this building today, we should also remember, splendid as it is, that it is merely a shelter and a shell. Far more important are the men, women, faculty, students, and the spirit of dedication — your dedication — to freedom with accountability for the use of that freedom…. This school will have an important role in the future of the great Pacific Northwest. It must and will produce leaders who will shape, perfect, and protect our precious freedoms.

❞

CHIEF JUSTICE
WARREN BURGER
U.S. SUPREME COURT
REMARKS AT THE
DEDICATION CEREMONY

DECEMBER 1982
UPS GRADUATE SECURES
U.S. SUPREME COURT
CLERKSHIP

❝

Gay Gellhorn '82 recently was accorded the highest honor a new law school graduate can receive: Appointment as a clerk to the United States Supreme Court. A magna cum laude graduate of Radcliffe College who received an M.A. in teaching from Harvard University, Gellhorn will begin her clerkship for Justice Thurgood Marshall in July 1983. She is the first Puget Sound law graduate to be selected for the prestigious post.

❞

AN EXCERPT FROM NOTES
ON ALUMNI UNIVERSITY
OF PUGET SOUND LAWYER
WINTER 1983

FEBRUARY 1983
TENTH ANNIVERSARY
CELEBRATION ATTRACTS
CAPACITY CROWD TO
PANTAGES CENTRE

❝

If we in legal education do not find out what is happening in the profession, if we do not take into consideration in our curriculum, in our teaching methods, and in our programs, the fundamental changes that are occurring, then we shall find ourselves educating students equipped to operate in a society which has vanished and a profession which does not exist.

❞

DEAN FREDRIC C. TAUSEND
FROM HIS PROLOGUE TO THE
REMARKS OF U.N. AMBASSADOR
JEANNE KIRKPATRICK

MAY 1987
LARGEST GIFT EVER:
LAW SCHOOL RECEIVES
$1.75 MILLION

❝

An individual who has asked to remain anonymous has given $1.75 million to create an endowed professorship in legal education. The donation is the largest single gift in the history of the Law School, and is the most significant thing to happen to the school since its 1980 relocation to downtown Tacoma's Norton Clapp Law Center.

❞

AN ANNOUNCEMENT BY
UNIVERSITY PRESIDENT
PHILIP PHIBBS
AT SPRING COMMENCEMENT
EXERCISES

JUNE 1990
PUGET SOUND FACULTY
MAKE "TOP 50" LIST

❝

The University of Puget Sound has been ranked among the top 50 law schools in terms of scholarly productivity of faculty members. The Faculty Scholarship Survey, published annually by the IIT Chicago-Kent Law School, analyzes the number of articles published per faculty member in the nation's 20 leading law journals. Puget Sound is the only law school in the Pacific Northwest to make the list.

❞

EXCERPT FROM AN
ARTICLE IN CASE NOTES,
AN ADMISSION PUBLICATION
OF THE SCHOOL OF LAW

NOVEMBER 1990
PUGET SOUND CITED
AMONG "AMERICA'S 56 BEST
LAW PROGRAMS"

❝

Our law school has been listed in Top Law Schools: The Ultimate Guide, a first-edition book published this month by Prentice-Hall. The publication provides extensive information on only 56 schools, or fewer than one-third of all law schools in the country. While my colleagues and I retain a healthy skepticism when it comes to lists of this kind, it nevertheless is gratifying to see Puget Sound as one of only two Northwest law schools included in a bound-to-be bestselling book.

❞

FROM A NEWSLETTER
WRITTEN TO SPECIAL
LAW SCHOOL FRIENDS BY
DEAN JAMES E. BOND

AUGUST 1991
FIRST UPS GRADUATE
TO SIT ON STATE
SUPREME COURT FINISHES
HIS FIRST YEAR

❝

After nine months on the court, several fellow justices say Charles W. Johnson '76 has won their respect with his energy and legal smarts, bringing to the court a valuable and fresh perspective. 'Charles Johnson was an instant Supreme Court justice,' said Justice Charles Z. Smith. 'He had an impression of what the Supreme Court was, and he had an idea of how he wanted to affect the court.'

❞

REPORTER JIM SIMON
WRITING IN THE
SEATTLE TIMES

The firm advises commercial clients on all aspects of their businesses, from creation and financing through operation and sale. The primary areas of business practice are formation, acquisitions and divestitures, taxation, private securities and finance, contracts, real estate, trademark and copyright, antitrust and trade regulation, employer/employee regulations, estate planning, and probate.

The firm's litigation practice includes commercial litigation, public contracts, securities and antitrust, intellectual property, subrogation, collections, employment law, wills, and trusts.

Representative clients include Marsh & McLennan, Blue Cross of Washington and Alaska, Diagnostic Ultrasound Corporation, Group Health Cooperative of Puget Sound, McCaw Cellular Communications, Inc., and Omni Enterprises, Inc. The firm also advises many small-business clients and women-owned businesses.

Besides the areas of practice, people who work at the firm frequently cite a congenial office environment as a factor for working there. "You realize the importance of the people you work with, as well as the importance of the work you're doing," says Thomas.

"The atmosphere is important. There is already enough stress in the practice of law," says Monroe. "It doesn't make sense to add to it with the atmosphere of the office. You'll hear a lot of laughter in the hall. We put a high premium on a sense of humor and on people with balance in their lives and interests outside of law."

University of Washington School of Law

The University of Washington School of Law opened in 1899 (after an earlier Washington Law School failed to grant a single degree). John T. Condon of Seattle was selected as dean, at a beginning salary of $1,500 a year (and served until 1926). The Law School opened in upper floors of the University Building tract at Fourth and Union, with a two-man faculty of Dean Condon and George McKay, who schooled twenty-six students in the first class.

In 1903, the Law School moved from downtown to the present campus. The school was nomadic in its early days, beginning with quarters in the Denny Hall attic, and moving from building to building on campus, including Lewis Hall and the Meany Hall basement. In 1933, the Law School moved to a new building, John T. Condon Hall on the UW Quad. By that time the faculty had increased to 10 members, and registration was 344.

The current Condon Hall was completed and occupied in 1974. When the building opened, its architecture, designed by Romaldo Giurgola, was the subject of some discussion in Seattle, because the bright white concrete was then a new idiom to the city. The *Seattle Times* lamented its "inhuman concrete," but famed architect Victor Steinbrueck called it "the best modern building in the city." Aesthetics aside, the building thus far has proved sufficiently solid and roomy to accommodate the Law School's needs. Additions are likely by the late nineties.

The Marian Gould Gallagher Law Library contains more than 435,000 bound volumes and volume equivalents of microfilm. The library has one of the most extensive collections of Japanese law materials in the U.S.

In the last half of the 1980s, the thirty-eight permanent members of the law school faculty published about ninety essays or matters, and labor/management relations. articles and twenty-two books, a quantitative record that ranked among the top twenty law schools nationally. Among the specialities in which the faculty has attained national distinction are comparative (Asian) law, environmental law, intellectual property, real property, taxation, legal writing, marine law, legal ethics, education law, and labor relations.

Wallace Loh became the eleventh dean of the UW School of Law in May 1990. The first Asian-American to head a law school in the U.S., Loh was born in China and grew up in Peru. He attended Grinnell College in Iowa and earned a Ph. D. in social psychology at Michigan and his J.D. at Yale.

Each fall now, an entering class of about 150 begins the study of law on the UW campus. The total enrollment for 1990-91 was 523. Dean Loh has plans to work in partnership with local law firms and businesses to train attorneys in the skills that will be needed in the nineties. Loh plans to maximize the school's strengths, especially in its Pacific Rim and high-technology emphases. The UW already has one of the preeminent Asian-law programs, including what is generally considered the best Asian-law library in the U.S.; 125 Tokyo attorneys are UW graduates. At the UW, one in nine students is Asian-American, and the entering class in 1991 was 36 percent minority—second only to UCLA as the most diverse law school in the country.

Established graduate programs are in Asian Law, and Law and Marine Affairs. A Center for Cooperative Law has been set up with a mediation clinic where students get hands-on training in alternative dispute resolution. Other special programs include trial advocacy programs, criminal and civil clinics, moot court and mock trial programs, and the Washington Law Review.

Within the next few years, the UW will start several new highly technical, scientific programs, including one graduate program in the law of sustainable development, essentially land development and Third World development. There will also be a master's program in international environmental law.

Loh also says that specialization tracks will be in place in two or three years, consistent with trends in the profession as a whole. On the horizon, Loh sees an American Indian Law Center, training the next generation of Native American leaders.

"The common denominator to all these plans," says Loh, "is to have a vibrant law school that helps the economics of the region."

The practical component of this exciting future-gazing is a partnership with local law firms and businesses. The school plans to ask lawyers to get involved as advisors and mentors. "This is not sheer altruism, we need their support," says Loh. "I don't conceal this; we want their financial support. But they get something, too. We are a farm team, and they're going to get graduates with a leg up."

Loh also plans to propose something even more unexpected, a required program of public service work. "This is a trickle-up theory of moral responsibility in the profession," says the dean. "You do it by inculcating the next generation of lawyers."

Wechsler, Besk, Erickson, Ross & Roubik

This five-attorney firm was formed in 1988. All members emphasize family law, including marital dissolution and child custody proceedings. The attorneys in the office are Mary Wechsler, Lawrence Besk, Duane Erickson, Katharine Ross, and new member Linda Roubik.

The attorneys knew each other through work in other firms and in family law professional associations. Duane Erickson is the current chair of the Family Law Section of the Seattle-King County Bar Association; Linda Roubik and Mary Wechsler are both former chairs of the section. Mary Wechsler has also chaired the Washington State Bar Family Law Section.

The firm was formed after the partners had worked together and found themselves compatible. "We had a similar philosophy about service and standards," says Erickson. Also, since the family law area is often the domain of sole practitioners, the partners believe that they filled a niche by creating a firm that could handle more family law cases and share expertise. With the increasing complexity and specialization of family law, they believe in the benefits of such concentration in one field.

The nature of family practice is emotional and the attorneys inevitably find themselves shouldering their clients' emotional burdens. "You have to strike a balance," says Wechsler. "You'd be no good

if you were totally devastated. But you also have to provide client satisfaction, and the main factor in that is that the attorneys show clients that they care about them."

This is one of the most visible of legal areas. Everyone, whether personally or through relatives or friends, seems to come in contact with family law. The attorneys in the firm believe that it is very important to work through professional organizations with the courts and the legislature regarding perceptions of justice and impact on the public.

The attorneys share the view that family law is a fascinating area and that this is the ideal practice if you went into law in order to work with people. As Linda Roubik states: "Clients put their lives in your hands. We learn so much about a client's entire life, including children, finances, property, debts, gifts, past history, and future expectations. The field is very challenging since family law practice includes so many legal areas such as real estate, taxes, business valuation, parenting plans, child support, medical insurance, pension plans and domestic violence. We gain wisdom and perspective from working in this field and appreciate the many difficulties our clients are going through."

The firm members also take pride in their pro bono work. "It is an obligation," says Wechsler. "The circumstances just hit you sometimes, that a person needs help."

The partners stress the value of developing and maintaining a good reputation. The firm obtains all of its work from referrals. They also emphasize the need for positive interpersonal dynamics in a small office.

Wechsler says the firm might expand by a few people, but the partners are essentially satisfied with a small operation. "Some of the mid-sized firms seem so unwieldy. This is a compatible group of people. It works so well," she laughs, "we hate to mess it up."

INDEX